Genesis for Ordinary People

Genesis for Ordinary People

Unwrapping the First Book of the Bible

Paul Poulton

RESOURCE *Publications* · Eugene, Oregon

GENESIS FOR ORDINARY PEOPLE
Unwrapping The First Book Of The Bible

Wipf & Stock
An Imprint of Wipf and Stock Publishers
199 W. 8th Ave., Suite 3
Eugene, OR 97401

www.wipfandstock.com

ISBN 13: 978-1-62564-930-0

Manufactured in the U.S.A.

Isaac (Abraham's son), Isaac Newton, and Isaac Poulton—all inspirational in their own way.

Contents

Introduction

GENESIS IS LIKE NO other book, its stark beauty stands alone in literature, ancient or modern. The economy of its phrasing, the artistry used to convey its objective, and the compelling nature of its subject matter leaves many people with the conclusion that the text of Genesis is special, authoritative, and sacred.

Yet the book of Genesis is being scrutinized. Scientific data continues to accumulate, and the history of the universe and life on earth is being quantified by a huge expansion of knowledge. What is the person who is teetering on the precipice of faith or doubt to do with the stockpile of facts presented by the scientific community? How can young people reconcile a belief they are taught by some Christian people against the body of information they receive as part of their education? These are the questions that need to be answered if successive generations are to have strong faith in the opening book of the Bible, and consequently the God who breathed upon its words. The days of those who say they believe in the literal truth of Genesis seem to be numbered; their rebuttals to scientific documentation have too many leaks and appear unable to hold water, their pleas to be allowed onto a scientific platform ignored, and the mountain of evidence presented against their cause is proving too large to scale.

All believers in the Bible are creationists; no one group can commandeer that name. We all believe that the Bible is truth. Saying we believe in the literal truth of the Bible is true but we also have to recognize that the Bible uses parables, poetry, and sometimes hyperbole to explain that truth. Would people who say they believe in the literal truth of the Bible sever their hand as Jesus said they ought to? No, they understand that Jesus was making a point in a dramatic way.

Introduction

Genesis is a strong book and able to withstand the conclusions of both enthusiastic believers and hostile adversaries. We are told that God is keen for us to read his words and understand how they apply to each human being, and the first book he presents us with is Genesis, so there's something important about the opening scenes shown to us. Every author knows the power of the opening chapter of a book and I'm sure that God is no different. But Genesis has a lot more to offer than just its opening chapters; there is adventure, intrigue, and a drama that begins to take shape. The story holds our interest like a gripping detective adventure, like a well-produced film where attention must be paid to detail and dialogue. If we read it correctly, with innocence and reason, we find that it tells us what we need to know about the world we live in and about the grand design for the human race, as well as the central theme of the Bible.

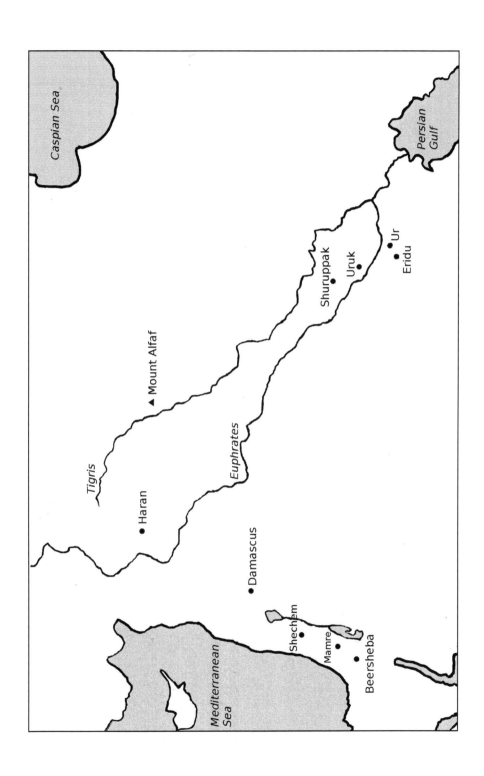

CHAPTER 1

Proverbial Wisdom

HERE IT IS:

> It is the glory of God to conceal a matter, but the glory of kings to search them out. (Prov 25:2)

Given the limited capability of the ancient Hebrew language used in Genesis and the fact that God does not readily give us all the information we might like in order to satisfy our curiosity, it is not surprising that people come to different conclusions of how God created the world we all inhabit.

The question of why God would conceal a matter has a few answers, and one of them is that trust comes first. We need to have faith even when we don't understand. There are examples of this throughout the Bible: Abraham was asked to sacrifice his son Isaac and although he may not have understood such a senseless and shocking order, he obeyed, trusting when he didn't understand. Jesus himself said, "Blessed are those who have not seen and yet have believed." It's important to have faith. It is also good to remember that God has given us a mind, and he expects us to use it. We find that when we have the "mind of Christ" our thoughts support our faith in God rather than undermine it. Implicit in the proverb is the hope that men will "search out" what has previously been concealed.

Viewpoints on Genesis vary wildly from people who laugh and pour ridicule on talking snakes, magic fruit trees, and two progenitors of humankind who only began to populate the earth 6000 years ago, to those who tell us that the universe itself is only 6000 years old because, they say, "The Bible says it is." The two viewpoints are diametrically opposed. Those who scorn Genesis tell their fellow disparagers not to have any dealings with the biblical-literalists, not to take them on in debate, lest you give them oxygen to help keep their naïve and dangerous doctrine burning. Not everyone listens though and sometimes a well-publicized debate takes place that has the feel of a big boxing match, where the public at large are the judges and polls over the next few days will reveal who won on points or maybe even a knockout.

My teenage son and his friends are still at school and I'm somewhat surprised how knowledgeable they are about the universe we live in. They are taught in line with the received knowledge and facts that have been passed on since I was at school, except there is a lot more information available now. I have to work at being informed and cannot rely on my schooling because education moves on. I sometimes wonder about the disparity between the data young people are aware of and the preaching of some preachers who tell us the Bible contradicts the lessons being taught in school. Who are they to believe?

Some time ago there was a movie that attempted to uncover a rather serious conspiracy in the scientific community. It may be with a note of relish that believers pointed out that the journalist uncovering the plot in the film was a non-Christian. The film is a welcome companion to a theme that some quarters of the church seem to hold, namely that the scientific establishment has an agenda to discredit the scriptures. It may be true to say that there are some scientists who do in fact look for evidence to discredit Christ and the Bible, but it seems likely that the vast majority of scientists are not trying to match their science up to anything other than truth. Scientists in turn accuse some Christians of also having an agenda, after all it is the church that has a prerequisite script to follow, whereas the scientists point out that they themselves have no agenda save seeking out the truth of the physical universe we all live in. I guess that scientists find it hard to take the church seriously when some Christians sound like dodgy conspiracy theorists that resort to scare mongering to score points for their cause.

The job of those who are called biblical-literalists must be getting harder by the day. There's only so far one can neutralize mounting evidence, especially as the precise nature of the equipment used to gather information gets sharper and more refined each year. In the face of facts, trying to provide counter arguments to support their view of the scriptures places them in the same position as the Medieval Church who believed the sun travelled around the earth. Copernicus (1473–1543) who was himself a canon of the church, upset the church by writing that the earth orbits the sun. This was a contentious conflict at the time, even Martin Luther called Copernicus "a fool who went against Holy Writ" and an "upstart." Today we all take the solar system as common knowledge even though the Bible tells us that the sun rises and the sun sets. We've adjusted our view of the way the Bible teaches us things, as the Apostle Paul says, in malice be children, but in understanding be men. We still believe the Bible but have a bit more light than our medieval brothers and sisters and for some of the light we have to say thanks to Copernicus and others who stood firmly on the side of truth, even though it cost them, some times dearly.

Yes, we must trust God even when we don't understand, but because we are made in his image we have a duty to search things out so that we can understand. "Come now, let us reason together" (Isa 1:18). He conceals a matter; humans search it out. We don't give in at the first few hurdles because things have begun to get hard. We may feel like taking the easy option and say we don't understand how Genesis and science coexist so let's just have faith. Faith is good and without it it's impossible to please God, but just as God spoke to Jeremiah we may find that he speaks to us. "If you have raced with men on foot and they have worn you out, how can you compete with horses?" (Jer 12:5).

When God conceals something he's not trying to trick us, he does it for our own good. But if God has concealed something then we can be sure he's done a good job of covering it, because God does all things well. There will come a right time for men to search the matter out, and we could be in one of those times now.

When we are looking for something we need to keep our eyes open. We understand the Bible because of what we see around us. When the Bible talks about a tree, we understand what it is saying because we have seen a tree and so relate to its narrative. This principle happens time and again. We connect to the book of Genesis because we have seen snakes, we know how embarrassing it feels to have no clothes on, and we all know what it's like to be tempted, so we relate well to the story. If we take it a step further, we now know that stars are enormous balls of gas in space and by using the earth's orbit and a little trigonometry we can work out how far away they are, up to about 400 light years. For stars further than that we can use the star's color spectrum and other means. Under today's light-polluted skies the most distant star that can be seen with the human eye is Deneb, which is located around 1550 light years from us. This means that when we look at it we are seeing it as it was 1550 years ago, because it has taken the light that long to travel to us. There are stars much further away than that though; from the Hubble Telescope's newest camera glimpses of the most distant galaxies have been seen. Furthermore, the methods geologists use for dating have become refined and self-checking; there are many different radiometric dating methods, and other testing means available such as ice cores and sedimentary rock. So with data from scientists, archaeologists, and geologists we have additional information to consider when we read how the universe came to be.

Sometimes, someone's belief in the face of impossibilities tells us more about the person who has the belief than their beliefs themselves. We must trust God when we don't understand, but there comes a point when facts become so replete that we have to question why we don't understand. It's not God we question, those of us who have faith in him and know him, know he can be trusted. And any amount of materialist theories aimed to shake our faith in God fail to do so because faith does not come to us via that route. So our faith is not in question, but when God has spoken and there seems to be conflict with the facts around us it's time to read again what God has said.

CHAPTER 2

Synchronization of Science and Scripture

So what does Genesis say?

> In the beginning God created the heavens and the earth. (Gen 1:1)

In his *God and Religion*, the British philosopher Bertrand Russell said, "There is no reason to suppose that the world had a beginning at all." And some atheists held that viewpoint a few years ago: "Why couldn't the universe have always existed?" But scientific evidence has overtaken them and not too many people say that nowadays; science and Genesis tell us that there was a beginning to the universe. Genesis tells us that God created it. Materialists don't like to say exactly what happened before the universe came into being. They call it a singularity, but it's hard for them to rule out a creator. Most people seem to agree that the universe had a beginning.

"God created the heavens and the earth." Notice that the heavens came first then the earth. That also rings true to most people. We have begun to pick up light that has travelled to us from galaxies 13.2 billion light years away. As science advances and techniques become more refined, the estimated age of the heavens gets more precise. The age of the earth is younger: 4.5 billion years. One question that springs to my mind straight away is, "Why would God want to wait such a long time before creating the earth?" But then I check myself for thinking God is a man. It seems a long time to me, but God is outside of space-time because he made it. Also, there could be many hidden factors in creating a universe that I'm not aware of, factors that space and time manufacture. I watched the men who built my house with admiration. I noticed they would sometimes wait for things like glue to get to just the right consistency before they joined two pieces of wood. If I had butted in and tried to tell them to, "Get on with it," I'm sure they would have put me in my place by telling me they knew what they were doing. It took time, but now I'm living in the house they built. But God can do anything he wants to, right? Yes he can, and if he chooses to take his time building the heavens and earth then all I have to do is look on with admiration and wonder.

But how do we know for sure how old they are? One answer is that men who know more than me tell me they are. Of course I could disbelieve them just like I could disbelieve that there's a country called Norway.

"But people have been to Norway and seen it."

"You may say that, but I haven't been to Norway or seen it."

"But people wouldn't make it up."

"Wouldn't they? They all might be trying to fool me into believing there's a country called Norway when there actually isn't."

The person who refuses to believe in Norway is telling us more about himself than any reasonable argument for why the country of Norway might not exist. Perhaps someone he admires has told him that Norway doesn't exist, and he trusts that person's opinion. Then we have to admire his loyalty, but it might be good for us to suggest that maybe the person who told him that Norway doesn't exist, actually didn't say that, you probably misheard him. Maybe he was from the northeast of England and you heard him say, "Norway, it doesn't exist." But because of his accent he was really saying, "No way, it doesn't exist." We could suggest that it's probably best if he goes and asks the person who said it what they actually meant. If the person isn't around, then maybe he could investigate the subject for himself. Do some research and study and see what you come up with.

Secondly, and most importantly, where there's size there's time. As soon as a space is created then the possibility exists for an object to travel from one side of the space to the other, and travelling takes time. Hence space and time is now called space-time—it's one thing. God made this "one thing." If it has size then it has time, you can't have the one without the other. When we say the universe is big, we mean it has lots of time.

The sheer size of the universe is sometimes raised as a barrier to belief in a creator: How can this massive universe be designed simply to accommodate a tiny planet called earth? Why is the universe so big? And we all agree that the universe is big, so how can something so big be designed for us here on this little planet that orbits an average size star in an average size galaxy?

Some structures have to be precise and strong or they will not survive long. When they are constructed they need to have large foundations in order for them to remain stable. You may have seen a TV transmitter standing tall on the skyline. Ropes are attached to help it stay upright; they themselves are secured into blocks of concrete, which in turn are housed in stable ground, which may be surrounded by reinforced piles that have been driven into the ground. Can you see what is happening? In order for the mast to stay in position, other parts must be in positions that are further away from the mast itself. The universe is held together by gravity—one of the four fundamental forces in the universe. We all feel the effect of atoms attracting each other, scientists are not entirely sure why they attract each other, but know they do.

We stay on earth because gravity is attracting us to the earth's surface. The sun is also attracting each human being on earth, but because we are further away from the sun and its gravitational pull is weaker, we don't get drawn towards it. But the planet we are standing on is drawn towards it, our planet is held in orbit because it travels around the sun. Imagine swinging a rope with a weight attached to the end round and round your body. If you were to let go of the rope the weight would shoot off in a straight line, but as long as you hold on to the rope you keep the weight the same distance from your body, similar to the way the sun holds on to the earth. The moon also has a gravitational pull on earth, which causes the tides to move. The bigger the mass of atoms, the greater the gravitational pull. The gravitational pull of dense objects in the universe can even stop light escaping from them.

So, how far does gravity's arm reach? Gravity is described by imagining a cannonball on a trampoline (e.g., imagine that our sun is the cannonball and the elastic sheet is the rest of the universe), which weighs heavily upon the trampoline's elastic sheet and causes a dent in the middle of the trampoline. The rest of the elastic sheet is also altered slightly. The center of the sheet is curved quite dramatically but the further away from the center you get, the less and less the sheet is affected by the cannonball. But no matter how far away from the center of the sheet we look, the sheet never quite gets back to the original state it was in before the cannonball was sitting on it. There are equations that give the figures in black and white if we want them. Isaac Newton put it like this: "$F = G$ then M_1 and M_2 over R_2." This means, the Force of Gravity equals the Gravitational Constant, ($6.7428 \times 10-11$) M_1 and M_2 are Mass 1 (our sun) and Mass 2 (another star, say 13 billion light years away), R_2 is the distance between M_1 and M_2's centers of gravity.

If we do the sum we notice the value is not zero, gravity extends across the universe, because it never reaches zero. In other words, when the solar cannonball is in place, the universal trampoline never gets flat again, even at it edges. So, like the TV mast that needs a series of interacting foundations, our solar system is influenced by the pull of our galaxy, which in turn is affected by the pull of other galaxies which are influenced by yet other galaxies, and so on. We don't know exactly how big the universe has to be in order to keep this tiny bit of it stable enough to house the wonders of our planet, but we do know we feel the influence of all matter in the universe, so therefore it is important for each bit of the universe to be there. If some of it were removed, then in some way, however small, it would make a difference here, in our neck of the universal woods. So in that respect the whole universe is made for this tiny planet.

Let's move on. "Darkness was over the surface of the deep, and the Spirit of God was hovering over the waters" (Gen 1:2). Although scientists and geologists are strong on some things they seem to be a lot weaker on others. For example, how the earth was formed is scientifically a lot less precise. Though some scientists may venture a guess at it, guessing is not what scientists are good at. After all, how 98 chemical elements made their way to this one planet is not easy to quantify. Earth's core is complicated and how it came together is still a puzzle to scientists. Sophisticated x-ray technology may give us a few clues: the formation of earth's foundations seems to be a multistage process that involved the earth's core and mantle growing in an intricate sequence over time. The LORD asked Job where he was when the foundations of the earth were being laid. When the scriptures talk about the earth's foundations, the foundations are really there. And implicit in the phrase, "when the foundations of the earth were being laid," is the fact that foundations are layered and laid down in sequence. But what scientists, the public, and Genesis know is that the surface of planet earth has lots of water.

"God said, 'Let there be light,' and there was light" (Gen 1:3). "God called the light 'day' and the darkness he called 'night'" (Gen 1:5). This is the first mention of the word "day" in Genesis. God called the light day. Light has a name: day. It's not easy to work in the dark; we usually work in the day. The darkness, God called "night." This is important because the next bit in Genesis tells us that there was evening and there was morning— the first day. Now people talk about the creative days in Genesis a lot, and quite often some of those people say, "God created the universe in six literal days." Whenever people start to add words to scripture it rings alarms. They seem to enjoy using and even placing emphasis on the word literal. But it's not there in Genesis. In fact there seems to be something we ought to think about here and not rush to conclusions. If God means he is working in a period of light called day, I would have to be careful about telling him that his period of light called day must coincide with the period of light I call day. Einstein has already taught us that time is relative to the person experiencing it. After the six days in which God worked, he took a break on the seventh day and rested. Later in a psalm we read that some people will never enter God's rest, which implies that he is still resting from his creative acts. And in a way I can see that, yes, the universe is complete; God has done his work. Why shouldn't he rest from it? I built a kitchen once, it took me about two weeks but when I'd finished it I enjoyed standing back and looking at it. Maybe it's a similar thing for God. And it lets us know that the period of light he is enjoying now is still ongoing.

The other point is that day is such a fluid word in Hebrew or in English. For example, "In my granddad's day it took two days to travel to Cornwall because you could only travel in the day." That's a simple example of how the word day can be used in three different ways in the same sentence.

Jesus said, "As long as it is day, we must do the works of him who sent me. Night is coming, when no one can work" (John 9:4). He was talking about the night when he would be taken and killed. But the day Jesus spoke about lasted three years. That sounds like a long day.

To add another point, each of the creative days ends by saying, "there was evening and there was morning." There seems to be something cryptic about this. God had just named the darkness night, so that word was available to use, but the word used is evening, which is twilight; it's not yet dark but it's not exactly daylight either. The other word is morning, which begins at sunrise, but it's not as bright as midday. Either way there was light and light is called day. If we take a look at planet earth from space, we can see evening and morning taking place on either sides of the globe quite clearly. When Genesis talks about evening and morning taking place in a creative day, the evening and morning are both consistently there, which leaves room for a creative day to be as long as it needs to be, because evening and morning are there with it all the time. With today's technology, our generation can see this now, and begin to realize how Genesis reveals scientific data in its own way. The text in Genesis could have said, "There was night and there was day," but it didn't, it said, "there was evening and there was morning." It says that for a reason, it's the evening and the morning that are the frontier of night and day as they move around the planet and that frontier was there for all the live-long day.

There's an idea that if the word "day" is connected to a number in the Bible, such as "first day" or "day two" then it always refers to a 24-hour day. In Hosea 6:2 the poetic language of the prophet tells us he is not talking about 24-hour days, yet he numbers them. "After two days he will revive us; on the third day he will restore us, that we may live in his presence." Hosea is using a poetic figure of speech as a way of appealing to his compatriots to return to the LORD. And yet there is also a prophetic element concerning the resurrection of Jesus, so here we see the Bible use the word "day" in two different ways. For Jesus it was three solar days, for the Israelites it was an unspecified time.

The universe is a large place, and at some points time moves faster or slower depending on where you are. Time on the sun is slower than on earth but time on the moon is faster than on earth. Where there are dense stars time moves very slowly indeed. Psalm 8:3 says, "When I consider your heavens, the work of your fingers, the moon and the stars which you have set in place," we don't presume that God made the heavens with fingers such as we have. No, this is a human way of saying how God made the universe. The psalm also says, "You have set your glory above the heavens" (Ps 8:1). So that is God's perspective on the universe, he is above it all, outside of space-time. How is time measured for God? He can use it as he pleases; he made it.

> A thousand years in your sight are like a day that has just gone by,
> or like a watch in the night. (Psalm 90:4)

So which way are we to suppose Genesis uses the word "day" for God's creative work? We have to use the knowledge we have of how the world around us works, just like when Genesis tells us about a tree or the stars. We understand exactly what a star is from what we have been told by astronomers. Some people in the past may have thought that stars were pin holes, not too far away, where bits of celestial light shone through a black canopy, but now we have a little more knowledge of how the world around us works. This knowledge doesn't make us any better than our forebears but it does help us to understand the scriptures. Scientists tell us that the age of the earth is 4.54 billion years old. We can try to convince ourselves that their calculations or equipment are wrong or that maybe they are trying to fool us, or we can believe them. If we choose to believe them then that gives us the answer of how we are to view the way Genesis uses the word "day."

On God's next day of work we read that earth's atmosphere began to lift. At any one time there is about 37.5 million billion gallons of water in the vapor phase. This is enough water to cover the entire surface of the earth (land and ocean) with one inch of rain.

Once some of the water on the planet had been lifted by volcanic gas pressure the tectonic plates began to move and form continents of land, which were pushed up and rose above the remaining water. The plates move very slowly, about the same pace as a fingernail grows. They may not have always moved at that speed but when tectonic plates move, "steady as she goes" is the order of the day. They have to move slowly because there is massive friction involved and such immense forces could easily chew up the world. It's a bit like three or four men trying to move an expensive grand piano. How do they move it? The answer is, very slowly and carefully, inch by inch sometimes. That was part of the work God did on the third day.

God also caused vegetation to start, which is good because algae and plants could then produce oxygen that will be needed to replace any volcanic gases that helped to lift the clouds. Plus oxygen will be needed by creatures yet to appear. Time would be required for the vegetation and algae to produce all the oxygen that was needed for the next phase, but the time could be put to good use because the creatures that God was planning to make in phases five and six would need energy, particularly when they reached the twentieth century AD. There would be quite a lot of them and they would need to travel and move large quantities of freight over great distances quickly. Ninety-eight tons of buried plant material is needed to produce enough fuel for each gallon that we put into our cars. So this creative day was a good one because God was planning ahead.

How much oil is used in cars, aircraft, and machines, etc., in one day on planet earth in the twenty-first century? The answer is roughly 3,570,000,000 gallons. I'm thinking that this equates to a lot of buried plant material for just one day's fuel consumption. So how much buried plant life would be required for 100 years? The internal combustion engine was first invented in the mid-1800s and they were being widely used by the end of that century. That all equates to a lot of plant life and it takes time for plants to grow and then get buried until layer after layer of plants and algae start to produce oil, but that's okay because God has time at his disposal, and he doesn't get impatient either, unlike us.

On the fourth day God made lights appear in the sky. This doesn't mean he created them on this day; there is a word for create in Hebrew and there is a word for made. The lights were created earlier just like the land was created earlier but God made the land appear on day three even though it was there on day one. On day four the atmosphere became thin enough for the sun and moon to appear through it. It had thinned because fresh water was needed for plant life, the 37.5 million billion gallons of water in the atmosphere around the planet is recycled 40 times each year in what is known as the hydrological cycle. This means a water vapor molecule has an average residence time in the atmosphere of only nine days: the sudden shower of rain you were caught in last week had evaporated into the atmosphere approximately nine days before. The huge amount of water is processed through a cycle of evaporation, condensation, and precipitation all over the globe. The hydrological cycle is driven by solar energy. Evaporating water does require energy; in fact it takes 577 calories of energy to evaporate each gram. So the sun was doing a good job in shining to help with the evaporation.

The next two working days God is busy first with living creatures in the waters and secondly with birds that fly, then animals that live on land, and finally humans. This fits in well with what scientists tell us, although they don't all agree on the order of what came first but we are told that the fossil record is overwhelming. Some churchgoers struggle with thinking that God may have made species slowly over time. But we are also told that, "The vast majority of Christians who are active in biological research have no problem incorporating evolutionary theory with their belief in God as Creator."[1] All "creative processes" are exactly that: a process. For instance when I am in the recording studio putting a song together I do it in many stages. At various points we run off a mix of the song up to that point to take home and listen to for a day or so. Eventually we arrive at the finished product, a quality song. I still have all the earlier mixes around the house that I can still listen to at any time and they are still interesting in their own way. In a similar way those who believe God used evolution say we can see a record of God's process of creation with our own eyes as we look around us and see the lower forms of life and continue all the way up to humans. Apparently Genesis 1 does a good job of describing the evolutionary process.

The creation story in Genesis of how life began has a number of "leaps" in it. So does the naturalists' story of how we all got here. The first big leap

1. Alexander, "Can a Christian Believe," lines 38–39.

is: how did inorganic matter turn into organic matter? The naturalist will say that billions of permutations bridged the yawning chasm between inanimate dirt and a living, reproducing life form. Genesis tells us that if God had not said, "Let the earth sprout vegetation" (Gen 1:11 nasb) then the leap would never have been bridged. Some biologists seem eager to come up with a form of synthetic life. We have seen DNA designed on a computer then transferred into pre-existing bacteria, and we have even seen metallic based cell-like structures called iCELLS that remain inorganic, but work is progressing to see if they can be encouraged to replicate. Proof of abiogenesis (the study of how inorganic matter turned into organic matter) remains frustratingly elusive for the naturalist, but not for those who believe Genesis. The lesson for the biologist and for the man in the street who has an interest in the subject, is that non-life does not naturally turn into life; God must speak for that to happen. And now we see all sorts of attractive vegetation around us each day. The first gulf has been bridged quite beautifully.

The second jump is between vegetable life and animal life, another leap that was successfully negotiated with the words, "Let the earth bring forth living creatures" (Gen 1:24 nasb). Most people would agree that large leaps and then many smaller leaps took place before we can arrive at where we are today. Each leap improved upon the one before it: a procession of life becoming more able and capable, all kinds of tiny flowers to all sorts of shrubs and trees; all kinds of creatures, finishing off the creative process with human beings. Biological life is a wonder that never ceases to amaze us; TV programs about the natural world are always popular because we love to see "life" at work.

We can easily sit back and admire our position as human beings in the higher echelons of the biological league on earth. For instance amoebas are very small and can't cover much ground when they move. They also struggle with direction. But dogs can move around much better because they have four legs to carry them from one place to another. On the downside they have to carry things in their mouths (which can't always be pleasant, although the dogs themselves never seem to mind). Apes, on the other hand, can get around well, plus they have the added advantage of having hands in which they can hold things, which is certainly more effective than putting items in your mouth. But a disadvantage with monkeys is that they can't talk very well and limit their communications to screams and oohs. Yet humans can move around well, carry things in their hands, and communicate exceptionally well through speech. Yes, us humans are certainly close to the highpoint of God's good creation. And we could content ourselves in that fact alone but it would be wrong to do so, because we have a higher calling to the rest of the inhabitants of planet earth. They may be content with their biological lot but we are not. Life started low and got higher with each successive leap, and human beings, though we were made a little lower than the angels, are called to reach up to where we can breathe that same spiritual air. For we have something lower biological life does not have—we have spirit. We read that God said, "Let the earth produce living creatures," then said, "Let us make man in our image." Yes, we share a common chemical base with all biological life, but we also share a common spiritual base with spiritual life. God is spirit and we are made in his image.

Genesis is eager for us to grasp that we are made in God's image because we have a nice learning aid in the form of a poetic verse.

> So God created man in his own image . . .
> In the image of God he created him . . .
> Male and female he created them. (Gen 1:27)

It's important that we grasp this point. Believers in the Bible have to part company with materialists, naturalists, and humanists if they tell us that humans are no more than a biological machine, albeit a very sophisticated machine. I recently watched a nature show on TV. The presenter was Steve Backshall who has become a hit with children and their parents who watch BBC's *The Really Wild Show*, a show about animals. The TV show is great. Steve got me thinking when he showed some interesting footage of himself with chimpanzees, partly because I love to watch the chimps, (if I go to a nature reserve I could watch the apes all day and not bother with the other animals) and partly because we are told that chimps are our closest living relative who share about 98 percent of our DNA. Steve showed us some chimps that actually use tools, (after a manner of speaking), they got some wood and smashed it down on a nut to break the shell, and they then ate the nut.

The human spirit is what separates us from animals. We have creative thought; animals have instinct. This is the point where Christians differ from naturalists. All animals have instincts that enable them to live and survive. We have instinct but we also have spirit and it's the mind of man that uses our brain to sometimes override our instinct, hence we curb our sexual instinct until the circumstances are right, or at least we ought to. However animals only have instinct; we could look on it as God's gift to them. Each animal seems to have a special instinct, one in which it excels. For instance when I was at my friend's house, he went into the kitchen to make a drink and left me on the sofa listening to the weather forecast on the radio. I noticed the weather reporter repeating something he had said about 15 seconds before. When my friend Steve came back in the room and I mentioned it to him, he said, "It's not the radio it's my budgie." Sure enough I went over to a birdcage in the corner of the room and there was a budgerigar repeating what he had heard earlier on the radio. I was fascinated and laughed.

Such is the gift some animals have. Dogs are excellent at sniffing things out, which is very useful for law enforcement. Some animals are strong, which is important for farming, particularly before the industrial revolution. Foxes are cunning, cheetahs run fast, bees dance to explain direction, birds build excellent nests, pigeons find their way home, and apes ape. Apes copy things they see, it's deep inside them to do that. So saying that chimpanzees can paint or use tools is no different than saying budgies can tell us the weather forecast; these skills are instincts that God placed within them. Naturalists like to make a point that chimps are really no different than us, just one step lower down the chain of life forms. Christians point out that whatever views we have about the way God created life, he did create life and that humans are in fact a lot different to the ape family because God has put spirit into us and we were made in his image.

Genesis tells us that living creatures were produced from the ground. "Let the earth bring forth living creatures after their kind: cattle and creeping things and beasts of the earth after their kind" (Gen 1:24 nasb).

Again we find that science and Genesis are not in conflict. We said earlier that all 98 naturally occurring chemical elements of the periodic table made their way from the stars to this one planet and placed themselves neatly into the earth's crust; 59 of those elements found their way into the human body. The earth's crust is rich with them. We are all made of stardust. The phrase sounds like a line from a poem or song, but there is some solid science behind this statement too: almost every element on earth was formed at the heart of a star. It's the dust from the stars that made the elements that made the earth that we are made from. The heavens were created first, remember?

Genesis doesn't present us with fanciful myths of how human beings were lowered to the ground by the gods; the opening book of the Bible stays true to the physical process that scientists inform us shaped the universe.

Men who did not have a vast reservoir of scientific knowledge wrote it, yet in its own way Genesis stands solid and accurate when compared to modern scientific insight.

CHAPTER 3

Three Levels

THE SECOND CHAPTER OF Genesis begins:

> Thus the heavens and the earth were completed in all their vast array. (Gen 2:1)

To make sure we know that it is the stars, moon, sun, planet earth, and all its varied life forms we have just been reading about, the words "in all their vast array" are used. The work is complete, a job well done. Then God takes a break and gives us an important principle to live by: if God takes a day off then we who are tiny in comparison should take a day off too. But what about the length of God's week, isn't it a lot larger than our week? Well it would make sense if it were because God is a lot larger than we are, the heavens themselves cannot contain him. Our week is probably commensurate to our size, we are small so our week is small, but the principle still holds that we need to take a day off equivalent to our human frame.

Then in Genesis chapter 2 we come to a phrase that's used frequently throughout Genesis: "these are the generations of." It's used to explain someone's family line, and who is related to whom, and how they are related. It seems odd, but the first time this phrase is used it's not about someone's family, or at least not at first glance. It's about heaven and earth's generation. How can heaven and earth have children?

If the earth is made from the dust generated by stars and we are made from the earth then there is a way we could look at it to suggest that we are heaven and earth's offspring. We have heard of the phrase mother earth, a name that some religions make quite a lot of. But I don't think that's the point here. There is something else we ought to consider.

When Jesus taught his disciples to pray he told them to begin with "Our father who is in heaven." It's important to understand that the early chapters of Genesis teach us about the universe we inhabit but also teach us something important about the spiritual world we inhabit. Remember that God put spirit within humans, so we cannot live by bread alone.

The astute reader of Genesis may slowly become aware of another meaning as they read its narrative. When a person reads it a number of times they may become aware that there are more meanings. The book is written in a very clever way, not dissimilar to the way C. S. Lewis wrote the Narnia stories with levels of meaning—there's the story itself, and later people began to realize there was a secondary meaning to the stories, and recently it was discovered that there was actually a third level. People can view the creation story in Genesis in a similar way. So far, we've been looking at the story itself, which we will continue to do. Some people like to think about the story itself, others about the way the story reveals what science has taught us, but maybe there is another level that we can look at it from. Moses, who is credited with writing quite a lot of Genesis, was a poet, and a good one, his writings contained not only an aesthetic quality but also a prophetic vein running through them. One of the ways we can look at the opening chapters of Genesis is to look for the poetic and prophetic aspects of the creation narrative. Such as when the serpent deceives Eve and so God says, "I will put enmity between your offspring and hers; he will crush your head, and you will strike his heel." We understand this means something prophetically, but at the time it was written people might have struggled to understand what exactly it referred to. The devil did strike Christ's heel, because Jesus had a nail go through it, but at the same time Jesus crushed Satan's plan when he rose from death.

So let's take a brief poetic view of the opening of Genesis. On the first day God said, "Let there be light," he then separated the light from the darkness calling it day and night. This opening picture sets the scene for a parallel used throughout the rest of the Bible. The darkness came first but God has called us out of darkness into his marvelous light. We are children of the day and children of the light. We do not belong to the night or to the darkness, said the apostles Peter and Paul.

On day two, there was a dividing of the waters. God made an expanse, and separated the waters that were below the expanse from the waters that were above the expanse. God called the expanse heaven. This is important for us to know; some things are above and some things are below. It's good for us to keep this in mind as we live our lives and as we read the scriptures. Daniel saw four beasts coming up from below out of the sea. John was told to come up higher and he saw a rainbow around the throne in heaven. Jesus ascended into the clouds. This doesn't mean that if we look hard enough into space we'll see him, but it does teach us that there is somewhere higher than this earthly plane we live on.

On day three, dry land appeared with trees bearing fruit with seed in them. Later in the story we find out that one tree in particular was called the tree of life; it stood in a garden that God had planted. God told Adam he was free to eat from any tree in the garden including the tree of life (only the fruit from one tree was prohibited). But no one got to eat from the tree of life, or did they? Jesus proclaimed himself to be "the life" and said, "I tell you the truth, unless you eat the flesh of the Son of Man and drink his blood, you cannot have eternal life within you" (John 6:53 nlt). So maybe we can still eat from the tree of life, it's not without reason that we are encouraged to "taste and see that the Lord is good."

Day four and God made a great light and a lesser light to shine on the earth. Strangely or poetically the word sun is not used here and neither is the word moon. But Jesus did say, "I am the light of the world." Jesus had a relative called John about whom Jesus said John was a shining light. Two lights: one greater, one lesser. There were also stars and Jesus told each one of us not to hide our own lights. Paul reminded the Philippians to shine like stars in the universe.

On days five and six God created fish, fowl, livestock, and creatures that creep along the ground. Then he made man in his image and told him to rule over the beasts and over every creeping thing that creeps on the earth. But there was one creeping thing that turns up in the story quite soon after this. The man and woman were suppose to rule over it, but the opposite happened, the creeping serpent ruled over the woman and man, which highlights the fact that man needs saving from our own condition. We needed someone who was strong enough to rule over the serpent.

So when Genesis chapter 2 says, "These are the generations of the heavens and of the earth" it's good to bear in mind the spiritual and poetic aspects of the story we are reading. God is in heaven and we are on the earth. A generation happens when there is a coming together of two parties opposite to each other: male and female. Genesis begins to tell us that there is a generation where heaven and earth come together and offspring ensue—a plan for heaven to come to earth. And if we look along the chain of time the New Testament tells us that the Son of Man came from heaven to the earth. Already here in the early chapters of Genesis we begin to see there is a plan afoot: a plan to bring heaven and earth together right there in the first book of the Bible. In the last book of the Bible we read that the dwelling of God is now with man. If we tread carefully and search the matter out we will begin to see just how intricate and wonderful the plan is.

CHAPTER 4

Humanity

THE KING JAMES VERSION says:

> These are the generations of the heavens and of the earth when they were created. (Gen 2:4)

As we have read Genesis chapters 1 and 2 we have got used to the phrase, "heavens and earth," maybe without even realizing it. Chapter 1 begins with, "In the beginning God created the heavens and the earth." Chapter 2 begins by using the same phrase, "Thus the heavens and the earth were completed in all their vast array." We have been talking about the heavens and the earth in all their vast array when suddenly, without warning, the phrase is turned around and reads: "in the day that the LORD God made the earth and the heavens." We said earlier that biblical Hebrew has a small number of words—under 9000—compared to modern English which has over 450,000, so when there is a change in phrasing we ought to take note because it is probably there for a reason. The language may have had some limitations but there are still ways of making a point. We are not talking about the "heavens and earth in all their vast array" anymore we are talking about "the earth and heavens." Suddenly we are no longer considering the astronomical point of view, but from a location on the earth looking up at the heavens. The writer of these words never had the benefit that we have of knowing what our planet or the solar system actually looked like, and yet Genesis does a splendid job of explaining the universe. But now the text moves on and it turns "heavens and earth" around so the earth is first. If we stand on the earth it means we are in a particular location. In this location, of which the narrative is talking about, we read that no shrub of the field had yet appeared and there was no rain, neither was there a man to work the ground. Wherever this location is on the earth it is dry and arid.

We could suppose that the entire planet was dry but I don't think we are talking about the whole planet here for several reasons. Firstly, chapter 1 has dealt with the planet and it has been completed as part of the vast array.

Secondly, we are no longer talking about "heavens and earth" but "earth and heavens," or as we might put it today, "earth and sky."

Thirdly, the modern mind usually thinks of the globe when we say "the earth" but to the people in those days that image wasn't there. They saw the landscape of where they were standing with the horizon a few miles away, and the sky—earth and heavens.

Fourthly, we are actually told where this location is a few sentences further on. It is in the east, in an area called Eden in southern Mesopotamia, modern Iraq. If you've seen pictures of Iraq you will know it's a dry place, there's not a lot of rainfall. But in those early days something happened that caused water to stream into the area.

The people who lived in Mesopotamia over 4000 years ago shared stories about someone who caused the waters to flow, which made the area fertile. That's why God chose that spot to plant a garden. There were four rivers that helped with the supply of fresh water, which brings me to the fifth point of why we are not talking about the whole world here but a location in the world and that point is fresh water. If no rain had fallen anywhere in the world fresh water would be in very short supply. Water on land naturally flows downwards following the course of least resistance until it eventually winds up in the sea. If water didn't evaporate the seas would fill up with no way of getting the water back up onto the high points of the earth. Plants need fresh water; salt water is bad for plants (unless it's sea weed). We get fresh water mostly from seawater that evaporates and falls back down to earth. Gravity then causes it to run down mountains and into valleys and then on into the sea, where it becomes salty again, but the minerals in it are left behind when it evaporates again. As we have said earlier, this happens forty times a year.

Genesis 2:5 mentions that God had not sent rain, not that it had never rained anywhere on the planet. Knowing this helps the reader to understand that not only is this area arid but also the garden of Eden period is pre-diluvian. We can infer a warning in the text: there is a time to come when rain would fall upon this arid land and when it did there would be serious consequences.

In 1987, a group of geneticists published a study in the journal *Nature*. The researchers examined the mitochondrial DNA taken from 147 people across all of today's major racial groups. The geneticists concluded that every person on earth right now could trace his or her lineage back to a single common female ancestor. The study sounds as if it is running parallel to what we have heard some people tell us of the Genesis account, until the geneticists go on to tell us that this certain female who was named Mitochondrial Eve lived 200,000 years ago. She, of course, is not to be confused with Eve who came from Adam's rib.

We know that Genesis chapter 1 tells us that at some point on God's sixth working day he said, "Let us make man in our image." If the days of God's working week were long, as we have said, and God's creative process was a sculpting of living creatures until they got closer and closer to what God intended, then there came a point when God said, "Let us make man in our image," because up to that point living creatures however close to being human they were, were not made in God's image. There are remains from earlier human type creatures and their names usually begin with Homo. Genesis talks about God making creatures after their "kind" which is a group marked by common characteristics; these days we say "genus," humans are from the genus Homo, we are called Homo sapiens. All of the earlier models died out, we can see evidence of them but they are dead. They have been wiped out perhaps by the Ice Age or climate change or for some other reason. In a local park near to where I live there is a large rock that doesn't belong in our area's natural geological rock strata. There is a plaque on the boulder that tells us sheets of ice brought the rock from North Wales in the last Ice Age. It's possible that the Neanderthals struggled with the changing conditions brought by increasingly cold temperatures.[1]

There came a point when God put his finishing touches to the human frame as we know it: he included human spirit. He placed something immaterial in each human being, making us more than a cloud of atoms. We not only had a brain in our heads but also a mind with which to reason; we still possessed our instincts but also had compassion, humanity, and a conscience. Homo sapiens are made in God's image. "God blessed them and said, 'Be fruitful and increase in number.'" Then, the King James Version and the American Standard Version of the Bible say, God told them to

---

1. Mayell, "Climate Change Killed Neandertals," lines 1–2.

"replenish the earth." The Hebrew word for replenish is *male* and replenish is a legitimate way of translating it; it can also be translated "to fill." If Homo erectus, Homo antecessor, and Neanderthal man, etc. were wiped out then replenish would be a good word for Genesis to use, because to replenish something means to refill it.

When Paul was speaking to the Athenians about God some modern versions of the Bible say he said, "From one man he made all the nations, that they should inhabit the whole earth" (Acts 17:26). In the Greek text it states, "He made of one every nation of men." The text doesn't actually say the word "man." It could mean one stock, one earth, or as some manuscripts say, "one blood." Scientists tell us that as well as Mitochondrial Eve there is a Y-chromosome Adam. They say that all men living now have a Y chromosome descended from that one man. All mitochondrial genomes today should be traceable to a single woman, a mitochondrial Eve. Whereas the Y chromosome is passed from father to son, mitochondrial DNA is passed from mother to daughter and to son. So if we think that God made mankind 6000 years ago or a lot further in the past, Paul is correct either way. The point Paul is making is that all mankind is made from one substance; we are all the same. No one nation can say they are any better than any other nation. We are all equal; we are all made in God's image. The Lord may have different jobs and tasks for us all, just like he singled out Adam and Eve for a special purpose.

Then God gave the humans he had made every seed-bearing plant on the face of the whole earth to eat and every tree that has fruit with seed in it. This happened in chapter 1 of Genesis where we are still talking about all of the earth, not just a location on the earth. That's why verse 29 says, "the whole earth" or "all the earth." When we get to chapter 2 of Genesis, we are talking about a garden that God has planted in a certain location and most of the chapter is about what happens in and around the garden. The garden was an arid place at first, no men went there because it was dry and nothing would grow, but God watered the area and it became fertile. There was a good reason that the Lord was doing all this planting and preparation. Something very important was about to take place.

When God mentions that he made man back in chapter 1, he made man in the plural sense; God made humans, he made them male and female. In chapter 2 God breathes into a human and places him in the garden. Some people struggle with chapter 2, skeptics say Genesis chapter 2 was written by someone else who had a different story than the guy who wrote chapter 1, because when you read it in Hebrew chapter 2 says man is made first and then the animals, but in chapter 1 it was the other way around. Some supporters of the Bible say, "It's just a retelling of chapter 1 and the added English words are there to help us understand the tense." But chapter 2 stands up on its own without anyone needing to prop it up. Man was made from the ground and so were the animals; it's not just Genesis chapter 2 that reminds us about that. Abraham called himself dust and ashes (Gen 18:27), and in times of sadness people in the Old Testament would throw dust on their heads. It's a reminder that we are all made from the dust of the earth and to that dust we must return. God places a man in the garden who, like all men, had come from the dust of the ground. But God did something special to this one man, he breathed into him and something from God went into him. He became living and when we say living, he really did live, he lived to be 930 years old. And furthermore, God said to him something different because previously in chapter 1 God had said to both male and female that every tree that has fruit with seed in it would be theirs for food. But now in the garden he instructs this one man that there is a tree that he must not eat from.

Genesis essentially moves forward in chronological order. Genesis chapter 2 is a natural progression from chapter 1, not a retelling of chapter 1. If we are totally honest when we've read the first few chapters of Genesis without thinking too much about them, we get the feeling that although we are reading about Eden and its garden there are other people around too. Let's look at Adam and Eve's son Cain. Cain was thrown out of the area because he killed his younger brother Abel. He was distressed not because he'd killed his brother but because he was being driven from the land and was afraid that anyone who found him would kill him. It seems a little strange to worry about that if the only people around are your mom and dad. Even if Adam and Eve had more children they would be few in number compared to all the space in which Cain could hide throughout the whole earth. We don't read of anyone else being expelled from the land except Cain; it was his punishment.

Cain went to live in the land of Nod and we then hear he has a wife. It sounds like his wife came from Nod. There is a thought that Cain married his sister, but we read that Cain lay with his wife after he'd got to Nod. It seems unusual that a man and wife wouldn't sleep together until they'd travelled a distance and set up a home. Cain may have wanted to wait because he was being responsible, but that doesn't seem in line with what we know of Cain. We know he got downcast and let his face show it, we know he got angry, and we know he was a murderer. So expecting Cain to "do right by his woman" may be expecting too much. It looks like she came from Nod. Cain's wife got pregnant and while she was expecting the child, Cain was already building a city. Don't you need a lot of people for a city to exist? Also when Adam and Eve ate from the tree God told them not to eat from they were ashamed because they were naked. Usually husbands and wives are not ashamed to be naked in front of each other, so who were they ashamed to be naked in front of enough that they sewed fig leaves together to cover up? I don't think the answer is God because when he came along they hid themselves. The fig leaf coverings were for some other reason.

Let's take a look at the short poem that Genesis chapter 1 gives us:

> God created mankind in his own image,
> in the image of God he created them;
> male and female he created them.

Some English versions write it as:

> God created man in his own image,
> in the image of God created he him;
> male and female created he them.

Notice the singular word "him" in the English version. But the Hebrew Masoretic text uses the word "them." But even if we go for the word "him" it is still talking of humans in the generic sense because of the qualifying statement at the end of the verse, "male and female he created them." Science and Genesis are again in agreement.

Chapter 5

Good with Words

ADAM, WHO HAD GOD'S breath in him in some special way, could not find a compatible companion.

> But for Adam no suitable helper was found. (Gen 2:20)

Adam, who walked around naked, a strong perfect example of humanity, a human who was so well biologically developed that he would live 930 years; he must have been handsomely proportioned, a wonder to behold. Adam, the clever man endowed with enough wisdom to name all the animals in the area and look after a garden with many and varied fruit trees. Adam, this Adam, had looked, but could see no one to match his nature and capabilities. It's a common theme; a young man will look for a woman with whom he is compatible. If there's no one around he feels comfortable with he'll stay single. For Adam there was no one else around who had that special touch from God that gave him these special qualities. So God had to step in and take things into his own hands. He put Adam under anesthetic and took a piece of this special man and made a special woman. This was a part of heaven coming to earth because through the seed of this couple Christ was to be born. We begin to see the phrase often used in Genesis, "These are the generations of" actually taking place. This generating of Adam and Eve will lead to heaven and earth touching each other, because chapter 2 starts this episode by saying, "These are the generations of the heavens and of the earth."

When God made Eve the event was special in that she was made from another channel to most people. If we believe in God then we can accept that Eve, Adam's wife (as opposed to Mitochondrial Eve) was made in an advanced molecular biologically engineered way by God, probably utilizing Adam's stem cells.

Eve was like Adam, she was going to live long; they were given the title "living" by God (Gen 2:7). She had a certain innocence that made both of them nonchalant about walking around naked. She was taken from Adam—bone of bone, flesh of flesh. Then Genesis immediately draws a lesson for us all from it saying, "Therefore shall a man leave his father and his mother, and shall cleave unto his wife: and they shall be one flesh." The lesson was acted out in a most dramatic way.

There were animals that were alive, and humans that had been made in Genesis 1 who were alive too, but Adam and Eve had something that God had breathed into them that gave them the title "living beings." Clay tablets have been found from ancient Mesopotamia that speak of long-living people. We have stories of a man called Adapa who was created as chief among men, he was endowed with special wisdom, and he had been warned by a god not to eat a certain food. He is summoned to appear before father-god and given a garment to wear, and though he could have acquired eternal life he missed out. There are a number of other parallels with Genesis and we have to allow for mythological embellishments that get passed down from storyteller to storyteller each adding their own little bit, but it seems the core of the story we find in Genesis is there in the Mesopotamian stories too. Some people may think the Bible is no different than the myths; the stories got embellished and changed. But the Bible is a book we can trust. It was Moses who first started talking about a "book"; it crops up in the first few books of the Old Testament, as if there was something special about this particular book.

Many of the stories contained in the "book" have their beginnings in Mesopotamia. The Sumerians lived in the southeast of Mesopotamia, where the rivers meet up and then enter into the Persian Gulf; their land is called Sumer. The Akkadians lived further upstream of the Euphrates and Tigris Rivers in a northwest direction; they were based around the city of Akkad. The city-states of Sumer and Akkad rose from the Ubaid culture, which settled in the arid land of southern Mesopotamia about 5500 BC. Cities sprang up here with names that became well known, such as Ur, Eridu, and Uruk.

Agriculture benefited by the use of irrigation systems. A complicated system of canals was constructed and maintained. The Mesopotamian people were industrious and excelled in a number of areas. They were particularly good writers and we still have many of their documents and journals that were written on clay tablets, even though they were written thousands of years ago. We know that there is a correlation of writings about creation and a flood, plus other parts of the Genesis narrative that were written by the Mesopotamians and not Moses. In fact Moses wrote many years after the Mesopotamian writers, which leads some people to say that Moses plagiarized earlier stories when he wrote in Genesis. And it's true that stories about how one man built a boat and saved some people and animals from drowning in a flood existed long before Moses talked about them. In fact there are several ancient stories about a flood.

In the Sumerian King List, kings who lived before the great deluge lived very long lives. In the Epic Of Gilgamesh the man who built the boat released a dove and a raven from the boat to see if the waters had receded. We read the same things in Genesis, although they don't agree at all points, maybe partly because it's the nature of journalists to report events from their personal point of view. What the Bible claims to do is tell us things from God's point of view. What seems certain is that the people of Mesopotamia talked about what had happened to previous generations because they had heard it from their parents who heard it from their parents, etc. . . . We all know that human forgetfulness, exaggeration, or worse, lying, can twist stories. The area I live in now is having a friendly debate about a local landmark that got its name in the late 1800s. There are three distinct stories of how the landmark got its name and no one is quite sure which one is correct although there is a common theme that runs through all of them. This situation goes to show how a story can get altered in only 140 years.

Abraham first met God in Mesopotamia; he then journeyed northwest to what is now southern Turkey, then turned south to Canaan and Egypt. The journey was a common trade route in those days. Abraham would have known all these stories of what had happened to previous generations and would have passed them on to his family. Abraham may have began to record these events himself, as he was a businessman and we know that traders found writing useful because we still have many records of trade from that area written on clay tablets. But even if he used word of mouth or what is known as "oral tradition," he took the job seriously. He passed on to his family all he knew about his family's history and all he knew about what God had told him. A few hundred years later Moses formalized the "book" because the Lord was interested that his side of the story should be told and gave Moses that task. The assignment of preserving these words was a full-time job for many of the subsequent generations; the scribes were an important part of Jewish culture. God had chosen Abraham and his family for a number of reasons and one of them was to preserve the record.

In the book of Romans in the New Testament Paul asks, "What advantage then, is there in being a Jew?" He answers his own question by saying, "Much in every way! First of all, they have been entrusted with the very words of God." So that's how Paul saw it, he put the preservation of God's words at the top of the list of special advantages for the family of Abraham, Isaac, and Jacob, words that go back to early Mesopotamia where God first planted a garden. God took men whom he trusted and spoke with them. They used their own knowledge of history, and anything they didn't know but needed to, was told them by God who was able to correct any errors that may have crept in. Because as well as human fallibility in recalling something that has happened there was also someone who made it his business to actually cast doubt on the words that God spoke. He spoke to Eve in the garden saying, "Did God really say . . . " calling into question the words that were spoken by God. It's no wonder that all the early records of what happened in the garden, the Flood, and other stories from Mesopotamia differ from the Bible and differ even from each other, because it was someone's work to confuse the issue. But "God is not the author of confusion." God gave Abraham and his children a job to do and they rose to the task. We have preserved for us a body of writings that is sometimes called the "Holy Scriptures," in fact Paul himself referred to them in that way. Holy comes from the same root word as "whole," the dictionary puts it like this: "that must be preserved whole or intact." And these writings have, by and large, been kept intact and whole by the family of Abraham, because that was a job that was given to them to do. The scriptures are like no other book we've ever known, they are a direct connection with the past, and they affect the present, and project into the future.

CHAPTER 6

Son of Man

ADAM HAD A WIFE made from one of his ribs.

> The LORD God fashioned into a woman the rib which He had
> taken from the man, and brought her to the man. (Gen 2:22 nasb)

Usually when two people get married they both have a different genetic
make-up, and their children are a 50 percent mixture of both parents, but
Adam and Eve had the same genes because Eve was taken directly from
Adam. Each cell in the body contains 23 pairs of chromosomes. One chromosome from each pair is inherited from your mother and one is inherited
from your father. So when Adam and Eve had children they would inherit
Adam and Eve's composition; they generated offspring like themselves.
Adam couldn't marry any woman who happened to be around the area
because they would have different DNA.

God had planted something into Adam and consequently into Eve
because she inherited Adam's flesh and bone. God planted a seed in Adam
and when God talks to the serpent we get to hear that the woman has a
seed inside her. Seeds can stay in the ground for a long while before they
germinate, many years sometimes. God breathed into Adam, then years
later the Holy Spirit, when the time had fully come (Gal 4:4), overshadowed
Mary and the seed that had been planted in Adam began to grow in Mary's
womb and God sent his only begotten Son into the world. We plant seeds in
the ground, and man was taken from the ground. God took a heavenly seed
and planted it in the earthly Adam. The noun Adam is also the masculine
form of the word *adamah* which means "ground" or "earth." It also means

"man" who was taken from the earth. God breathed into Adam planting a seed, he then overshadowed Mary and the seed was fertilized. Those are the two strands of the divine DNA from heaven that began to replicate in a young girl who gave birth in Bethlehem. The process had a beginning and it had an end. Adam was an ordinary man who had something placed into him by God, Mary was an ordinary woman who had the seed she was carrying fertilized by God. Heaven was touching earth. Jesus, who is called "The life" (John 14:6), passes that life on to us all.

> To all who received him . . . he gave the right to become children of God. (John 1:12)

> These are the generations of heaven and earth when they were created. (Gen 2:4 kjv)

God represents heaven and Adam represents the earth. The generating line of Adam and Eve is important because it leads to Christ. Satan would try to extinguish this line through direct murder or mixing it with other DNA, or even mixing it with "other flesh." This attack on the line of generation continues right up to just before Christ was born, when King Herod commands that all the male boys up to the age of two in the vicinity of Bethlehem should be killed.

We tend to think of Eve's creation as immediate but her formation may not have been that way. The text intimates that when God had finished fashioning the woman he brought her to the man. We are not told how long the fashioning took. Modern stem cell research is still in its infancy yet we are learning that there is amazing potential in being able to fashion cells though it takes time. Scientists in Australia have already grown the first kidney from stem cells.[1] God fashioned Eve, somewhere private, and then brought her to the man when the process was complete. But it was not only Adam who was interested in the woman.

We get to read about the devil fairly early in Genesis, he is given a name called "the serpent." The name is appropriate because snakes have a forked tongue and Satan speaks deceptively. Snakes are cunning, waiting camouflaged, looking for prey, and then they suddenly pounce, injecting poison into the system of their victim. So a serpent is a fitting title. Ridicule is sometimes poured on the story of Eve being tempted by a talking snake: "How can a snake speak?" "Snakes don't have a larynx or vocal chords!" But that's not what the text is talking about. We said earlier that humans

1. Pearlman, "Kidney Grown," line 1.

are close to the highpoint of God's creation, and that's true but we are not the highpoint, because there are creatures that surpass us. We are made a little lower than they are. They don't need a material body to live; they are spirits—angels. However, if they want to make an appearance in the material universe that we inhabit then they are able to appear as men.

There are stories of angels who appear as men in the Bible. (And myths outside the Bible of a similar nature where gods visit earth.) In the Bible Samson's mother tells his father that she'd met a man who she thought was an angel. Some time later she met the man again and ran off to find her husband, Manoah. When the skeptical Manoah met the man himself he said, "Are you the one who talked to my wife?" It wasn't until later that day when the angel did something that humans can't do that Manoah realized it was an angel. This tells us that angels have the ability to take a step down and appear in a corporeal form. I guess it's the opposite of when a human being dies and we cast off our mortal frame but our spirit remains. What we garner from these stories is that angels are pure life, without material restrictions, spirits who can dip into the material universe and appear, as they wish, as men. God grants them that ability. I know a few people who believe they've met an angel although I have never met one myself, as far as I'm aware. We are told to treat all people with respect because sometimes people have entertained angels without realizing it. Manoah was one such person.

Satan was created as an angel and could stand and talk to Eve face to face; he could take on flesh like any other angel. He could appear to Eve as a man. Genesis, with some scorn, labels Satan a serpent along with the beasts. Jude in the New Testament says some people have gone the way of Cain; they are like brute beasts. After Satan tempted Eve he tempted Cain. The LORD God warned Cain that sin was crouching at his door but that he must master it. Satan crouches waiting to pounce on unsuspecting victims. Serpent is the name given him in Genesis because it fits his character well.

We get to hear the dialogue between the serpent and the woman. Eve is tempted and falls into the trap. She eats from the tree that God had told Adam not to eat from, gives some of the fruit to her husband and he eats it too. This isn't the first sin that we read about in Genesis, the first sin is committed by the serpent when he tempts the woman. And then it is the woman who sinned before Adam, then Adam himself sinned. This is a good picture of us all because we have all sinned. But sin goes even further back and we don't read about that until we get to the New Testament.

Now I need you to stay with me here. I may have to quote a couple of scriptures. Remember that it is the glory of God to conceal a matter, so if we want to be kingly and search things out, we have to stay with the thread. We see through a glass darkly, we know that, but sometimes it's not quite so dark as it has been in the past, because God gives us light.

Romans 5:12–13 says, "Therefore, just as sin entered the world through one man, and death through sin, and in this way death came to all people, because all sinned—To be sure, sin was in the world before the law was given, but sin is not charged against anyone's account where there is no law."

So sin was already in the world but until we had a specific law, men couldn't see it for what it was. The first law that we read about is when God told Adam not to eat from the tree of the knowledge of good and evil. "And the LORD God commanded the man, 'You are free to eat from any tree in the garden; but you must not eat from the tree of the knowledge of good and evil, for when you eat from it you will certainly die.'" The scripture we read from Romans tells us that sin was in the world before this command— "To be sure, sin was in the world before the law was given," but sin is not charged against anyone's account where there is no law. So here is the first man who is given a specific command to follow but he breaks it. The law reveals what is in the heart of man. God has granted us free will and each man has turned to his own way. The book of Romans goes into some detail telling us that it is the law that highlights sin. Adam is representative of us all, not only those who were after him but those who were before him too. That's why he's called Adam; his name also means "man," which can be used as a singular or plural word. Men and women need saving. God steps in and starts putting the great plan of man's salvation into effect right here with Adam and Eve.

Sin entered the world through one man, though we know it was in the hearts of men before Adam broke the law God gave him. But it wasn't known as sin until there was a command. Romans 7:7 says, "I would not have known what sin was had it not been for the law." And verse 13 continues, "in order that sin might be recognized as sin."

So Adam let us see the debt we are all in, and through Adam's line God is going to send a second Adam to pay what is owed.

According to the Bible, "The first man Adam became a living soul. The last Adam became a life-giving spirit. Howbeit that is not first which is spiritual, but that which is natural; then that which is spiritual. The first man is of the earth, earthy: the second man is of heaven" (Cor 15:45–47 asb).

As we said, Adam means "man." So when Christ is called the Son of Man the entire generating line all the way from Adam down to Jesus is being recalled. Christ is the second Adam with a direct link to Adam himself. Of course there were generations in between; when Christ is called the second Adam it doesn't mean that he was born straight after the first Adam, no, but something that God put into Adam made its way through the line of generations to Jesus. God's breath or Spirit deposited something into Adam so that he was called a living soul. The Hebrew word for soul is *nephesh*; it's used in the Bible for animals as well as humans. What's important about Adam's *nephesh* is that God breathed into him and he was called "living." There were other creatures who were also living but Adam was called living in a special way because of God's breath. We don't read of God breathing into any of the other creatures, even when man was made in Genesis 1. Other humans had God's breath, but it seems the garden was an illustration of what was happening in the world at large. Humans outside the garden were made with spirit inside them; we know this because they were made in God's image and part of that image includes spirit because God is spirit.

God's breath is what separates us from the animal kingdom. Job 32:8 says that, "It is the spirit in a man, the breath of the Almighty, and gives him understanding." Adam was taking part in an object lesson; we all have God's breath but the act of God breathing into Adam was highlighted. Adam stood out because of God's breath transforming his body into a living organism that would stay alive for 930 years; his body was a superb piece of biological hardware. Hebrews 10:5 says, "when Christ came into the world, he said . . . a body have you prepared for me." Jesus Christ's body was to be the perfect sin offering, it was to be a sacrifice without spot or blemish. Adam and his line had the mark of sin because he was the first man to break the law that God gave. So the Son of Man carried the sins of men in his body on the tree (1 Pet 2:24).

When Christ is called the second man ("The first man is of the earth, earthy: the second man is of heaven") it doesn't mean that he was the second man, just the same as when Adam is called the first man, it doesn't mean he was the first man created. Adam was the first man in the line to Christ. He had the "living" title that would ultimately lead to the second man. All other men weren't living in the same way as Adam. Adam could have lived forever but as with the Mesopotamian story of Adapa he missed his chance. The day Adam ate from the tree of the knowledge of good and evil he sealed his fate. That was the day he made certain death would be his to endure. But there was another man who was to come along the generations of Adam's line who wouldn't miss the target. He would have eternal life and he would give eternal life to those who received him. Adam could have helped the human race lift themselves higher, but he fell at the first hurdle. The LORD had informed Adam that he would die if he ate the fruit from the tree of the knowledge of good and evil. Adam and everyone after him who were in the line to Christ failed, they all tasted of the knowledge of good and evil and were unable to use the "life" that had been planted within them. That fruit is hard to resist, using the knowledge of good and evil for our own advantage is something we all do, we all sin and fall short. All, except one: the man Christ Jesus. We see again how the garden of Eden is an example of the wider world. The story depicts how we have all fallen short of the mark.

As well as the tree of the knowledge of good and evil there was another tree in the center of the garden called the tree of life. If someone ate its fruit it had the capability to give them eternal life. After Adam disobeyed the command, God said, "The man has now become like one of us, knowing good and evil. He must not be allowed to reach out his hand and take also from the tree of life and eat, and live forever." This is important because we note that until Adam ate from the tree of life he didn't have eternal life. There is a thought that seems popular at the moment that there was no death at all until Adam sinned, because, as we read, death entered the world through sin. This doctrine says that animals didn't die until Adam sinned neither did human life get extinguished, no death at all.

Firstly, if we think about this for a few moments we'll see that it's not the way things were. If there was no death of living creatures before Adam broke God's command, what about the smaller creatures who lived in Adam's stomach who live off the food we eat inside our intestines. We need good bacteria to help break down our food. If those bacteria didn't die and pass through his system Adam would get bloated pretty quickly, because living creatures had been given the ability to increase and multiply. Also if there were no death what would happen if, let's say, a big boulder fell from a cliff and landed on a human? The boulder would squash the human flat. It sounds to me like a flat human would be dead. Maybe he would be able to bounce back like a cartoon character but that seems nowhere close to the rules of physics we all experience. What about if his arm was severed? Or if a huge tree fell on him and he was accidentally dismembered into small parts, would all the little bits gather back together like in the movie *Terminator 2*? And if they did how long would it take them to do so? In the period where they were gathering themselves together back into the shape of a person wouldn't the person be dead? The fossil record going back for many millennia is replete with animals and humans who have died.

Secondly, Romans tells us that sin was already in the world before the law was given but sin wasn't revealed as sin and the sin wasn't imputed to men; it wasn't held eternally against us, but it was in the world and because of that so was death. Similar to a man who is in court for a crime, the judge may decide to let the man go free because he has shown remorse and has to face the consequences of his crime, which could be very hard for the man to live with. So the judge feels that the evil the man has committed carries its own penalty. Sin was in the world and because of that, men died, but the sin was not charged to their account. There was a man to come who would in fact pay the price for those sins.

Thirdly, it has also been said that when God had completed all he had made at the end of the sixth day "it was very good." So if it was very good then there couldn't have been any death. That would mean that spiders weaving their webs and catching flies didn't happen. Or cats catching rats was not good either. If creatures however small or big didn't die the world would become overrun. I was listening to a gardening program on the radio a few days ago and a man was talking about greenfly (aphids). He'd worked out that if greenfly didn't die we would soon be up to our waist in them. If animals didn't die swarms of birds would soon block out the sky because they are fulfilling God's commission to "be fruitful and increase in number." If the death of animals is a bad thing then shouldn't we all be vegetarians? If it was not good then, it is not good now. People eat animals: we eat brute beasts, creatures of instinct; we don't however, eat other people who are made in God's image because that is unacceptable. God made the food chain and it works well; it is good.

Furthermore, people die too. Adam wouldn't have lived forever in the natural state that God had made him, he needed to eat from the tree of life to live forever, and it was in his natural state that Genesis tells us, "was very good." Precious in the sight of the LORD is the death of his saints (Ps 116:15 kjv).

CHAPTER 7

Security Staff

> Remember the days of old; consider the generations long past.
> (Deut 32:7)

It is not always easy for us to see exactly how things happened in the garden because there is some concealment involved. But we do get a few glimpses into how an event could have unfolded. Windows sometimes open elsewhere in the Bible. In Ezekiel 28 (nasb) we read, "Son of man, say to the leader of Tyre." So Ezekiel speaks to the leader of Tyre. Then a little later on we read, "Son of man, take up a lamentation over the king of Tyre." Then Ezekiel speaks not to the king this time but "over" him. Tyre was a place of injustice and iniquity and so this time the message goes straight to the spirit of the power of the air. We quickly realize that it is the serpent who is being addressed.

> You were the seal of perfection, full of wisdom and perfect in beauty. . . . You were in Eden, the garden of God.
> You were anointed as a guardian cherub, for so I ordained you.
> You were blameless in your ways, from the day you were created, till wickedness was found in you.
> So I threw you to the earth.

Through this little window we get a glimpse of his work before he became known as the devil. He was a guardian cherub. The garden of Eden was a protected place, people may have seen it from a distance and they knew that the region had been irrigated. They may have even helped with digging canals from the Euphrates to the general area. But the garden itself was a special place and if anyone were allowed in, it would be by invitation only. The garden had a security team.

If you go out to a hotel or a venue there may be security staff there. If you worked in the same building, after a while you would get to know the security guards and probably talk to them, they may tell you how to get the coffee machine to work properly and pass on other bits of useful information. That could be a picture of how the woman got to talk so intimately with the serpent. Adam seems to be close by while Eve's conversation with the serpent is taking place and he doesn't seem unduly alarmed. Eve gives him some of the fruit straight away. It's as if he's used to the presence of the guardian cherub and has been listening to the conversation. When God has told the serpent that he'll go on his belly from now on, other guardian cherubs seem to have taken his place. God placed cherubim on the east side of the garden to guard the way to the tree of life. Part of the serpent's work may have been to discourage Adam and Eve from the tree of the knowledge of good and evil, but instead he did the opposite. Sin was found in him and he lost what he had.

The serpent talked with the woman, and then the LORD God talked to the serpent. The consequences of what God said to the serpent meant he now had to crawl on his belly all the days of his life and eat dust. God wasn't talking to snakes here, he was talking to Satan the devil, and the devil would no longer be able to stand on the earth. God gives license for angels to appear as flesh, Satan's license was revoked; he would be like a snake that cannot stand because it has no legs to stand upon. He would eat dust all of his days. Jesus said, "When an impure spirit comes out of a person, it goes through arid places seeking rest and does not find it." Unless someone gives Satan a home to live in he has to travel through dry waterless places. Satan came to Jesus while he was in the wilderness, a fitting place, but Jesus gave him no sanctuary.

The LORD God then said to the serpent:

> I will put enmity between you and the woman and between your offspring and hers; he will crush your head and you will strike his heel.

Straightaway God is talking about the woman's offspring. This is God's important plan and he is keen to protect it. God sees the woman as having a seed, the seed is already in the woman, God planted it. He first breathed into the man and then made the woman from the man. What was in the man was in the woman too. The life that they carried touched their bodies also. When Jesus walked about on earth he would touch people and healing and strength would flood into them. Once, a lady who was ill pushed through a crowd of people to reach him, she thought, *If I can just touch the edge of his garment.* When she reached out and touched him she was strengthened and healed. Jesus felt something leave him and started to ask the crowd who had touched him. Adam came into contact with the life, Eve too; both were in contact with the life. She was a long-liver, physically superb, and strong, God had made her as a helper to the man as he worked in the garden full of trees, she needed to be strong. Trees are hefty things, and some may say "no place for a woman," but not this woman, the work was well within her capabilities. She was carrying something important; she was "living."

It's also important for us to note that the LORD God said to the serpent that he also would have offspring. How can that be? Who can have the devil for a father? Jesus said to the Jews who were trying to kill him, "You are doing what you have heard from your father." They said, "The only father we have is God himself." Jesus replied, "If God were your father you would love me. . . . You belong to your father, the devil, and you want to carry out your father's desires. He was a murderer from the beginning, not holding to the truth, for there is no truth in him. When he lies, he speaks his native language, for he is a liar and the father of lies." They picked up stones to stone him but he slipped away. However, sometime later they got their chance to strike. The LORD had said that the serpent would strike at the heel of the woman's seed and Jesus suffered a Roman crucifixion where nails are driven through the heel. But Christ was able to deal a crushing blow to Satan because he rose from the dead and is alive forevermore. At every turn he told the devil to get behind him, and even when the serpent gave it his best poisonous strike by amassing a hostile crowd and stirring them up to threaten the Son of Man with death, Jesus still held fast.

Then, back in the garden, after the LORD had spoken to the serpent he spoke with the woman and went straight to the subject of childbearing.

> Unto the woman he said, "I will greatly multiply thy sorrow and thy conception; in sorrow thou shalt bring forth children."

The usual interpretation of this is that women now have to bear children in pain. And some versions of the Bible mention pain when translating this verse. It's true that women do bring children into the world in pain.

But let's look at what the LORD said a little more. When he spoke to the serpent he talked about the woman's seed. When he spoke to the woman he again spoke about offspring, but this time the LORD uses the plural word children. We know that the woman's seed referred to Jesus when the LORD spoke to the serpent, so let's think about that. The woman didn't actually give birth to Christ, it was Mary who did that. The Gospel of Matthew traces the lineage of Jesus through David's royal line on through to Joseph who adopted Jesus. The royal line passes from father to son—a prince becomes the next king. Luke however, traces a different line that can only be the line of Mary the mother of Jesus. Jewish tradition didn't include women in its genealogies so Joseph, Mary's husband is named at the end of it. But the line itself ends with Mary represented by Joseph who is the son (in-law) of Heli (Mary's father). That's why Joseph appears in both genealogies. When Mary presented her son Jesus at the temple, a righteous and devout man named Simeon spoke to Mary and told her that a sword was going to pierce her soul. Mary's son was killed. Eve also had a son who was killed. Sorrow was in store for both women. "I will greatly multiply thy sorrow and thy conception." As well as sorrow, the LORD also talks about the woman's conception being multiplied, Mary's conception was multiplied to the degree that she was still a virgin when she conceived.

Then the LORD spoke to Adam. Adam had been working in the garden of Eden, which was irrigated by streams (and possibly canals according to archaeological work at the Euphrates River in southern Iraq). That was going to change, all the fruit picking and managing the fruit trees was coming to an end. The garden was to be left with no one managing it. Now Adam would have to eat plants or crops that grew in the earth and not from trees, and he was told that he would eat bread by the sweat of his brow. In southern Mesopotamia the story they had of the man Adapa, whom the god Enki endowed with intelligence, and was made a chief among men went on to bake bread, "With the bakers of Eridu, he does the baking." Adapa isn't the exact same name as Adam but we have to remember that dialects and language alter from one area to another. In Hebrew Adam is pronounced Adama, which is quite close to Adapa. A little further north in Akkad, they have the name Adamu that crops up in some of their genealogies, maybe because parents like to name their children after a renowned celebrity. The clay tablets on which these stories are written also tell us where Adapa baked this bread. It's a place called Eridu, which is in southern Mesopotamia in Sumer. The Sumerian King List cites Eridu as the "city of the first kings."

> Therefore the LORD God sent him forth from the garden of Eden,
> to till the ground from whence he was taken.

Adam became a tiller of the ground. Wheat cultivation was now his new job. In Adam's day the process of turning wild grass into wheat was a relatively new technique. The early farmers of Mesopotamia played an important role when they repeatedly harvested the stronger stalks and larger grains of grass and then sowed only the stronger grains, which eventually led to the creation of domestic strains of wheat. The Iraqi's have excavated Eridu and have found remains of wheat and barley ovens for baking bread. They found 19 levels of occupation at Eridu going back to 5000 BC with some extremely fine quality pottery just above the soil where the occupation finishes. A tale of the garden has been found at Eridu in which a weaver or gardener is cursed by the great god for eating of the fruit of the forbidden tree in the garden after being told not to.[1]

The LORD God banished Adam from the garden and set cherubim on the east side of the garden to guard the tree of life. We know the garden of Eden was near the rivers described in Genesis chapter 2. The ancient cities in southern Mesopotamia, Eridu and Ur were located near the junction of the rivers we read about. Edin is a Sumerian word meaning "plain." Genesis 2:10 tells us that water flowed from Eden to water the garden, which informs us the garden was in the vicinity of Eden but not at its center. River can also mean "canal" in Hebrew. There is a canal that is written about on the Gudea Cylinders, which can be viewed in the Louvre in Paris: the reference is to the "edin canal." The two terracotta cylinders were found in the ancient city of Girsu, north of Eridu. Eridu could have been the place that Adam went to live after he left the garden and because of his qualities he would have been looked on as chief among men. Because the Mesopotamians were prolific writers we can read their side of the story. According to some of the clay tablets upon which they wrote, Eridu was reputed to have in its neighborhood a garden, a holy place, in which there grew a sacred palm tree. This tree of life appears frequently in the Mesopotamian artwork, often with two guardian spirits standing on either side.[2]

The *Ancient History Encyclopaedia* tells us that most probably Eden in the Genesis narrative is modeled on Eridu. It is situated close to the river Euphrates and a canal had been dug to provide fresh water to areas

1. Mark, "Eridu," lines 21–22.
2. G. Smith and Sayce, *Chaldean Account*, 84–85.

northwest of Eridu.[3] They have a story of a god who "caused to flow the water" and they called him Enki the Water-Lord. The Sumerian Paradise Myth says, "Enki . . . filled the dikes with water, He filled the ditches with water, He filled the uncultivated places with water. The gardener in the dust in his joy . . . , He embrac[es] him.[4]

When excavations at Eridu took place over 1000 graves were found from the fourth millennium BC. Two hundred of these were looked at in detail; the men and women had been laid in rectangular tombs constructed of sundried bricks. Buried with them was beautifully painted pottery. One woman had been buried in a skirt with an ornamental belt with a six-inch fringe of black and white beads.[5] The people who lived in the city-states of Sumer grew crops and they also grew fruit trees and date palms. Because of the lack of reliable rainfall they used irrigation ditches that channelled fresh water from the Euphrates, Tigris, and their tributaries. The irrigation channels needed constant maintenance.[6] The early Mesopotamian writings mention canals being dredged and smaller canals being cleaned to establish growth. So when we read that Adam worked in the garden of Eden there really was some work to do. It's probable that help was needed, which is why we get the feel that other people were around. Mesopotamia means "(land) between rivers" and is known as the Tigris–Euphrates basin. Both rivers start their journey in Turkey, then travel through Syria and Iraq, and join up to flow into the Persian Gulf. The first civilization in human history was that of the Sumerians. This civilization was up and running smoothly by the mid-fourth millennium BC, with the appearance of the first cities on the Mesopotamian flood plain. There were scattered villages around before that and nomadic tribes roamed the area. In the third millennium BC we hear of the Amorites who were a nomadic people and were well known to the Mesopotamians, who called them the Mar.tu. The Mesopotamian's penchant for writing means that we get to hear what they thought about the roving Amorites, and the civilized Sumerians didn't seem to think too highly of them.

"The MAR.TU who digs up truffles . . . who does not bend his knees (to cultivate the land), who eats raw meat, who has no house during his lifetime, who is not buried after death . . . They have prepared wheat and

---

3. Safer, "Eridu," 28.
4. Kramer, "Sumerian Myths," 39.
5. Lloyd, "Oldest City of Sumeria," 303.
6. Allan, *Dawn of Civilization*, 56–58.

gú-nunuz (grain) as a confection, but an Amorite will eat it without even recognizing what it contains."[7]

Archaeological excavations in Mesopotamia have revealed human settlements dating to 10,000 BC and they indicate that the fertile conditions of the land between two rivers allowed an ancient hunter-gatherer people to settle in the land, domesticate animals, and turn their attention to agriculture. But something happened in southern Mesopotamia, God stepped into human affairs and the area has since become known worldwide as the "Cradle of Civilization."

So Adam leaves the confines of the garden, but before he does the LORD God made garments of skin for the couple. Previously Adam and his wife had sewed together fig leaves as a covering. How durable these garments were we don't know, and how many garments and for how long they wore them we don't know either, but maybe when the Mesopotamian writers spoke of the man in the garden being a weaver, perhaps this is what they were referring to. However God had superior means of clothing them. It's been widely acknowledged that in order for Adam and his wife to be clothed in animal hide an animal had to die. It was a sacrifice of blood. Excavations in Turkey have found a settlement called Catal Huyuk going back to 7000 BC, where fine wood ware and textiles were found. This was a city that traded with other people groups. The people lived in homes of about 300 square feet that were made of mud bricks and plastered walls. Many shrines were unearthed too but there were no signs of any animal sacrifice.[8] God introduced animal sacrifice. "Without the shedding of blood there is no forgiveness" (Heb 9:22). Adam would have noted this because it was a practice that continued throughout Adam's offspring. Noah, Abraham, Isaac, and Jacob built altars. When excavators reached the lower levels at Eridu, they found an altar that looked like a typical altar upon which an animal would be sacrificed. It had lateral niches, and a central table. Humans sought after God with shrines but it wasn't until Adam arrived that the creator began to show us that if we want a relationship with him we must come on his terms. He loves justice and equity; injustice places us in debit, we fall short of the standard God intends for us being made in his image, and all debts must be paid. We can easily think that God saved us from our sins when Jesus died in 33 AD, and it is true, he did, but it is better

---

7. Chiera, *Sumerian Epics*, plate nos. 58, 112, parentheses in original; Chiera, *Sumerian Texts*, plate no. 3, parentheses in original.

8. Hamblin, *First Cities*, 54.

for us to realize that God started the process back in the fifth millennium BC. The chain started with Adam and finished with Jesus. The structure is manufactured and assembled by God to bring humanity into a relationship with himself.

CHAPTER 8

What Is Your Name?

BACK WHEN THE MAN is taken to the garden God says, "It is not good for the man to be alone." Then we get the phrase:

> "I will make for him a suitable helper." Now the LORD God had formed out of the ground all the beasts of the field.

However, that's the English translation, if we read it in Hebrew the word "had" is not there. The verse simply says:

> "I will make for him a suitable helper." And formed the LORD God out of the ground every beast of the field and every bird of the air and brought (them) unto Adam.

People who are skeptical of Genesis quickly say, "In chapter 1 the animals are made first but in chapter 2 they are made after the man." And, then they say, "The reason for that is because the two chapters are juxtaposed next to each other by two different authors who had two different ideas of how God created life." Their theory is that Genesis is actually put together by three groups of people, the Yahwists, named because they always call God YHWH (Yahweh), commonly referred to by scholars as "J"; the Elohists because they call God by the formal title of Elohim (God), they are known as "E"; and lastly the Priestly authors known as "P."

If we read Genesis chapter 2 alone in the Hebrew language we could end up thinking that God made man first and then made the animals, and the reason he made the animals was to show the man that there was no suitable helper among them. But we don't read Genesis chapter 2 by itself, we read it after we've read chapter 1, and in chapter 1 we know that God has already made the animals. That's why some modern English translations of the Bible insert the word "had" in chapter 2 so that it reads: "Now the Lord God *had* formed out of the ground all the beasts of the field." The more formal English translations stay true to the Hebrew text expecting the reader to piece it together himself. The same phrase structure is also used of the man in chapter 2: "The Lord God formed man from the dust of the ground and breathed into his nostrils the breath of life and man became a living being." If we can say that God had made the animals, we can also say it of the man. So when chapter 2 is talking about the arid place where no shrub or plant of the field had yet appeared, and streams (or as the Septuagint says a "fountain," some translations say a "mist") watered the surface of the ground, we could easily equate "And the Lord God formed man from the dust" with "And the Lord God *had* formed man from the dust," just like he *had* formed the animals. If we look at it like that, humans would have been on the earth for many centuries; God made them all from the ground. God took one of those men and breathed into his nostrils and he acquired the individual title of "living." So if that's what happened, how old was Adam when God breathed into him? Also at what stage of development did God create Eve? Genesis gives us some reasons that may give us the answers to those questions that we can look at later.

Back in time, in the early days of Mesopotamian civilization, God introduced himself to man. But how did that happen? We have said earlier that angels can dip into space-time and appear as men. These angelic visitors acquire a body that has atoms and molecules, but the particles in their bodies (as far as we can assume) did not come from the dirt of planet earth.

According to Einstein, energy and matter are different forms of the same thing, so when matter and antimatter annihilate each other, they actually create energy. The reaction also happens the other way around, energy can turn into matter. If angels have a life-force that's allied to energy, then accessing a body made up of matter shouldn't be a hard task. Energy can turn into matter without destabilizing the universe by introducing a new substance into it. The essence of an angel is spirit, but it is spirit that has energy. Psalm 103:20 says, "Praise the Lord, you his angels, you mighty ones who do his bidding." David in the psalm tells us that angels have strength; in fact he singled it out as one of their special attributes. We don't see angels most of the time; the material world is not their natural habitat. They seem to prefer their own environment, but when required they can appear, and they can appear as men. Angels and humans are a bit like opposite sides of the same coin.

> Angels are spirits allied to energy, and energy can turn into matter—humans have a spirit allied to matter, and matter can turn into energy.

The picture presented to us in Genesis is that God planted a garden close to the rivers. Just how God did the planting is left to our imagination, but it does suggest some sort of anthropomorphic representation of God rolling up his sleeves and getting stuck into some satisfying gardening. It may not have been that way but there are stories where it seems that God walked around the Fertile Crescent, which is a crescent-shaped area that extends from southern Mesopotamia to Egypt. Assyria and Canaan are also a part of the middle section of the crescent. The technical name for these appearances of God is "theophanies."

While Abraham was sitting at the entrance of his tent in Mamre, Israel, he saw three men standing nearby. He seemed to recognize at least one of them and asked them to stay for lunch. Abraham stood under a tree while they ate. (There is a tree called the great Oak of Mamre and the tree is thought to be over 4000 years old so could have been the same tree that Abraham stood under.) As the story progresses we become aware that one of the men is God. After they had eaten and continued their journey Abraham walked along with them and had a debate with God. So when we talk about God planting a garden maybe he really did, and planted it in much the same way as we would, perhaps with some help from the angels who helped with the irrigation ditches. God makes rare visits to earth in a material form, and if earth has been in existence for 4.54 billion years and humans for thousands of years before civilization as we know it began, then his appearance in early Mesopotamia would be a very welcome sight.

So where does Jesus fit into all this? If God can just materialize as a man, why was Jesus born from a human woman? Part of the answer is that when God or angels appeared as men, they weren't actually human men. They were men with all the abilities that men have, even the ability to reproduce, hence the stories of the nephilim, but they weren't a part of the human race. To save the human race God had to become a part of it; humanity had to be cleansed from the inside. So Jesus was born of Mary, he was Emmanuel—God with us. And he is not ashamed to call us brothers. He was born into our family that we may be born into his.

But doesn't the New Testament tell us that no man has ever seen God? Yes it does say that, and the reason is that God is Spirit, and humans cannot detect spirit with the optic nerve. We can relate to God because we ourselves have a spirit. And sometimes God relates to us and uses a body to do it. God walked around Eden and spoke with men.

After Adam had decided to weave together some fig-leaved garments, he heard the sound of the LORD God walking in the garden in the cool of the day. When we see the word LORD in capital letters in the Old Testament it usually signifies that God's name is being used, which is Yahweh. (I've adopted the same rule for this book.) Originally we only had four letters for it—YHWH, it is called the tetragrammaton, and it is a proper noun. Genesis chapter 2 starts to use it from verse 4, which is where the section about the dry ground and the water begins. When we meet someone it is normal to find out their name quite early in the conversation, so we can call each other by name. After Adam heard the sound of Yahweh walking in the garden he hid. Yahweh called out to him. This is a scenario that could take place in most people's lives. We hear someone coming who we want to avoid so we make ourselves scarce. They call out to us. We soon get to the point of embarrassment knowing the person looking for us knows we are hiding and the pretense is over, we'd better just come clean. Yahweh asks Adam if he has eaten from the tree he was told not to eat from. Adam is quick to point out that the woman Yahweh put there in the garden with him gave him some fruit from the tree and he ate it. What we see from this exchange is that Adam felt free to talk to Yahweh in a manner that is matter of fact, even perhaps hinting that a portion of the blame should be on Yahweh for putting the women there with him in the first place. Again this is a normal exchange that two men in a place of work might say to each other. One of them has been found doing something that's not within company policy, and as he looks for mitigating circumstances to get himself off the hook he may implicate his fellow worker in his misdemeanor. This shows us the kind of relationship that Adam had with Yahweh, he felt at liberty to speak in such a manner. If we skip forward a bit in the story, Yahweh said to Cain, "'Where is your brother Abel?' 'I don't know,' he replied. 'Am I my brother's keeper?'" How did these men get to speak to God in that way? Adam was pushing it a bit but Cain was patently flippant.

When Moses first went to look at the burning bush to see what was going on with it, he heard someone call his name from within the burning bush. Moses responded, "Here I am." Then the voice said, "I am the God of

your father, the God of Abraham, the God of Isaac and the God of Jacob."
At this, Moses hid his face. God revealed himself to Moses in a different
way to that of Adam and Cain.

We know that the history of man's relationship with God has been
a gradual revealing of the glory and majesty of God, the revelation didn't
happen all in one go. The Bible follows a similar route, time passes before
we get to see God the Son walk among us, talk to us, and show us his beauty,
humility, and love, and reveal the Father to us. Philip said to Him, "Lord,
show us the Father, and it is enough for us." Jesus said to him, "Have I been
so long with you, and yet you have not come to know Me, Philip? He who
has seen me has seen the Father; how can you say, 'Show us the Father?'"
God, it seems, hadn't revealed his glory to Adam or to Cain. By the time
Moses was alive, God's glory was beginning to shine through. Moses took
precautions not presuming to stare at God and hid his face. In fact God
later tells Moses he had not previously made himself known by his name
Yahweh. Adam knew the actual name Yahweh, but the glory and meaning
behind the name had not been revealed to him. "I am that I am," Yahweh,
Almighty, the self-existing.

Jesus also came in humility; he too was spoken to in a disrespectful
manner. Adam, Cain, and those in and around Eden knew Yahweh as a
gentle, kind person who, although he was strong and clever, could be spoken to as though he were simply a man.

In some parts of the academic schooling system the three groups
of scribes who are thought to have assembled Genesis consider Genesis
chapters 1—2:3 to have been arranged by P and chapter 2:4 to the end of
chapter 2 by J, because in chapter 1 God is called God, but in chapter 2
he is called LORD God. It's been said that the anthropomorphic imagery
of God walking around has embarrassed later exegetes. P and E, who are
thought to have compiled Genesis, may have wished they'd never let the
Js near the text in the first place if that's the way they are going to portray
God. But we can see quite plainly that God made the universe in all its vast
array in chapter 1, but in chapter 2 he begins to relate to men, and men
have a convention among themselves where they call each other by name. If
Yahweh was tolerant enough to put up with Adam and Cain's discourteous
comebacks, then it looks like he would be happy to call people by name and
be called by name.

CHAPTER 9

The Living Label

> Adam named his wife Eve, because she would become the mother
> of all the living. (Gen 3:20)

WE CAN SEE AT least two meanings in this statement. Firstly, in the New
Testament we are told that not every breathing human is alive. "When you
were dead in your sins . . . God made you alive with Christ" (Col 2:13). Eve's
seed would eventually be born, he in turn would pass his life on to as many
as received him; but not all men receive him. The men who were trying to
kill Jesus were told their father was the devil; they were his offspring not
offspring of the woman. To be living we need the "life," and Jesus is the
"life." The "life" that was deposited in Adam made its way into his offspring
too and somehow they received the benefits of it, they were recipients of the
fallout of having the "life" in their family tree. They lived long, were strong,
and were handsomely proportioned with a certain amount of intelligence,
which is what we would expect if the creator of the universe had breathed
something into their first forefather. We can think of it as God lighting the
fuse in Adam that burned through his genetic line until it got to Christ,
who was the consummation of it, and the power was released into the world
through Jesus. Those who are born into Christ's family inherit the power
of "life." Christ was killed but he had too much power to remain dead. He
passes this power on to us too; we are beneficiaries of it. Sometimes the
"life" touches our mortal bodies through healing or special strengthening
or blessing. And furthermore, remembering that spirit also means breath,
if the Spirit of him who raised Jesus from the dead is living in you, he who

raised Christ from the dead will also give life to your mortal bodies (Rom 8:11). Jesus came from Eve so she is the mother of all the living.

Secondly, God had given Eve the "living" tag, so her immediate biological offspring would also carry that label. We know exactly what route the "living" label took because Luke records it for us. Seth was next in line to receive it. Abel inherited it and so did Cain, but Cain killed Abel and it appears that Cain married a woman from Nod or elsewhere. So the strength, wisdom, and long years that were assigned to being "living" would be diluted if he married a human who was short-lived. The phrase that Genesis uses, "These are the generations of" is not used of Cain. The phrase is important—it is called a *toledoth*—a generating. We get to read about Cain's descendents but not with that heading. Adam's *toledoth* skips over Cain and goes straight to Seth as the next in line (Gen 5:3), even though Cain was born first.

Abel, Adam and Eve's second son, kept flocks. Dr. Denis Alexander, an evangelical Christian and editor of *Science and Christian Belief* says, "The Genesis account portrays Adam and Eve as Neolithic farmers. It is perfectly feasible that God bestowed his image on representative *Homo sapiens* already living in the Near East to generate what John Stott has called *Homo divinus*, those who first enjoyed personal fellowship with God."[1] Dr. Alexander points us to the important theme that Adam and Eve were representing all humans. The duo did have God's image, as all humans have it, what happened to Adam and Eve is played out in its own way by humans across the planet whatever era we live in.

Dr. Alexander alludes to Adam's family finding themselves in the Neolithic period. There is documentation that northern Mesopotamia had farmers around 6000 BC but southern Mesopotamia started to use farming from about 5500–4800 BC.[2] Adam had lost his position in the garden so he grew and cultivated crops and made bread. His son Cain also worked the land; Abel kept the herds.

Although the family had fallen from the height at which they were made, Yahweh is still nearby and can be approached. We start to get the picture that Yahweh made himself available. We sometimes hear of a CEO of a company who makes it hard for anyone to get close to him, he's too busy or maybe too important for ordinary people to approach. Not so with Yahweh, there is a gentle kindness, he does not treat us as our sins deserve.

1. Alexander, "Is it Possible," lines 71–75, emphasis in the original.
2. Owen, "Mesopotamia," 4, 7.

Jesus, who was of course one in essence with Yahweh, said, "Love your enemies, do good to them, and lend to them without expecting to get anything
back. Then your reward will be great, and you will be children of the Most
High, because he is kind to the ungrateful and wicked." This gives us a little
insight into the compassionate and tender nature of Yahweh. Although the
garden was now out of bounds, the area around the garden, the local plain
called Edin (in the Sumerian language) and the local city called Eridu, must
have been a pleasing and pleasant place to live. Though we know some hard
work would be called for as Yahweh had declared, "By the sweat of your
brow." Adam would now need to toil for food. He was no longer in the well-
watered garden, he would have to find a way to irrigate the land and keep
on top of ploughing, sowing, cultivation, and eradicating weeds and thistles
that would naturally grow—the trees in the garden were much easier to
maintain. But fresh water was not too far away and Yahweh was not too far
away either, adding to the security of the peaceful way of life the people of
Eridu enjoyed in the warm gentle breeze. They would have lived a simple
life with houses made from either sundried bricks or reeds from one of the
nearby marshes. The reed houses can still be seen in the same area today,
built in much the same way as they were all those years ago.

Abel brought some nice cuts of meat from his flock to Yahweh. The
smell of lamb cooking with the juices and fat is a pleasant aroma, especially
if you are hungry. Yahweh was pleased with Abel's gift, it had a nice aroma
yes, but that is not the reason that Yahweh was pleased with it. He found it
an acceptable gift because it was a drama sketch or parallel of his Son, who
would become a sweet smelling sacrifice on the cross. Cain brought some
produce from his work on the land. Yahweh was making a point here, if we
want to have a bona fide bond with God then we must come without bag-
gage, our debts must be paid. Christ will pay our debts and that is our first
priority as humans. Yahweh is putting first things first by accepting Abel's
gift because it is a message to us all. Cain didn't receive the same favorable
reaction that Abel did to his gift. Cain got very angry!

Perhaps because the benefits of being part of Adam's offspring were
lofty, if the axis turned then the negative aspects could be very low indeed.
This looks like it's a mood swing of grand proportions, so much so that
Yahweh, being the Father that he is, took Cain under his wing and said,
"Why is your face downcast?" Most of us have been spoken to like this by
someone who is older and wiser than we are. "What's the problem here?"
God goes on to tell Cain that if he lives righteously he will be accepted,

there is nothing to worry about, God has made provision for us all. Yahweh was showing friendship to Cain. If we fail to warn someone who is heading for trouble, what kind of a friend are we? So Yahweh gives Cain some excellent advice, especially knowing that there's a serpent crawling around looking for prey. God entreats Cain to be strong, coupled with instruction for him to master the feelings of jealousy and anger he is struggling with: "Because sin is crouching at your door and desires to have you." A stark warning; what else could Yahweh do?

We have freewill, it can be a marvelous gift or a heavy burden, we must choose. And Cain chose, with malice aforethought he pretends friendliness and leads Abel to a spot where he thinks no one will see, and kills his brother. Later Yahweh comes along and asks if Cain knows where his brother is. Then we get to hear Cain's curt and discourteous reply. He seems to be using a colloquial expression of indignation that he's heard people say. We have similar expressions in the modern world. Then something happened. We don't know how much Cain knew of Yahweh's abilities, maybe if he'd have known a little more of Yahweh's power he would have at least feigned respect, albeit more through fear than love. Little did Cain seem to know that Yahweh can hear cries from beyond this material world, Abel, though taken from this scene of space-time, was able to appeal. Yahweh, as if startled, exclaims to Cain, "Listen!" (Gen 4:10 niv). Can Cain hear it too? I think we can safely say that Cain could not hear it, but Yahweh certainly could. Justice and holiness are a part of God's nature, without it we cannot see the Lord. "Make every effort to live in peace with everyone and to be holy; without holiness no one will see the Lord" (Heb 12:14). Cain had made no effort; in fact the opposite was true and now he would not see the LORD. Corruption is not a part of God's kingdom and Cain, like his parents, has not been able to follow God's command. Abel's blood was crying out to God. The "life" is in the blood (Lev 17:11). Abel was from Adam's stock, which had the sublime "life" in it. How much more would this blood cry out for justice?

So far, of all the people God chose to breathe into, all but one have let him down. The only one who has brought joy to the Lord is now dead. Cain can no longer stay on the ground that received his brother's blood, he can no longer work the local fields. He is going to be a restless wanderer. Cain protests: "Behold, thou hast driven me out this day from the face of the earth; and from thy face shall I be hid; and I shall be a fugitive and a vagabond in the earth; and it shall come to pass, that every one that finds me shall slay me" (Gen 4:14 kjv). We can see from this statement what Cain meant by the "face of the earth" or "face of the ground." He meant the locality in which he had been living. He would now be a wanderer on earth.

Secondly, he was greatly worried for his life. He thought he had got away with murder, but Yahweh had hidden resources to help with detecting crimes. The area in which Cain lived was becoming civilized; there were laws and there were sentences when laws were broken. We know of Mesopotamian legal systems from around the late third millennium BC.[3] There would have been others of an earlier date, as laws tend to get built up over time and amended as they are put into practice. The code of Ur-Nammu is written on tablets that we still have today, the first law being, "If a man commits murder, that man must be killed." This is why Cain was worried for his life. Southern Mesopotamia had the first recognizable civilized city-states where people manifested the cooperative effort necessary to make urban life possible. The early Sumerian cities were characterized by a high degree of social and economic diversity giving rise to artisans, merchants, priests, bureaucrats, and for the first time in history, professional soldiers.[4]

It's plausible that Abel was well liked in the local communities. Local people would have known him as one of the wise and long-living people, who wasn't afraid to work hard as a herdsman. Now that the news was out he'd been killed they were likely to want to drag the perpetrator off to court to be tried. So Yahweh put a mark on Cain. It was common practice for people of Mesopotamia to wear a stamp or cylinder seal that was made of colorful hard stones. They were worn suspended from wrists, and were pierced through so they could be hung from a necklace too. They were used as administrative tools and identity seals; the stamp would leave an impression on soft clay so the information it contained could be distributed to an area easily, much like we use a photocopier today. The cylinder could be rolled along soft clay so that the picture, symbol, or writing that was on the cylinder would leave its impression, the clay would harden, and a document would be the finished result. Women wore their husband's seals to the grave, and men did likewise, more as a romantic gesture than anything official. This important administrative practice had its origins in central and northern Mesopotamia as early as 7000 BC.[5] Later in Genesis we find

---

3. The Code of Urukagina is widely accepted as the first recorded example of government reform.

4. Realhistoryww.com, "Ancient Man . . . Sumerian Cities," lines 4–6.

5. Ur et al., "Early Mesopotamian Urbanism," 593.

that Jacob wears a seal that's attached to him by a cord. And the book of Job also makes mention of clay taking shape under the imprint of a seal.

Cain's case had been to trial and judgement had been made and sentence passed by the highest judge in the land. So it was probably something like a stamp or seal that Cain had put upon him, so that if someone tried to take him before local judges he had a legal document to say he'd already been tried. There's a similar picture in Deuteronomy where God says, "These commandments that I give you today are to be on your hearts. Tie them as symbols on your hands and bind them on your foreheads." The Hebrew word for "symbol" is the same word as "mark" that's used for Cain. But would God write on a piece of stone and give it to someone? Well, some years after the incident with Cain that's exactly what happened, God wrote on two tablets and gave them to Moses.

Cain's mark didn't secure his life; it was only an aid. God had said that if anyone killed Cain he would suffer vengeance seven times over. Cain travelled away unable to see Yahweh anymore as his sentence dictated. Cain's punishment didn't include the loss of special attributes assigned to Adam's family, he didn't lose his intelligence or strength as we read that the next project he undertakes is to build a city, which he called Enoch, named after the child that was born while he was building it. The record of Cain's line ends with Lamech's family, who was also a killer and threatened unparalleled vengeance on anyone who tried to bring him to justice. It could be that Lamech killed Cain as well as others, hence Lamech took upon himself Cain's mark poetically squared—seven times turned into seventy seven times. Or perhaps Lamech had killed that many people that Cain's "seven times" was nothing compared to his achievements. Lamech also broke with the established order that God had shown to Adam and Eve of one man marries one woman, which was also the custom of the surrounding people. Lamech's son Tubal-Cain instructed men in the ways of forging metals (so Lamech had a good supply of weaponry), his two other sons taught how to look after livestock and how to play music. Lamech and his family appear to know how to make themselves rich, and how to make war, and how to make merry, but nothing of fellowship with Yahweh.

CHAPTER 10

Back to Square One

MURDER IS SUCH A heinous crime; it leaves us thinking about how many people would have come from Abel's line if Cain hadn't wiped them all out. Cain's line was not faring well.

> A man who is laden with the guilt of human blood will be a fugitive until death. (Prov 28:17 nasb)

The "life" was still with Adam and Eve; it looks like Abel could have carried it forward but Abel had gone, and along with him his posterity. God's plan was back to square one. The serpent's plan was working, he must have thought, *So far, so good.* Adam's offspring were different to the offspring of the surrounding people groups who had normal life spans. Bones have been found from the fourth millennium BC indicating the age of those buried in Sumer was 60 to 65 years old and many younger than that.[1] The kings on the Sumerian King List lived many years but the common people did not. A man was considered in his prime at the age of 40, a man of 70 would be considered as living a long time, 80 was old age, and if someone lived to be 90 it was extreme old age.[2]

According to a translation of a Babylonian tablet in the British Museum, Cain was considered the king of his city.[3] If Adam's line was different to the regular people and they were considered as chiefs among men, wouldn't the Bible mention that there were sons of Adam and also sons of

1. Churchin, "Old Age in Sumer," 61–70.
2. Vivante, *Women's Roles*, 97.
3. British Museum, Babylonian tablet no. 74329.

men? Yes I guess it would, and that is what we do in fact find. There are a number of instances of it. Psalm 8:4 (kjv) says, "What is man, that thou art mindful of him? and the son of man, that thou visitest him?" The first "man" mentioned in this verse is common man (Hebrew word *ish*) but the "son of man" mentioned is the son of Adam. The two words for "man" are different. As the psalm points out, it was Adam and his children who were visited by God. Furthermore Jeremiah says, "No man will live there, nor will any son of man reside in it" (Jer 50:40 nasb). The first use of the word man is regular man, (*ish*), but the phrase "son of man" is actually son of Adam. As we have said, Christ is the son of man (i.e., his lineage can be traced all the way back to Adam).

Adam and *ish* can both be translated as man. For instance, when Eve gave birth to Cain she said, "With the help of the Lord I have brought forth a man." She used the word *ish* for man even though Cain was from Adam's line. When the word Adam is translated as man it can be plural or singular. When God first made man as recorded in Genesis chapter 1 the word Adam is used, but it is used in a plural sense. When we get to chapter 2 we see it being used in a singular sense about one particular man (Adam) who is representative of all men. So once we have been introduced to Adam the man, that influences how we think of him and his offspring, and some parts of the Bible pick up on that theme.

In the course of time Adam and Eve had another son. Eve named him Seth, saying, "God has granted me another child in place of Abel, since Cain killed him." Adam and Eve were no longer in the garden of Eden. We know that cherubim had been placed on the east side of the garden to stop Adam and Eve from regaining admittance, which indicates that Adam and Eve travelled east. About six miles to the west of Eridu is an area that is irrigated by water from the Euphrates River. In the Greek version of the Old Testament (called the Septuagint, which was the version that the New Testament writers quote from most often) the word "fountain" is used to describe how the garden was watered. The phrase "fountains of the deep" was a saying that the Mesopotamians used to describe the irrigation ditches and canals. The "deep" was a deep river.[4] The Septuagint uses the phrase "fountains of the deep" in Deuteronomy 8:7 when talking of streams that will flow into the Promised Land. Ezekiel used "deep" to mean river (Ezek 31:4) although deep can mean ocean or sea too. Modern maps show an area to the west of Eridu that is now part of the marshland called Lake Hammar.

4. Clay, *Hebrew Deluge Story*, 63, 67.

Several news agencies over the last few years have reported that a severe drought was threatening Iraq's southern marches. The site is known as the traditional site of the garden of Eden. The flat plain is said to have had an influential role in helping to raise civilization to a new level. The reports went on to say that the drought was debilitating the area that is now little more than a large area of cracked earth.[5]

If you take a look at Internet maps you can see canals and tributaries from the river Euphrates that feed the area. We can also understand that the area without the water feeding into it is a dry hard place to live, which is how it was before the LORD God brought water to it in Genesis chapter 2.

We read in Genesis 2:10 that a river (or canal) flowed from Eden and watered the garden. Then we read how "from there it divided." It makes good sense that "from there" refers to Eden not the garden. There was a conjunction of four rivers not too far from Eden. (We know two of them because they are still flowing: the Euphrates and Tigris. Landscapes and weather patterns change over time and the rivers Pishon and Gihon are no longer flowing in that area, although there is speculation about dry channels which can be located by satellite that look like they could have been the rivers spoken about in Genesis chapter 2.) Digging canals would have meant hard work, but the design and planning would not be so difficult. The landscape was basically flat with a very slight descent in a southeasterly direction. The descent could have been utilized for canals to some extent. The canal would be lined with bitumen to prevent the water being lost to the porous nature of the dry ground. Bitumen was in plentiful supply from the Euphrates.

Adam would be greatly helped by having a community around him. When Adam left the garden he probably lived in Eridu, which was founded sometime before 5000 BC, and would have been up and running as an efficient community by the time he wanted to raise his family there. Eridu was a prosperous city, with nice brick houses and surrounding fields where crops would grow and herds could graze. It was located not too far from the Persian Gulf so fish were in plentiful supply. It had a temple to one God and an altar. Fine pottery has been found in Eridu, deep down at the lowest level of excavation just above the virgin soil. The decorative designs on the ceramic vases are geometric, using chevrons, triangles, and zigzags.

5. Harte, "Drought and Dams," lines 9, 629; Abbas, "Drought Threatens Peace," line 656; Gamel and Salaheddin, "Drought Strikes," line 869; Wayman, "Lack of Water," line 224.

They wouldn't look out of place in a modern home. Eridu was homely and settled, although the surrounding landscape did not yield its crops easily and it took hard work to get water to them. The hard work was rewarded by a comfortable city in which to live. Seth would have been born there as well as Seth's son Enosh.

We then read that at that time men began to call on the name of Yahweh (Gen 4:26). Yahweh does not appear to be as accessible as he was before, that's why men were calling for him. Previously the LORD had been the one calling for men. He called to Adam, "Where are you?" He made inquiries about Abel, "Where is your brother Abel?" But now it's the other way round. The Sumerian King List tells us that the kingship was first at Eridu but after the second king the kingship was taken to Bad-tibira, which means "wall of the copper worker(s)," or "fortress of the smiths." Bad-tibira was near Uruk, which could have been the city that Cain built (taking into account the language and dialect changes). Uruk was located just over 25 miles from Eridu in a northwesterly direction. Bad-tibira was a little further northeast of Uruk. The Uruk period started around 3800 BC, which fits in with the timing of Genesis. If Cain's line had been intermarrying with the short-lived people then their life span would start to dwindle down, but Adam and Seth still had the benefits of living long, so although Lamech's sons were several generations further on than Seth and Seth's son Enosh, Lamech and his family could have been living when Enosh was. If Lamech's family lived at Bad-tibira rather than with Cain at Uruk then Tubal-Cain's forging of iron and bronze could have taken place at Bad-tibira, which was a fortress of the smiths; and shows that the weapons forged were put to use, perhaps following Lamech's leadership. The relatively peaceful way of life at Eridu was about to be disrupted as Uruk began to find its feet. As well as the king list telling us that the kingship was transferred from Eridu there is also a change in the pottery just above the fine pottery found at Eridu, which usually lets us know that there was a change of population and maybe an occupation by an opposing force. The new pottery was similar to that found in Uruk, which tended to be of a lesser quality, looking like it was mass produced. The threat of Cain's family taking over Eridu may have been another reason that men near Edin and Eridu were calling out for Yahweh.

After Abel's death the line to Christ had not moved from its first recipients, but now Seth had been born, and it was on its way once again; then Enosh was born taking it further up the line. The serpent would not be pleased with this state of affairs, so it's not surprising that as Cain's city flourished and his descendents practiced violence that Satan would be on the lookout for an opportunity to stop the seed from germinating, the seed that he had been warned would crush his head.

Uruk had temples to a god called Anu and a goddess named Inanna. Unlike Eridu's deity, who later Sumerian scribes called Enki, the common translation of which is "Lord of the Earth" (the Sumerian "En" is translated as a title equivalent to lord or king, and "ki" means earth). There are later stories of Inanna the goddess of Uruk going to Eridu in order to receive the gifts of civilization, leaving the impression that Eridu was taken by an opposing force and tribute paid to the leadership of Uruk. Lamech did have a daughter called Naamah. Whatever the state of affairs, like Joseph who escaped from Herod's malevolent plans, Adam also managed to keep his family safe.

The Sumerians used the prefix En to denote a ruler as in Enki. Seth named his son Enosh, which indicates he was a ruler, and Cain also named his son Enoch—both names have the prefix En. If Seth was Eridu's first ruler and Enosh its second, then it was after Enosh that the change at Eridu occurred. The first ruler at Eridu is called Alulim, which doesn't sound like the name of Seth, but names and titles are different things. Alumin means "stag."[6] Persian fallow deer are few in number these days but the people in Eridu knew what the commanding appearance of a stag looked like and titled their first ruler after one. If Adam was Adapa of the later Sumerian writings, then Adapa and Alulim weren't the same people. This is also attested by a letter found at an excavation at Sultan Tepe written by Adapa to Alulu (also called Alulim), the first antediluvian king.[7]

Josephus the Jewish historian tells us that while Cain and his children were indulging in every form of vice and violence and growing rich by ending the simple life, Seth was virtuous and had a talent for the science of astronomy. Adam told Seth to inscribe his findings on two pillars, one of brick and the other of stone. The reason for this was that Adam predicted a coming flood and didn't want his son's work to be lost to following generations. Josephus then tells us the inscribed stone of Seth's astronomical work was still there in his day in the land of Seiris. Much conjecture has ensued about the location of the pillars. The brick pillar may not have survived the Flood but the stone pillar was made out of stone for the purpose of surviving the deluge. But where is it now? I am fairly certain that copies of Seth's

6. Hallo and Simpson, *Ancient Near East*, 32.
7. Hallo, "Antediluvian Cities," 62.

work would have been made even if we struggle to find the original. It is interesting to note (although we can't be certain) that in 1821 a sandstone circular slab was removed from Dendera, Egypt, a stone depicting what John H. Rogers in the *Journal for the British Astronomical Association* described as "the only complete map that we have of an ancient sky."[8] Joseph Fourier, a mathematician and physicist estimated that the age of the stone was 2500 BC, but others put a later date on it. The ancient "sky at night" map, which can now be seen in the Louvre in Paris, is an accurate configuration of the planets among the constellations that occurs about once every thousand years. It calculates both when a solar eclipse and a lunar eclipse occurred. The journal states that, "The Dendera Zodiac seems to be a complete copy of the Mesopotamian zodiac."[9] Mesopotamia is, of course, where Seth would have done his studying of the night-time sky.

8. Rogers, "Origins," 10.
9. Ibid., 10.

CHAPTER 11

The Flood

EVE WAS CREATED FROM the rib of Adam, which is a very close gene pool.

> This is now bone of my bones and flesh of my flesh. (Gen 2:23)

We don't know where Seth got his wife from but it could have been his sister. It would be many years before Moses would tell people not to intermarry with close relatives. We know these days that the two strands of DNA from both parents help correct any flaws in each other so the baby to be born will not have any genetic errors accentuated. Where one strand may have a defective gene the other strand fills in for it. If close relatives marry then the offspring may not have those flaws covered because both strands of the DNA may have the same flaw. If so, what God placed into Adam and Eve was being preserved in their line but being lost from Cain's line.

From Adam to Noah there were ten men who fathered children. Genesis chapter 5 lays them all out neatly as part of Adam's *toledoth*. Cain isn't in it, but Seth is. The seventh generation begins with Enoch, and we read that Enoch walked with God. Adam hid from God when he heard him walking in the garden. God's desire to "walk" with us is there for us to see. When someone walks in a garden, usually their footsteps are soft and not always audible, so perhaps Yahweh sometimes made a noise when he walked, it could be that he sang as he walked, it's a nice thing to do when someone is out for a leisurely stroll. There are verses in the Bible that mention Yahweh's inclination for singing and one of them let's us know that the LORD God will rejoice over us with singing (Zeph 3:17). If it was singing that Adam could hear then Adam may have recognized the melodic voice from someway off, which gave him and Eve time to hide. Whatever it was, Adam wasn't normally afraid to walk with God because the creator of the universe brought peace and goodness along with him. Adam would ordinarily enjoy walking with God in the beauty of a balmy evening, enjoying the shade of the green-leafed garden. They may have sat down next to a pool of water and Adam would ask how all this came to be and Yahweh would have first told Adam how he made the heavens and the earth, explaining it poetically using the days of the week.

Adam passed the creation story on to Seth who passed it on the Enosh; the story was written down and passed though the family. When we read Genesis chapter 1 we could be sitting in on a conversation that first took place in the glory of the garden that Yahweh had planted. This was a precious, peaceful, and productive time for Adam. Jesus wanted to pass his peace onto his disciples, saying, "Peace I leave with you; my peace I give you. I do not give to you as the world gives. Do not let your hearts be troubled and do not be afraid" (John 14:27). This was the peace that was around a person when they were in the presence of Yahweh.

There may be a window we can look at the garden through in Psalm 32:7. David tells us that Yahweh sings songs of deliverance; immediately after David tells us this it looks very much as if a verse from one of Yahweh's songs is written down for us to hear:

> I will instruct you and teach you in the way you should go;
> I will counsel you with my loving eye on you.
> Do not be like the horse or the mule,
> which have no understanding
> but must be controlled by bit and bridle
> or they will not come to you.

If Adam related the songs that he heard Yahweh sing, it's not inconceivable that they would be passed along the line to David, who then put music to them. If so, we could be listening in on a song that Yahweh first sang to Adam. We also get to see that Yahweh's songs had some instructional value too. In fact singing is a good way to learn, because the tunes help fix the words in our heads. The picture we are getting of Yahweh is one of a loving father who sings to his children.

Cain's line and possibly some of Adam's other children were unruly; Mesopotamia at that time was getting more evil by the day, so when Enoch (seventh in line from Adam) walked with God it would have been a sweet connection for Enoch and Yahweh. Jude, in the New Testament, mentions a prophecy made by Enoch, it is not directly from the Old Testament but there is a book that was assembled about 300 BC called the book of Enoch. The book seems to have been accepted by the early church, but didn't make it into the biblical canon, neither is it a part of the apocrypha found in some Bibles. Jude quotes, "Enoch, the seventh from Adam, prophesied about them: 'See, the Lord is coming with thousands upon thousands of his holy ones.'" Enoch, according to the same section in the book of Enoch, said, "The Holy Great One will come forth from his dwelling, and the eternal God will tread upon the earth." Enoch made his own set of footprints next to Yahweh's. When Enoch reached the age of 365 God took him. What does that mean? It means what it says. Enoch didn't see death, God took him to where the angels and God reside. God walked with Enoch on earth and now Enoch walks with God in heaven. The early Sumerians also have a story of the seventh king on their king list who had a sage who ascended to heaven. Some people say that's where Genesis got the idea for Enoch, but it could be that the actual story of Enoch ascending to heaven gave rise to the Mesopotamian story.

But isn't it appointed unto man to die and then face judgement? (Heb 9:27). Yes it is, and we don't know what God has in store in the future, maybe Enoch will make an appearance along with Elijah or some say Moses—as the two witnesses of Revelation because both of the witnesses get killed, and if they get killed they will have fulfilled the appointment to die. Some things we have to leave with God because he has concealed them and we have to accept that we don't know and can't find out until it happens, meanwhile all we have to do is trust, it will become clear one day. Prophecy is sometimes there so that we can praise God after the event. Many missed the first coming of Christ even though the scriptures stated where Christ would be born, but when we look back and see how wonderful the prophecies are we are filled with praise.

Some of Adam's sons may have understood that there would be some judgement coming to the area because of Cain's family's evil behavior. Stories of the Mesopotamian flood abound. The Sumerian King List splits the list into pre-diluvian and post-diluvian. The Epic of Gilgamesh was a popular story in Mesopotamia, a number of copies of it have been found around the region. In the story we read that a man named Utnapishtim built an ark in the town of Shuruppak—Utnapishtim means "long-lived." Josephus tells us that Noah feared being murdered so he and his family moved to a new location. Shuruppak, a town about 65 miles northwest of Eridu and Uruk stood on the banks of the earlier course of the river Euphrates. Excavations at Shuruppak, now called Tell Fara, Iraq, have revealed flooding sediment that interrupts layers of pottery before the flood and layers of pottery after the flood. Other Sumerian cities also have flood sediment layers dated in the same timeframe, 2900 BC. Genesis 7:22 tells us that in the Flood everything on the dry land died. The Hebrew doesn't say the word "land" it simply says "dry." Everything that was on the dry died. The Hebrew word means dry ground like a desert; the Tigris and Euphrates Rivers are fertile areas, but once away from these two rivers most of the land is dry and harsh.

There was more than one reason for the Flood. If some men are given the ability to live long lives when people all around them are dying after about 70 years or so, there must be a temptation to think you are indestructible, especially if you have intelligence, a beautiful physique, and strength to go along with the many years. The temptation to look down on those who only live short lives must also be strong. Pride could rear its head in a big way. This feeling of power could, of course, bring some extremely bad behavior along with it. Adam's clan, all of whom had the breath of life that was first breathed into Adam, was getting out of hand, God said he was sorry he'd even put man (Adam's family) on the earth. We don't know how God dealt with the human race elsewhere in the world; we know that the world has been inhabited for well over 6000 years. I'm sure God has a way of reaching out to people wherever they are, but the main story of God reaching out to us humans starts in Genesis— it's here we discover how God stepped into human affairs in Mesopotamia using Adam and Eve as a starting point. The story would lead all the way to Jesus being born of a human woman. A baby, which couldn't be born blind, or infirmed, or with learning disabilities or any other disability, he had a job to do, he had to walk many miles, and speak to multitudes of people, he needed God's breath in him to speak such powerfully sharp words that they would slice through disingenuous hypocrisy. As a boy of twelve he astounded the learned men in the Temple. This child was destined to help us, lead us, shepherd us, heal us, and to save us. He was the seed of the woman, born and grown into an adult.

God needed to remove Adam's children that had gone wild, who had misused the privilege of long-life and physical beauty. But there was another twist to the tale: the angels who at various points came into space-time with a material body got to see some of the women from Adam's family. These were not like regular human women, they had a special beauty and strength. They would make ideal mates for angels. If the angels could start to spread their own DNA that hadn't been created in the same way that humans had, then they could father some offspring on the earth themselves. This would fit very nicely into the serpent's plans too.

We don't know how many pure daughters of Adam's line were around, but judging by the length of time it took each of the fathers to actually father a child, then there probably wasn't a large number. Genesis 6 says that the sons of God took whomever they chose. That sounds to me like they took as many as they wanted. If the serpent could take all the women in Adam's line and impregnate them with flesh other than human flesh then the promised seed would not see the light of day. Mythology has stories relating to giants, or gigantes as they are called in Greek myths. Genesis tells us they were "men of renown," hence the myths about them. If we look at the name it may yield some information: *nephesh* is soul, we all have it, the animals too, it means life. One way to look at it is Elohim, cherubim, seraphim, are spiritual beings while nephilim are a mixture of biological life and spirit life.

So something had to be done and the Flood was the answer. The "seed" would survive, which was important for the salvation of the world. In the Mesopotamian flood stories they mention that the "seed of life" and the "seed of mankind" were on the ark.[1] Noah and then Shem carried the "seed" that would lead to Christ's birth and both of them were on the ark. The Flood was mainly to free the earth of Adam's descendents, because they had gone seriously bad. Every thought and inclination of their hearts was evil all the time. Secondly, the hybrid nephilim could also be largely destroyed. But not all of them would be wiped out as Genesis 6:4 explains that some of them were around after the Flood too. But God sent the Israelites to track them down and one of the last of them to go was named Goliath who was killed by a boy named David.

The ark was most likely built at Shuruppak, according to Akkadian and Sumerian sources, which is also in agreement with the Sumerian King List, as Noah was considered a chief there owing to his long years. The waters came and the ark was lifted up from the ground 20 feet, the floodwaters also covered the hill country. Some English translations tell us the mountains were covered to over 20 feet (15 cubits), the Septuagint helps us understand

1. Budge, *Babylonian Story*, tablet 11:27; Jacobsen, "Harps that Once," line 153.

that the waters were 20 feet high and because Mesopotamia is a largely flat landscape, any hills there were also covered. The word for mountain in Hebrew is the same as hill or hill country. The Tigris-Euphrates basin is extremely flat and the gradient drops very slowly: 3 meters per kilometer in the long stretch to what is the current city of Bagdad, and the elevation of the rivers is about 30 km above sea level at that point. Then as they wend their way to the southeast they fall another 21 meters over 280 km, that's a very gentle descent indeed. The coast of the Persian Gulf was further inland in 2900 BC but the slope is still slight all the way to the sea. The area is an alluvial plain, which means periodic floods have always occurred every now and again. In spring the snows in the Turkish mountains would melt and the levels of the two rivers would be raised, and some years the rivers would break their banks because the area is so flat. There would be natural levees around where villages, towns, and cities could be built; they would be on slightly higher ground. The cities had to be built on the levees because the flood plains would be swampy for some time after a flood. Most hills in this region that are as much as 15 meters high are more than 95 km away from the river levees. Therefore, when Noah looked out of the one cubit gap between the upper deck and roof he would see only water in all directions. "And the waters prevailed exceedingly upon the earth; and all the high hills, that were under the whole heaven, were covered" (Gen 7:19). As Noah looked at the horizon, 360 degrees of it, the land was entirely covered in water. Josephus tells us that many refugees found safety from the flood on a mountain called Baris. Philo of Alexandria, who was held in high regard by the early church, tells us the floodwaters almost extended beyond the pillars of Hercules and the Mediterranean Sea. Although that's probably not correct, it does let us know that he thought the floodwaters had limits. Noah would have measured the depth of the waters, he was a builder, craftsman, and an excellent engineer, so measuring the depth of the waters as the ark floated upon them was something he would want to know and something he was capable of finding out. He concluded the depth to be 20 feet.

If torrential rain fell in Mesopotamia, and on the mountains of Syria and Turkey, and also in Saudi Arabia and Iran, the tributary streams from these countries would all contribute their volumes of water to the flood plains of the Tigris and Euphrates Rivers. We know from the Genesis account that there was a southeast wind because the ark travelled northwest, so if the waters of the Persian Gulf were being blown upstream onto the flat lands of Mesopotamia, the rain water and elevated river levels would have nowhere to drain. The cities that were built on the turtleback natural hills would soon be covered with water, and the people in the cities would have nowhere to run because the plains were covered too. The watershed for the two rivers reaches over 1600 km east to west from the Persian Gulf through to Syria and Turkey, and north to south 1000 km. Because Mesopotamia is narrower in its southeastern region the waters would be pushed into this area like a bottleneck causing the level to rise higher. This is the area where Adam's children lived, Cain's Uruk was there, and furthermore if Adam's children were there then so were the nephilim, because they wanted the daughters of Adam; they were all scattered around the cities of lower Mesopotamia. Excavations have revealed "flood clay" five feet thick at Uruk.[2] Flood deposits seven feet thick are also reported as far northwest as the ancient city of Kish.[3] The artifacts of human life suddenly disappear in the flood layers, but can be found below and above them. The consistent date for the flood deposits at the Mesopotamian cities of Ur, Kish, Shuruppak, Uruk, and Lagash is 2900 BC.

Every living thing on the face of the earth was wiped out. The "face of the earth" is the same phrase that Cain used when he said he was being driven from the "face of the earth." When Cain said, "face of the earth" he didn't mean the whole earth just the area of land he was on at that time, the part of the earth whose face he could see. Some people talk about a global flood, but this is another addition to what we have in the Bible, the word "global" isn't there, neither is "worldwide." There is evidence of a flood at that time in Mesopotamia but no evidence of flooding in Egypt, Turkey, Iran, or the Palestine region, with the exception of the Dead Sea.[4]

The ark came to rest on the mountains of Ararat. It's been much debated where these mountains are. "Ark-eologists" have done some mountain climbing looking for it. But if the waters only reached 20 feet from the ground in the Tigris-Euphrates basin, the mountain range it landed on isn't going to be very high. Berosus the Babylonian historian who lived around 290 BC said, "A portion of the vessel still survives in Armenia on the mountain of the Cordyaeans." The kingdom of Corduene was located south and southeast of Lake Van in Turkey. If we travel towards Lake Van from Shuruppak in a northwesterly direction the first small mountain we

2. Carleton, *Buried Empires*, 64.

3. MacDonald, "The Flood," 14–20.

4. Fischer, *Historical Genesis*, 125.

meet is Mount Alfaf, which rises to 1062 meters above sea level. The Bible itself may also give us a clue or two. Jeremiah spoke of the kingdom of Ararat. Greater Ararat reached down into northern Mesopotamia. The hills and mountains start about 18 miles northeast of the modern city of Mosul, Iraq, where there is a village called Bahzani, which lies at the foot of Mount Alfaf. The village is famous for its olive trees. When Noah let out a dove from the Ark it came back with a freshly plucked olive leaf, and Noah knew that the waters had receded. A portion of the ark still existed when Berosus wrote about it; he said people were scraping away the bitumen to use as amulets and antidotes. Noah, of course had been told to cover the boat in bitumen both inside and out.

Before the Flood the LORD had said he was grieved and stated, "My spirit shall not always strive with man, for that he also is flesh: yet his days shall be an hundred and twenty years" (Gen 6:3 kjv). This relates back to when God first breathed into Adam and his offspring, the benefits were great, with long-life being one of the advantages. But, as Jesus said, "From everyone who has been given much, much will be required." Adam's offspring were not coming up with the righteous goods that God required. So although there were a few people in the line who walked with God, the Lord was cutting the life span to 13 percent of what it had been. God may have let this happen naturally by some intermarrying with women who were not from Adam's line. Noah's son Shem lived noticeably shorter than his fathers, he lived 600 years but Noah lived to be 950. So, perhaps Noah married a woman who had mixed parentage, if the angels married anyone of the beautiful daughters of Adam's line "that they chose" then it's possible that there would be few left for Noah to marry. He could have married someone who was already in a mixed line, so she would live longer than generic humans but not as long as Noah. Or God could have reduced the benefits that Adam's line had without anyone marrying outside the immediate family. God's Spirit had been grieved with the men (Adam's line) that he had made, and he was not going to contend for them or bestow on them the physical benefits that he had done in the past. There would be a phasing out of the long lives. Some sort of paradigm shift occurred and God's Spirit was involved. God had breathed into Adam and the word Spirit is another way of saying breath, something of God's Spirit had endowed Adam and his family with qualities that were a sign to those around that Adam's family was carrying something important. But the pros were being outweighed by the cons; God needed to take action.

Towards the end of Genesis chapter 8 we read that Noah built an altar after disembarking from the ark and then he sacrificed some of the clean animals. Yahweh smelled the offerings and said he would never again curse the ground because of Adam's race. The word "curse" also means to treat lightly or with contempt. Never again would God bring such devastation through a flood. Nor would he destroy every living creature (Gen 8:21). When we read "every living creature" it doesn't mean all animal life on planet earth, because firstly the living creatures that live in water—whales, dolphins, squid, and all manner of fish—weren't destroyed. Secondly, the meaning is qualified in Genesis 9:8–10 when God Says, "I now establish my covenant with you and with your descendants after you and with every living creature that was with you—the birds, the livestock and all the wild animals, all those that came out of the ark with you." God was talking about all the living creatures that were on the ark.

As a sign of the covenant God produced a rainbow. Noah would have looked up into the sky where he suddenly saw it appearing. Rainbows have always appeared, ever since the skies cleared and sun, moon, and stars could be seen on the fourth creative day, but only God could arrange for one to appear at the precise time he was talking to Noah. In the future when Noah or his sons saw a rainbow it would remind them of the covenant: for a rainbow to appear it means the sun must also be shining and if the sun is shining the sky cannot be completely covered by dark rain clouds. (Although there would come a time when darkness would cover the sky and a curse would fall once again, but this time it would not be the ground that was being cursed but a man from Adam's line: the second Adam.)

Gilgamesh, who was a king in Uruk in 2600 BC (about whom the Gilgamesh epic is written) travelled to see Utnapishtim (Noah). Noah was still living in the region where the ark landed hence Gilgamesh calls him "Utnapishtim the Faraway." Gilgamesh tells him that now that he has finally got to see him, his features are not strange at all. Gilgamesh was under the impression that he would be a fierce looking man ready to do battle. But he finds Utnapishtim resting and lying down on his back. Noah would be about 900 years old at this point. The question that Gilgamesh really wants to ask is this, "(Tell me,) how joinst thou the Assembly of the gods?" This is the question people ask when someone has been in touch with God. Noah walked with God, he knew Yahweh. When Noah and his family with all the wildlife from the area got into the boat, it was Yahweh who closed the door. Noah was acquainted with God. In a similar way someone came to

Jesus and asked, "What must I do to obtain eternal life?" He supposed Jesus knew the answer.

Certain people in this life have been chosen to reveal God to the rest of us. Yes, we can all walk with God, maybe not the way Adam, Enoch, and Noah walked with God, but God did that to show us it's possible. God is Spirit and it's a spiritual relationship that we need to have with him. Some people say, "Show me God then I'll believe." It doesn't work that way. Rather, "Blessed are those who believe yet have not seen." Those are the people God seeks out. Certain men walked with God in a physical way that we all may walk with God in a spiritual way. Jesus said, "It is good that I go, because if I go the Counsellor will come." He told Mary after the resurrection not to hold onto him. Jesus was located to one place at one time; the Holy Spirit is with us all, all of the time. Gilgamesh may well ask Utnapishtim how he joined the assembly of the gods. It is a good question and one that the Bible gives us the answer to.

God uses ordinary men and women to tell his story and to proclaim "life" to people. Sometimes he does it through words and sometimes through an object lesson that reveals itself as an unfolding drama. Adam was an ordinary human taken from the ground just like all the rest of us, but God chose him to demonstrate something and to give us eternal life through his offspring. However, it was important that Adam's progeny didn't get filled with pride; they needed to remain humble and remember they were flesh like all humankind. That's why God said, "My spirit shall not always strive with man, for that he also is flesh." Yes, he also is flesh, the same as all men. God needed to remind Adam's line of their true position. Though God had blessed them with advantages regular humans did not enjoy, they were in fact ordinary humans. This lesson was brought home to them very strongly with a shortening of their life span.

CHAPTER 12

God Finds a Friend

WHEN GOD CREATED HUMANITY in Genesis chapter 1 there was a rapport between God and humans. We were made in his image; we had freedom of choice. God spoke to the humans:

> Be fruitful and increase in number; fill the earth and subdue it.
> (Gen 1:28)

We know this took place with findings of ancient man in many countries. God also told them to rule over the animals. Then God said, "I give you every seed bearing plant on the face of the whole earth and every tree that has fruit with seed in it. They will be yours for food. And to all the birds of the air and all the creatures that move on the ground—everything that has the breath of life in it—I give every green plant for food."

It has been said that before the Flood men or animals didn't eat meat. But we know there were carnivorous animals before the Flood and we also know that men ate meat too. Take Ötzi for example, he is a well preserved natural mummy; a man who lived around 3300 BC, which precedes the Flood date. He was found in September 1991 near the border between Austria and Italy. He is Europe's oldest known natural human mummy. His last meal consisted of red deer and goat; both were eaten with grain as well as roots and fruits. Ötzi was well inside the antediluvian timeframe. Fossils have been found all over North America and Europe of saber-toothed animals who were hunters, the saber-toothed animals went extinct over 10,000 years ago, which means they must have lived well before the Flood. Men and animals ate meat before the Flood. It isn't forbidden in Genesis chapter

1. What God indicates is that the support of the whole animal kingdom and human biological life is based on vegetation. When Noah was told to take animals into the ark he took seven of every kind of clean animal and two of every kind of unclean animal. This happened long before the Mosaic law started stipulating about clean and unclean animals, so what did Noah mean by clean and unclean? Humans worldwide have long been able to distinguish between the sheep and the wolf, the gazelle and the lion, or the dove and the vulture. Some animals eat vegetation and other animals eat other animals. Humans usually hunt herbivores. Noah probably took seven clean animals for farming purposes when they disembarked. He took two unclean animals for the purpose of keeping the area ecologically stable, because each animal has its part to play in the overall natural balance of flora and fauna.

The Flood occurred around 2900 BC according to geological dating. The biblical date agrees, if we use the Septuagint as the dating reference. The way calendars were assembled in antiquity were not the same way we assemble them today. The Babylonian and Hebrew calendars were based on a lunisolar year. Different cultures had differing ways of measuring time, it can get complicated with extra months being added to even things up with solar years. The phases of the moon played a much greater part in counting months and seasons in the ancient world. There's also an idea that tells us that an artificial year may have been used. That means the early Hebrews knew there were 7 days in a week. They put 4 weeks into a month (28 days) and 12 months in a year leaving 336 days in a year. There were a few possibilities for the way months and years could be counted, but as the world progressed solar years began to be the main way years were allocated.

The Greek translation of the Hebrew Old Testament known as the Septuagint first began to appear in the third century BC, and it quickly became the popular version to use. The New Testament writers quote from it often and use its chronology. There are some differences with the Masoretic text when years are quoted. The Masoretic text is the Hebrew text that was copied, edited, and distributed by a group of Jews known as the Masoretes during the seventh and tenth centuries AD. But if we use the Septuagint, we can work out the date of the Flood. To do so we need to pick a point in time that is accepted as being reasonably accurate such as King David's reign, which is said to have begun in 1010 BC. We know King David was 30 years old when he became king and he reigned for 40 years (2 Sam 5:4), then his son Solomon took over. First Kings 6:1 in the Septuagint tells us there were

440 years from the Exodus to the start of the work on Solomon's temple. (The Masoretic text says, 480 years, so if years of 336 days were being used that would seem to work out.)

Next, Solomon had been reigning for 4 years when the work began, so the year would be 966 BC. Let's add the 440 years, which then tells us the year of the Exodus was 1406 BC.

Paul in Galatians 3:16–17 tells us that from the promises being given to Abraham to the Law being issued there were 430 years. (The Law was issued in the third month after the Exodus.) The 430 years are confirmed by the Septuagint in Exodus 12:40 which lets us know that the time of the Israelite family's sojourning lasted 430 years including Canaan. (The Masoretic text doesn't mention Canaan, leaving some people to think the whole time the Israelites spent in Egypt was 430 years.) Adding the 430 years to the time of the Exodus lets us know that God first spoke to Abraham in Ur in 1836 BC.

Abraham was 70 years old when he first met Yahweh in Ur, when he first received a promise that the LORD would show him a land to settle in. Stephen talks about this too in Acts 7:2–3. So if we add 70 years to our total it takes us to the time of Abraham's birth in 1906 BC.

Abraham's father Terah was 130 years old when he fathered Abraham. So the date of Terah's birth was 2036 BC.

The Septuagint tells us through its genealogies how many years there were from the Flood to Terah, but we need to take something into account before we add those in. In Luke's Gospel we read about one generation, whose name is Cainan, who was born to Shem's son Arphaxad. It's fairly certain that Luke never wrote Cainan in his original Gospel, but that an early Christian copyist made an error. The Masoretic text doesn't have this generation in Genesis 11. And neither does early manuscripts of the Septuagint, we know this because Josephus quotes from the Septuagint which was widely accepted in his day (AD 70) and Josephus doesn't mention Cainan as the son of Arphaxad. Also the Christian historian Julius Africanus produced a chronology in AD 220, he also omitted Cainan even though we know he used the Septuagint. The copyist in question could negligently have looked a couple of lines down as he was copying and repeated the earlier name of Cainan who was the son of Enosh and included him twice. If that's what happened it had a knock-on effect because the Septuagint was widely used among Christians, so they included this extra Cainan in Genesis 11 in subsequent copies of the Septuagint because they had read it in Luke's Gospel. Theologian Dr. John Gill, who was known as an expert Hebraist, summarized the textual evidence in his Bible commentary.

> This Cainan is not mentioned by Moses in Ge 11:12 nor has he
> ever appeared in any Hebrew copy of the Old Testament, nor in
> the Samaritan version, nor in the Targum; nor is he mentioned by
> Josephus, nor in 1Ch 1:24.[1]

The Septuagint itself omits Cainan when it repeats the genealogies in 1 Chronicles 1:24. So it leaves us to conclude that a tired Christian copyist made a mistake inserting Cainan twice in Luke's genealogy.

So now we can go back to 2036 BC when Terah was born and add on the time the Septuagint tells us there is from the Flood to Terah's birth (but we'll subtract the 130 years assigned to Cainan). From Shem coming out of the ark to Terah's birth there are 872 years. If we add 872 years to 2036 years we get 2908 BC, which is the same timeframe the geologists get.

Noah seemed to enjoy his new location after the Flood, which was around 400 miles north northwest from where he started out in Shuruppak. Olives grew well in this climate and so did grapes. Noah enjoyed husbandry in this new area and was successful with vines. Noah drank some of the wine he'd made. Drinking had been a problem back in Sumer. Forty percent of barley grown was used for ale. The drunkenness of the Sumerians was even mentioned in the Greek stories: Dionysus the god of wine fled from Sumer in revulsion.[2] Now Noah was falling into similar ways, he fell down drunk in his tent. Ham, Noah's son, looked in on his father and saw him lying there naked. Instead of staying discreet about the matter, he started telling people. Shem and Japheth, Noah's other sons, got a long coat and walked in backwards to the tent and draped it over their father so they did not ogle but covered up Noah's shame—love covers over a multitude of wrongs. Noah cursed Ham's son when he found out. It sounds like Ham and perhaps his son Canaan, laughed, mocked, and jeered at Noah when they saw him drunk with no clothes, and then they brandished the news around and laughed about it to others. Shem and Japheth found this reprehensible levity shocking, and took steps to remedy the situation.

When Noah died, the Jewish book of Jubilees tells us that some of his family made their way back to southern Mesopotamia. The earlier cities of Uruk and Ur had been rebuilt, similar to how we would rebuild a town that's

---

1. Gill, *Exposition of the New Testament*, Luke 3:36.
2. Constable, *Age of God Kings*, 27.

been devastated by a severe flood or tsunami. Generally speaking Japheth and his sons moved west and north. The children of Ham moved south, although some stayed in Mesopotamia. Some of Shem's family started to move southeast to reoccupy the old cities. We know that Abram's father Terah, who was the ninth in line from Shem, lived in Ur, which was a little further north than Eridu.[3] Eridu never really got going again but Ur became a very prosperous city. Ur was said to be the largest city of those times. The people of Ur some 4000 years ago were intelligent designers, craftsmen, and creative artists, we know this partly because the British Museum has a room with quite amazing artifacts from Ur.

The people who lived in Sumer before the Flood may have had some understanding about God and a measure of truth. They spoke about a triad of male gods, of which Enki was one, Anu was considered the father, and Enlil the god of breath or wind. Similarly, as the Bible unfolds we read of the Father, Son, and Holy Spirit, it takes a while before we get to that point in the Bible because God's being is not easy for us to understand. But some shadow of understanding seemed to exist in those early days of Mesopotamia. We know that God had already spoken to men in general in Genesis chapter 1, and then in chapter 2 we read that God walked with men and that his name is Yahweh. Throughout the history of early Mesopotamia Yahweh talks and walks with some men. However, we also know there is a serpent at large, God allowed this, and men have to choose whom we want to follow, because choice is an important part of being made in God's image. The serpent corrupts truth—for our struggle is not against flesh and blood, but against the rulers, against the authorities, against the powers of this dark world, and against the spiritual forces of evil in the heavenly realms (Eph 6:12). As men gave in to the temptations on offer from the serpent, truth suffered. The further from God we roam, the less of truth is known.

After the Flood Ur started to become polytheistic, and although the city had rules and laws, there was less accurate knowledge concerning God. This of course could be dangerous and could get weird, especially where the afterlife was concerned. Sir Leonard Woolley, the excavator of the city of Ur said among the hundreds of tombs that he uncovered he found 16 elaborate "royal" tombs, all containing evidence of human sacrificial victims, with over 70 attendants in one tomb. It appears that when someone important died his retinue were also asked to die with him because he would need them in the afterlife. They may have gone willingly, there doesn't seem to be

3. Abraham was formerly known as Abram, and was renamed later in the story.

signs of a struggle; one young woman attendant was found still clutching her hair ribbon as if the poison or sedative she had taken kicked in before she had a chance to place it in her hair. This is a famous time in the history of Ur, culminating in the Third Dynasty of Ur under the control of King Ur-Nammu, the community was established around 2100 BC and was the capital city of much of Mesopotamia.

How many of Shem's family made their way to Ur we can't be sure about, but at that time in Sumer they all used the same language. There are over 6000 distinct languages in the world; languages traceable to Noah's children are from the same basic language tree.[4] Just before the second millennium BC, the people of Sumer started to build towers, probably because they were afraid of another flood. They built quite a few towers that are known as "ziggurats." There was a spectacular ziggurat at Ur and just like Genesis tells us, it was made of baked bricks. Each brick weighed as much as 33 pounds. The lower portion of the ziggurat, which supported the first terrace, would have used some 720,000 baked bricks, laid with bitumen, a naturally occurring tar most likely obtained from the banks of the river Euphrates. The resources needed to build the ziggurat at Ur would have been immense and it was a long-term building project. Ur-Nammu "was a prodigious builder. The most impressive monuments of his reign were ziggurats."[5] He wished to build the greatest ziggurat yet built at Ur.[6] Ur-Nammu started the project but died before it was finished. His son Shugli took the project over; it was being built around the time that Terah lived there.

Yahweh has not been seen for quite some time, the last we read is that he closed the door on the ark, or we might say battened down the hatches. Then he spoke with Noah after he had disembarked, and smelled the burnt offerings that Noah had prepared on the altar he'd built. But now suddenly Yahweh comes down to look at the city and the tower. How long Yahweh walked and looked at the city we don't know, it could have been days or weeks because the city was large: by the year 2030 BC Ur's population had grown in size to around 65,000 inhabitants. The remains of Ur have been subject to some extensive archaeological work that informs us that during the reign of its Third Dynasty the city had two-story houses; many houses had standardized dimensions. There were plumbing and sewage systems

---

4. Fischer, *Historical Genesis*, 170.

5. British Museum, "Foundation Figure of Ur-Nammu," lines 24–25.

6. Realhistoryww.com, "Ancient Man . . . The Ziggurat," line 9.

and even bathrooms in many houses. The streets had drainage and there was also, as Genesis points out, city planning. So along with the city's wide-ranging legal system, which took care of civil and family law, it was a recognizable civilized city.[7]

At some point Abram met Yahweh in Ur. When God speaks of Abraham later, in the book of Isaiah, he mentions Abraham, adding the words "my friend." Just like we might say to someone, "Hey do you know my friend Karl?" Abraham was Yahweh's friend, and the friendship was struck up somewhere. As Yahweh made his way around the streets of Ur he would have seen many of its inhabitants going about their business and Abram was one of them. Stephen in the New Testament tells us that God first spoke to Abraham in Ur, which is referred to as "Ur of the Chaldees" quite often, and Chaldees is the Greek name for the Akkadian area. Akkad was a city northwest of Ur and towards the end of the third millennium BC became the dominant political force in the area in what was known as the Akkadian Empire. It became known as the Babylonian Empire later. Nimrod, who was a descendent of Noah's son Ham, was the leader of a kingdom that covered quite an area of Mesopotamia: Babylon, Erech (Uruk), and Akkad in the land of Shinar. People sometimes speak of the "Tower of Babel," but Genesis never calls it by that name. Genesis chapter 11 speaks of a city and its tower, which was in a plain in Shinar. The Akkadians called the land Shumer and it looks like Shinar is the Hebrew equivalent. We know that there were a lot of towers built at that time; Genesis picks one of them to make its point. The pursuits and pride of the people of Ur and surrounding cities were not pleasing to God. Pride in our own abilities and standing do not comprise of the humility that God requires from us, so God took action: he confused "their lip."

Because the area was being repopulated after the Flood, God may have encouraged different people groups to infiltrate the area, and they would have used various languages so communicating may have been an issue. The precise nature of architecture and accurate building techniques required to construct the city and tower meant many managers and foremen needed to instruct their particular team of workers to follow exact instructions. And even though there were plenty of workers on hand, the chain of command may have proved too hard to implement, therefore work on the city remained unfinished. Well over 1000 years later Nabodinus, king of Babylon, worked on rebuilding the tower and adding some changes.

7. Stanley, "Ur," 382.

The tower can still be seen on maps, 10 miles southwest of Nasiriyah in Iraq.

Genesis has a succinct way of describing this episode: "Come let us build ourselves a city, with a tower that reaches to the heavens, so that we may make a name for ourselves and not be scattered" (Gen 11:4). Yahweh says, "'Come let us go down and confuse their language'. . . . So the LORD scattered them from there over all the earth" (Gen 11:7–8).

> Therefore its name was called Babel, because there the LORD confused the language of the whole earth; and from there the LORD scattered them abroad over the face of the whole earth. (Gen 11:9)

"Babel" is not from the Hebrew word *balal* which means "to confound." *Babel* is Aramaic meaning "the gate of God." If we look at the scripture just quoted we'll see that the emphasis is on the word LORD, which is mentioned twice. God came down to see the tower and so men called it the gate of God. Men had wanted to build a tower that reached the heavens; they intended it to be a gate into heaven but the LORD used it as a gate from which to mix men's language and then start a migration.

Interestingly when Jacob had a dream later in Genesis he saw the LORD at the top of a series of steps. Jacob exclaimed, "This is the gate of heaven." The men of Ur designed their own set of steps to reach heaven but God has his own stairway to heaven, and sometimes, even humans are permitted to climb it.

CHAPTER **13**

Move from Mesopotamia

> As for you, be fruitful and increase in number; multiply on the
> earth and increase upon it. (Gen 9:7)

THE AGE RANGE OF Adam's line was falling dramatically. People in the
Adamic family tended to have children after 100 years of age before the
Flood. Noah didn't have his three sons until he was 500, but that was un-
usually late even for Adam's line. We remember that God had originally
told humanity to be fruitful and multiply in Genesis chapter 1, but he did
not say that to Adam and Eve in chapter 2. Eve seems to have struggled,
and on the birth of Cain said, "With the help of the LORD I have brought
forth a man."

After the Flood God blessed Noah and his sons and told them to be
fruitful and increase in number and fill the earth. Suddenly the age when
couples started to conceive and become parents dropped dramatically. In
our English Bibles the age when a man became a father seems to be down to
today's levels, Shem's son Arphaxad was 35, which is back down to normal.
Others were in their early thirties; Terah's father was 29. (The Septuagint
has longer periods but still there is a lower age for childbirth than before
the Flood and a lower life span generally.) There were only ten generations
from Adam to Noah over quite a long span of years, which means that
keeping the seed safe was easier before the Flood. Now Adam's line was
fertile earlier, so more care would be needed with each link in the chain. In
the Septuagint Adam is 230 before Seth is born; Adam lived 930 years. If
we move the decimal point across one position we'll see the ratio compared

to regular human ages. So let's say Adam was 93 when he died, (instead of 930) that would mean Seth was born when he was 23 (230 moved across one decimal place). So if a 93-year-old man fathered a child when he was 23 that would be perfectly normal. As the ages of Adam's line fell so did the age they were able to procreate. By the time we get to David around 1010 BC, he lived to be 70 years old, so although he was in the line to Christ the overall life span had become normal.

Terah's family had the tragedy of losing a son, whose name was Haran, but not before Haran had become the father of Lot. Terah had two other sons, Abram and Nahor and also a daughter named Sarai, who was the offspring of a second wife. The Genesis story is now spearheaded by Terah's family, the direct line through to Christ, so the book focuses on how this family's gene pool was kept tight. There had already been many assaults on the line and attempts to break it up, mix it up, or halt it altogether but God had managed to keep the track to his Son's birth on course.

God had placed something in Adam that was making its way through the generations to Jesus. The thread started with God's Spirit and would be completed by God's Spirit, like a vein of gold running through the earth, which of course, is what it was, because men are made from the earth, and now we had something from heaven implanted within us. We know that Yahweh appeared as a man, but not as a human man, that came later. To be human means you have proceeded from a previous human in the human race. Perhaps when God breathed into Adam he placed the correct genetic code for himself to be born as himself as a bona-fide human being, with the same physical characteristics he had when he walked in the garden, closed the door on the ark, and spoke and ate with Abraham. In the New Testament the Jews said to Jesus, "You aren't even fifty years old. How can you say you have seen Abraham?" In Micah 5:2 (esv) there's a prophetic verse that talks about Christ's birth: "But as for you, Bethlehem . . . From you one will go forth for me to be ruler in Israel. His goings forth are from long ago, from ancient days."

Humanity has been on the planet for many thousands of years, they were not a large population compared to today but there were little clusters of human society spread throughout the earth. And as the first recognizable civilization began to emerge God was right there, making himself known to men, being there with us, helping us, and implanting something of himself within us. God was active in human society. His "goings forth" were from ancient days. Then some 4000 years later as the modern world begins with the large strides forward of the technically superior Roman Empire, God was there again, being born of a woman. We measure our dating system from that point, AD or some people say CE, Common Era, we can call it Common Era but it still means from the birth of Christ. Emmanuel—God with us. When Moses and Elijah spoke with Jesus on the Mount of Transfiguration, it seemed a very natural thing for them to do; it was as if they all knew each other because they had all met before and were having a reunion and a talk. In Hebrews 1:3 we read that, "The Son is the radiance of God's glory and the exact representation of his being." God was walking among us once again.

Abram was ten descendents down from Shem, and Abram would have heard stories from his relatives about God. We don't know where Shem moved, there's a chance he moved south to the Canaan area. His family had scattered but the stories and advice handed down about Yahweh were passed on, though not all sections of the family adhered to them because Terah was now getting mixed up with the polytheism of Ur. Later, in the book of Joshua, God says that Terah worshipped other gods. In the Genesis storyline as soon as Terah starts to get wayward God is ready to step in and redirect Terah's son Abram to pick up the truth and run with it.

The family left Ur; Terah, who had three sons, Haran, Nahor, and Abram, was probably happy to leave the place where his son Haran had died. Haran seems to be the firstborn, partly because he died first and partly because one of his daughters married his brother Nahor. We know Abram couldn't be the firstborn; his name is mentioned first in the Genesis list of Terah's sons because he was the most influential in the rest of the story.

Stephen, in Acts 7:4, tells us that Abraham left the town of Haran after his father died, and his father died at the age of 205. Genesis 12:4 informs us that Abram was 75 when he left Haran, making Terah 130 when Abram was born.

Haran was born when his father was 70 years old and we know that Abram was born when his father was 130, which would make Haran 60 years old when Abram was born. Haran's son Lot could have been born before that, so although Lot was Abram's nephew they could have been about the same age, which is maybe why they stuck together; they grew up together like brothers. In fact when they were struggling to find land for their herds Abram said to Lot, "Please let there be no strife between you and me, nor between my herdsmen and your herdsmen, for we are brothers." We can work out the ages of the family because Galatians 3:16–17 tells us that from when the promises were first made, to when Moses administered the Law, there were 430 years. Abram received his first promise in Ur, when God said, "I will make you into a great nation . . . and all peoples on earth will be blessed through you." This was God's original intention when he breathed into Adam.

Terah's family members were keeping their heritage very close. We don't know too much of what happened to Noah's other offspring through Shem, Ham, and Japheth even though they also were from Adam, but Genesis singles out the thread that is important for us to keep our eyes on. It's a little like watching an intricate movie where you must pay attention to the plot or you may miss something that later proves to be important.

Terah's family went to some lengths to keep their familial bonds tight. They made their way upstream of the river Euphrates. There may have been other people moving from Ur, the Lord had started to scatter them from that region, so the route they took would have most probably been with other migrants. We know that the prosperous city of Ur didn't finish the grand plans the people had made for themselves which began in the late third millennium BC.[1] Later, the rising empire of the Babylonians would absorb Sumer.[2] Abram had been told by the LORD to go to a land he would be shown. They would most probably have travelled along the common trade route heading northwest from southern Mesopotamia to modern-day Turkey. Travelling about 20 miles a day—the Tigris-Euphrates Valley was made for travelling—in about two months or so they came to the town of Haran, which has the same name as Terah's deceased son. It's located near the source of the Balikh River, a tributary of the Euphrates. The city had some links with Ur; the same moon god was worshipped in both cities. Terah and his family had probably made the journey before and had links with both cities, particularly, as tradition tells us, that Terah was a rather good craftsman who put his skill to work making idols.

The craftsmanship of Ur at that time was particularly artistic and aesthetically pleasing, as can still be seen. In the Mesopotamian room in the British Museum in London, thousands of people look at the "Ram in a Thicket" each week. In fact in 2013 some 6.7 million people visited the museum and the Ram is one of the focal points. The ram's head and legs are layered in hammered gold leaf, its ears are copper, the horns and the fleece on its shoulders are of blue lapis lazuli, and the body's fleece is made of

1. British Museum, "Third Dynasty of Ur."
2. Crawford, *Sumer and the Sumerians*, 1–28; Kramer, *Sumerians*, 40–72.

white shell. The figure's under parts are gold and its belly is silver plate. The tree the ram is caught in is also covered in gold leaf with gold flowers. The figure stands on a small rectangular base decorated with a mosaic of shell, red limestone, and lapis lazuli. The ram was made in Ur before Abraham was born and is beautiful to behold.

Some people say that the story of Abraham being told to sacrifice a ram caught in a thicket is based on an earlier theme which is highlighted by the figure now on display in the museum. However I look at it the other way round, God not only speaks to Adam's race, but as we have seen in Genesis chapter 1 he first spoke to man in general, and he continues to speak to us. The atheist C. S. Lewis was lead to Christianity because he seemed to read the gospel story in ancient myths that ostensibly had nothing to do with the New Testament: God is able to ignite the imaginations of all men. He loves all men whom he has created, whatever time they lived on earth. Men lost their way, and since we have learned sin, we need help. Adam was chosen to represent all men, to tell us a story, to take part in a play, a drama. The story of the garden of Eden is a description of us all; we have all fallen. We may not have been given such a specific command to follow like Adam received because the law is already in our hearts, it has been ever since we were made in the image of God. Adam and his wife broke the command given to them, which symbolizes how we have all broken the commands that God placed in our hearts.

The theory that humans have occupied planet earth long before Adam came along is not new, although now we have the science to inform us that some of the earliest cites like Jericho have been occupied since 7000 BC, and before that, many years before that, men have roamed the earth following God's commission for us to fill the earth. But even before we had the science to show us that man has been on earth for such a long time, theologians have discussed it, and books have been written. (Throughout the centuries some of the ideas were seized upon for racial propaganda purposes, which of course, is not what the Bible teaches. We all came from the dust of the ground, the message of scripture is that God is no respecter of persons, we are all equal in his sight.) Even the children's book *The Lion the Witch and the Wardrobe*—the well known Christian allegorical book from The Chronicles of Narnia—refers to the White Witch descending from Lilith, who was regarded to be Adam's first wife. Isaiah mentions Lilith and the Jewish Talmud goes into a little more explanation of how she ought to be regarded. Legend has also played a part explaining that Lilith was made from earth like Adam, not from Adam's rib like Eve. The man Adam didn't have a first wife, of course, but if "man in general" has a history before the man Adam then its easier to see how these stories came to be.

When I was a boy, I remember talking with an older Christian man about the long ages past before Adam. Also, my granddad's Bible has been passed down to me and I notice that the first chapter of Genesis has a printed footnote which says, "The first creative act refers to the dateless past and gives scope for all geological ages." Furthermore, Ellicott's well known Bible Commentary written in the 1800s tells us that, "A creative day is not a period of twenty-four hours, but an aeon, or period of indefinite duration, as the Bible itself teaches us."[3] The modern preoccupation with "literal" days of Genesis chapter 1 and rejection of earth's long ages could be a backlash from the well-publicized trial back in 1925 when a young teacher from Dayton, Tennessee, was fined $100 for teaching evolution even though it was in one of the school textbooks; teaching evolution was against state law at that time and remained so until 1967. A movie and a couple of TV dramas have been made about the courtroom proceedings, and it is the defense team who, even though they lost the case, come out looking sensible and fairminded. At the end of the movie, which is called *Inherit The Wind*, the defense lawyer picks up the Bible and Darwin's book, balancing them in his hands as if he was a scale. Then he puts the two together with a hard thud and walks out with them side by side in his right hand.

Rev. Dr. Malcolm Brown, who is the Church of England's Director of Mission and Public Affairs wrote in 2008 to the deceased author of *On The Origin Of Species* saying, "The Church of England owes you an apology for misunderstanding you and, by getting our first reaction wrong, encouraging others to misunderstand you still." Charles Darwin being unable to respond on this earthly plane, his great-great grandson Andrew Darwin did the responding for him. Andrew didn't take kindly to the apology calling it "pointless." The Associated Press published the headline: "Vatican wants to end battle with science." A Vatican project has been set up to help end the "mutual prejudice" between religion and science. The Vatican project was inspired by Pope John Paul II's declaration that the church's seventeenth-century denunciation of Galileo was an error resulting from "tragic mutual incomprehension." Galileo was condemned for supporting Nicolaus Copernicus's discovery that the earth revolved around the sun; church teaching at the time placed earth at the center of the universe. God can teach the

3. R. Smith, *Bible Commentary*, 13.

scientists something through the church and teach the church something through Science. Science can teach about physics because that is the skill God has given them and the church can teach about metaphysics because that is the gift given to them. Science teaches about the natural domain and the church teaches about the supernatural domain. It's possible that scientists go beyond their boundaries when they hypothesize about why things have happened and the church goes beyond its boundaries when it tells us how things have happened. Maybe it's Andrew Darwin's job to tell us what he has found out about how the universe works and the church's job to teach Andrew why he should receive an apology with grace.

Despite all our preconceived notions and fashionable doctrines God is still able to get his message across. The "Ram in the Thicket" that was made in Ur by an unknown craftsman is on display at the British Museum, and a second "Ram in the Thicket," also made in Ur can be seen at the University of Pennsylvania Museum in Philadelphia. They remind each one of us of the sacrifice that Abraham made, and consequently the sacrifice Jesus made. The skilled craftsmen in Ur are still having their handiwork admired and getting people to think.

Gradually the people of southern Mesopotamia, although they were a civilized group of city-states, lost their way, and they developed a preoccupation with predicting the future. People were given specific jobs of looking at the livers of animals, which were believed to tell people what decisions to make. The diviner's job would also be to analyze the flight of birds, another accepted form of divination. The king himself may have made decisions because of what those skilled at divining had told him. Of course, a society isn't going to last too long when decisions are made in such an arbitrary fashion. It's not surprising that the children of Israel were told to have nothing to do with divination.

So Abram was told by his newly found friend to leave Ur. By the time they reached the city of Haran they had travelled about 700 miles. It doesn't look like Abram's brother Nahor travelled with them at this time but he did at some point make the journey. Travelling 700 miles on foot or riding camels may seem a touch arduous to us today, but physical fitness was a normal part of life in those days. The human body is designed to move, and when it moves it responds to the movement by getting stronger. Today we travel in cars or public transportation, and many people work in offices, so we have to make a special effort to go to the gym, or run, or cycle to compensate for our modern way of life. In those days people worked in fields, did washing manually, and hunted for food. Travelling some distance was a regular feature of life. Plus we have to remember that Terah's family had special strength and length of days still inside their bodies. They still outlived regular human beings by some years; not all of the advantages of carrying God's seed had been taken from them. Abram was 70 years old when they left Ur; his father was 200 years old.

Abram's original intent was to follow the trade route around the Fertile Crescent down to Phoenicia and Canaan, but Terah, it seems, didn't want to go any further than the city of Haran. Terah probably had some standing in Haran, possibly because of his great age, strength, and maybe his artistic ability along with his previous links with the city. Many of Adam's descendents were thought of as chiefs or kings; there are stories of kings or pharaohs who take pride in having some sort of demi-god ancestor in their family line, whether that's through Adam's descendents or the nephilim we don't know. Abram stayed with the family until his father died at the age of 205. Word would have been sent back to Abram's brother Nahor in Ur about their father's demise and Nahor and his family made their way to the area of Paddan-Aram, which was the area in which the city of Haran is located. Nahor's family settled there and became prosperous. Abram then continued his journey, heading south from Turkey, taking his wife, his nephew Lot, people who worked for them in Haran, and his possessions, which could have included some animals. He would have to cross the Euphrates River. Four millennia ago the city of Ur was on the northern bank of the Euphrates (the river changed its course over time and Ur was abandoned). Abram could have stayed north of the river on his journey to Haran but the journey to Canaan would require crossing the Euphrates, which was no small matter. The root of the word Hebrew means to "cross over"; the name also ties in nicely with Abram's ancestor Eber who was born six generations before Abram. Eber also means to "pass" or "cross" or "the region beyond." Abram is the first person to be called a Hebrew.

This journey would be slower than the journey from Ur to Haran, but the Euphrates had known crossing points where the river could be waded. The reason they settled in Haran in the first place was probably Terah's decision. God had spoken to Abram in Ur, Abram related to his father what Yahweh had told him, and Terah had said, "Okay," probably because Terah had business opportunities in Haran and never intended to make the complete journey to Canaan.

When Abram left the city of Haran he took with him some of the wealth that had been accumulated—"a sinner's wealth is stored up for the righteous." There was another couple of rivers to negotiate as they were entering Canaan; Abram was becoming a cartographer, which would be useful for his children because they too would need to use the same route. Later, Abraham's grandson Jacob would make the journey to and from Paddan-Aram via the ford of the Jabbok River (a tributary of the Jordan River), which is most likely the same place that Abraham travelled. The Jabbok ford then leads nicely southwest on to a place where the Jordan River can be crossed; Abram would then be entering the country of his destination, Canaan. After the Jordan River crossing Abram would have then travelled 23 miles northwest along the Wadi Farah climbing up to Moreh in Shechem; there was a great tree there, a local land-mark. We then read, (Gen 12:6) with a hint of menace, that there were also Canaanites in the land. But, we are told Yahweh appeared to Abram. The visit was as if to congratulate him for reaching his destination after the long journey and to reassure Abram not to worry about the Canaanites because the land he was now in would be given to his seed. Abram had, of course, met Yahweh before, as some of his family before him had too. He knew what Yahweh looked like and their friendship started to take root. Abram must have wondered what his divine friend meant when he referred to his "seed" because even though Abram's name meant "exalted father," he had not as yet become a father.

God had managed to protect the seed prior to the Flood because there were only ten generations over quite a long space of time, but now that the family's life spans were falling the period between birth and puberty was also a lot narrower. So there would be more work for God to do in protecting the descent to Christ. However, there was a period of relaxation for the Lord because he was happy for Abram to live out his long years without Abram realizing what exactly he was carrying, and it meant the seed was safe. What was giving God an easy time was causing Abram some consternation; we know he believed God but he was perplexed as to how this offspring was to make an appearance. There in Moreh Abram built an altar to the LORD upon which an animal would be sacrificed, which, it seems, was a practice Adam had taught his offspring, and it pleased God.

Abram must have noticed that his friend Yahweh was a little preoccupied with the word "seed," but it seems Abram had not yet got the big picture of what was happening. God conceals things from us until the time is right for us to grasp what exactly is taking place. We sometimes put blinkers on horses because they can react in the wrong way to innocuous events, or sometimes the blinkers will help save the horse's life because we can lead them safely out of danger without them struggling. We can look back now and see what was happening to Abram and his family, but at the time they needed to trust in the Lord, and that trust would see them safely through to the completion of the great task they were about.

CHAPTER 14

Abram's Army

> By faith Abraham, when called to go to a place he would later receive as his inheritance, obeyed. (Heb 11:8)

ABRAM THEN HEADED ANOTHER 20 miles south to some hills that lay in between a town called Luz on the west and Ai on the east. (Luz would later be named Bethel by Abram's grandson Jacob.) Tents were pitched and an altar was built. Abram called on the name of Yahweh, though we don't read that Yahweh appeared this time, perhaps because God was fostering faith in Abram, teaching him to trust when he could not see.

Abram and his caravan continued their southward journey, leaving the hills between the two towns and passing the last town in Canaan, Beer-sheba, before they headed into the semi-arid area called the Negev, which is Hebrew for "dry land." There's not much by the way of water or food there and there was a particular shortage at that time, so Abram followed the "way to Shur" all the way to Egypt, which was where the Fertile Crescent comes to an end. Abram had travelled from one end of it to the other. The people of Mesopotamia must have heard stories about the people who lived on the far side of the crescent; some of those tales were not exactly true, as travellers sometimes like to make their stories sound a bit more exciting than they really are. But necessity drove Abram all the way to Egypt and these stories must have been weighing on Abram's mind because he told his wife Sarai to say she was his sister: Abram cried out, "They will kill me" (Gen 12:12). His view of the Egyptians being unlike "us civilized Mesopotamians" was probably based on the colorful stories of the villainous nature of Egyptians, which was without foundation. Egyptian culture dating back to 200 years before Abram was based on *maat*, which was the concept of truth, justice, law, morality, and balance. It's good for us to remember that God spoke to humanity in general when we were made in the image of God in Genesis chapter 1. Humankind has always had the shadow of God upon us, his reflection within us gets distorted sometimes and occasionally quite crooked but even in the worst of religions there is a faint resemblance of the actual truth. I'm sure that wrongdoing was among the Egyptians just as we also have crime and a justice system to deal with it; all civilized cultures do, that's why they are called civilized.

Abram told Sarai to masquerade as his sister because she was from Adam's stock, the women were "fair," in fact they were so fair that they had the beauty, strength, and long years to cause angels to fall. Had the Egyptians ever seen a woman like Sarai before? Abram wasn't sure and he didn't want to take any chances. Even though Sarai was now in her late sixties she had lost nothing of her splendor, and as Abram suspected, the Egyptians quickly spotted her and it wasn't long before she'd made it all the way to the palace to meet Pharaoh. However, God was not happy with Abram's deceit for two reasons: deceit is not part of his nature and secondly, Sarai was an important part of the royal line leading to God's son being born, which God was at particular pains to protect. Therefore, God inflicted serious diseases on Pharaoh and his household because Sarai was another man's wife. Pharaoh cried out to Abram, "Why didn't you tell me she was your wife?" Pharaoh shows his grasp upon morality by not only hearing what God says but also wanting to know why he should be led into an adulterous situation by Abram. He didn't want to commit adultery even if Sarai was stunning to behold, neither did he want to incur God's anger.

Abram had been given many animals and men and women servants by Pharaoh because of Sarai but now he is told to leave Egypt, although he is allowed to keep all he has been given. So Abram headed back through the dry Negev and then past the first town, Beersheba, and then turned north stopping from place to place: Hebron and Salem were on that pathway that forms a natural north-south route through the Judean hills, which Abram was slowly becoming familiar with. Lot also had flocks that were most likely from Abram who gave him a share of the animals bestowed upon him by Pharaoh. Lot was travelling along with Abram and the pathway they were travelling could not sustain the amount of animals they both had and arguments started to break out between Abram's herdsmen and

Lot's herdsmen. As we're being told this Genesis gives us a quick reminder that Canaanites, and also adds the Perizzites, were living in that area; they would also have animals that needed to graze, so a separation of Abram and Lot was the solution.

Abram was the complete gentleman that we suppose a great man to be. He left the choice to Lot, saying, "If you go to the left, I'll go to the right; if you go to the right, I'll go to the left." The pathway they were following was among rolling hills and as they travelled north they would see to their right the Jordan Valley, which led to the Dead Sea. The levels of the Dead Sea have tended to rise and fall throughout time, as I write this the levels are the lowest they've been for many years. Two basins hold the water, with the northern basin of the sea being deeper than the southern. From the advantage of the ridge-route Abram and Lot were travelling along they would see the gradual slope down to the plains both to the south and north of the Dead Sea. Lot saw that the area was well watered by the Jordan River and decided to head there with his entourage. The water was not so salty in those days and fertility would have been greater. It is also worth noting that the Dead Sea lies on a known fault-line—the Arabian-African tectonic plate boundary. The famous King's Highway ran along the east side of the Dead Sea area, the Highway was one of the trade routes used from Egypt through to the river Euphrates.

In the 1970s some 17,000 tablets were recovered from the courts of an ancient city called Ebla, which is in northern Syria. The tablets were written up to 500 years before Abraham's time. The cities that Lot chose to live among are mentioned on one tablet in the same order as mentioned in Genesis 14:2: Sodom, Gomorrah, Admah, Zeboiim, and Zoar, which are known as the cities of the plain (Gen 13:12).

Abram made his way a little further to the north and settled for a while in the meadows between Bethel and Ai where he had camped earlier. Abram was now without Lot, but not without the LORD who came to him after Lot's departure, and spoke with him once more. One of the subjects they talked about was the injustice and wrongdoing that was going on in the city of Sodom, though it may be rich, it was full of greed, iniquity, and promiscuity. The LORD was not pleased with what the cities of the plain were becoming. The prophet Ezekiel puts it like this:

> This was the sin of your sister Sodom: She and her daughters were arrogant, overfed and unconcerned; they did not help the poor and needy.

Abram reassured Yahweh that he would never let Sodom be in a position where they could dictate to him. Abram had given Lot a choice of going to the east or west and Yahweh then said to Abram that he should look north, south, east, and west, because all the land he could see would be given to him and his seed. Yahweh then suggests that Abram should walk throughout the length and breadth of the land. So Abram followed his friend's advice and moved his tents 18 miles south to Mamre near Hebron.

During this time Sodom and Gomorrah would have been prosperous business towns with traders often passing through. The five cities of the plain paid tribute to King Kedorlaomer. Kings in those days were not always as we imagine them today, they were chiefs or managers over a certain area, or men of renown. King Kedorlaomer was from the southeast area of Mesopotamia but further north than Ur, and it seems he was the traffic controller for the King's Highway.

The five cities of the plain wanted to control their own affairs and made a declaration of independence. The Mesopotamian chiefs who received the "road tax" gave it a couple of years but finally decided something had to be done to prevent the cities of the plain's rebellion from becoming permanent. So four of them, including King Kedorlaomer and the king of Sumer, Amraphel, joined forces and along with the necessary manpower, made a move on the cities of the plain. It seems the revolt had also been agreed upon by some of the other towns along the King's Highway, which gave rise to the Mesopotamian taskforce taking out several other towns en route. This action effectively removed all opposition from those living along the King's Highway, and also those who might have been called on to help defend when they started the main thrust of their campaign, which was aimed at the towns on the southeast shore of the Dead Sea. The Mesopotamian army was well versed in warfare as their own area had known battles and takeover bids for some time. Their strategic knowledge of military operations and the lay of the King's Highway, which was after all their responsibility, led the separatist kings of the cities of the plain into an ambush. With the Dead Sea being at a low point, mushy bitumen on the floor of the lake hindered some of the rebel soldiers, giving time for the rest of the rebel soldiers from the cities to run for the hills. The four invading kings got what they came for and carried off goods from Sodom and Gomorrah along with Lot and his possessions, as he was living there at the time. The chiefs of the cities of the plain hadn't thought things through and underestimated the strength and prowess of the authorities of the day.

One of the people who made it to the hills came and reported this to Abram the Hebrew. The whole countryside had been aware that a Mesopotamian force was in the area. Abram may have known the leaders of the campaign as he too was from southern Mesopotamia from a family that had standing in the area; only a few years had passed since he had been living there. King Kedorlaomer had probably descended from Shem's firstborn, Elam, they lived in the country of Elam whose borders extended into modern-day Iran. Abram probably didn't want to meddle with any trade-route agreements that existed between governing bodies, but the task force had taken a bridge too far when they included Lot and his possessions as part of the back-payment of arrears due. The Genesis text reads, "when Abram heard that his brother was taken captive," showing once again the close familial bonds in existence between the two men. Abram was a man of wealth and had always been a man who was respected; other sources outside the Bible speak of Abram as a great and just man, a man of understanding who first lived among the Chaldeans. And here we see Abram being forced into action by his "brother" and his brother's household being taken captive.

Abram was also from Mesopotamia where the Highways Commission had learned the art of enforcing their rule, and he too knew about strategic military action. We can now see just how large Abram's household was because he marshalled 318 trained men in his care. Abram had not idled his time away in the hills of Canaan, he had been passing on his knowledge and skills to those in his household. There would have been lessons and a timetable for training in the affairs of business and civil life, in the care of flocks and herds, and particularly in the art of war, which was necessary for the preservation of his family and compatriots from oppressors. Abram also had allies who lived nearby, one of whom was Mamre (after whom the town Abram was living in got its name). The taskforce was making its way back to Mesopotamia but progress wouldn't be fast. Among the procession would have been not only what was owed to the Mesopotamian chiefs but also the spoils of war, these were the spoils that Abram wanted to extract.

When Lot was seized, he may have explained to the coalition forces that he was new to the area and may have been willing to offer some proof, but by this time the excitement of war was upon the aggressors and they were not in the mood for listening. So they all started the long journey back to the "land between the rivers" heading along the King's Highway. A detachment of soldiers may have marched on ahead because all battles had been decided and foes overcome. By the time Abram had caught up with the company they were getting close to the northeastern town of Damascus. Abraham waited until it was night. He divided his men, and taking advantage of the darkness, they fell upon King Kedorlaomer's men unawares. Some were asleep in their beds, and others drunk, as Josephus relates, panic ensued and the Mesopotamian taskforce quickly scattered. Abram's game plan was a success; he gathered the captives along with their goods and led them back.

A runner would have been dispatched to take the news back to Canaan, where the townsfolk were eagerly awaiting news. By the time Abram and the liberated prisoners of war reached Canaan a welcoming party had assembled. The king of Salem was one of them; his name was Melchizedek. Abram and his household had been in the area a while, they had passed Salem before, so Abram was probably acquainted with Melchizedek. Genesis tells us that he was the priest of God Most High. The Bible tells us how God worked through one particular family to bring his Son into the world that we may be saved, but there are other stories going on too. God is working in many ways that we don't get to hear about. Just like God spoke with man in Genesis chapter 1, he is able to work in people's lives without us hearing much about it. Melchizedek is one example; we don't know how he got to be priest of God Most High, but God is always ready to surprise us with his goodness. Melchizedek brought out bread and wine and issued a blessing on Abram and God Most High the creator of heaven and earth. God had been with Abram and his men and delivered his enemies into his hands. Abram was pleased to give Melchizedek a tenth of what had been collected from the fleeing coalition forces. One tradition identifies Melchizedek with Shem but the New Testament (Heb 7:3) tells us he is without genealogy, yet Shem is not without genealogy. Shem lived long but he would have died in the third millennium BC and we are now in the second millennium BC. The pedigree of a Jewish priest was important in them taking office, but no such requirement was asked of Melchizedek, God chose him for his own good reasons.

The king of Sodom was also there, and no doubt pleased to see the victorious army return with so many goods. He offered to let Abram keep all the goods, Abram, remembering his talk with Yahweh about this very subject, refused and told the king why. Abram added one word to the title that Melchizedek had for God Most High and the word he added was Yahweh. Abram said, "I have raised my hand in an oath to Yahweh, God Most

High, Creator of heaven and earth, that I will not take a thread or sandal strap or anything that belongs to you, so you can never say, 'I made Abram rich'" (Gen 14:23).

CHAPTER 15

Signing the Contract

> The LORD appeared to Abram and said to him, "I am God Almighty; Walk before Me, and be blameless. (Gen 17:1)

ABRAM MADE HIS WAY back through the undulating green meadows to the town of Mamre, with the eponymous leader of the town walking with him. Abram had made sure the king of Sodom had given his friend Mamre the wages he deserved. Abram was making a few good friendships in his new land. His tents were pitched close to Mamre, he felt comfortable there among allies and friends and some distinguished trees.

Shortly after the excitement of the rout Abram spoke with the LORD again but this time not in person but in a vision. The friendship between the LORD and Abram had developed so much that Abram now felt at liberty to be frank with the LORD. Abram uses a new title for God that we've not heard him use before; there seems to be a hint of pleading attached to it. Abram must have noticed that Melchizedek was very respectful in the way he addressed God. Abram was familiar with Yahweh and when we are familiar with someone it's easy to be a little more informal, which is fine unless there comes a right time to show respect and we fail to do so. This time when addressing him Abram says, "Lord Yahweh," the Hebrew word for Lord is *Adonai*:

> "What can you give me since I remain childless?"
> Abram continues, "You have given me no children."
> God replies, "Look up at the sky and count the stars—if indeed you can count them."

Then he said to him, "So shall your offspring be."

Abram believed the LORD, and he credited it to him as righteousness.

The LORD then said, "I am Yahweh, who brought you out of Ur of the Chaldeans to give you this land to take possession of it."

Abram asked, "O Lord Yahweh, how shall I know that I shall gain possession of the land?"

A ritual is described in cuneiform texts from Mari in Mesopotamia dating from 1800 BC describing contracts that were entered into by cutting animals in half and the two parties contracting a treaty or alliance by passing between the halves. Genesis 15:9–18 describes a ritual for making a covenant or agreement between Yahweh and Abram. Abram cut in half several animals, and a "smoking fire pot with a blazing torch" passed between the halves. The covenant was now official: God was going to give Abram and his offspring the land he was now camped in. The LORD told him from the time he actually had his promised descendent (Isaac) there would be another 400 years before his descendents would be able to take possession of it, and part of it would include his descendents being in a land not their own, where they would be enslaved and ill-treated. Then in the fourth generation his descendents would come back to Canaan and could proceed to take the land. Four hundred years seems more than four generations, until we remember that God was talking to Abram and his line still had some length of years. God had said Adam's line would have a shortened life span to 120 years. Abram's hadn't got down to that yet, he lived to be 175, but his grandson Jacob died at 147. So when we look at it like that four generations for 400 years is about right.

The 400 years also reminds us that from Isaac's birth 30 years would have passed from the time Abraham first spoke to Yahweh in Ur. There were 430 years altogether between the first promise and the law being given (Gal 3:17). Abraham was 100 when Isaac was born leaving 30 from when God first spoke to Abraham; hence Abraham was 70 years old when he first met Yahweh in Ur.

Abram had been worried that his servant Eliezer would inherit all he had, but God told him that a son from his own body would be his heir. Over the next few weeks Sarai thought she may be able to take the matter one step forward by suggesting that Abram use his body to produce one: Mesopotamian custom allowed for a wife to give her handmaid to her husband as a surrogate mother. Pharaoh had given Abram and Sarai menservants and maidservants and one of the maidservants was a woman called Hagar. Some of Abram's frustration with the situation revealed itself and he agreed to the liaison. The Mesopotamians had many qualities for which we should be grateful: they taught the world how to write, cultivated crops, designed the arch, and invented the wheel, the plough, irrigation, and many other innovations. Their system of mathematics was sexagesimal, from which we derive the modern-day usage of 60 seconds in a minute, 60 minutes in an hour, and 360 degrees in a circle. They also had the rule of law and sought to secure social justice throughout the land. But to the modern mind, asking your husband to sleep with one of your handmaidens is bound to end in tears. Somehow Abram and Sarai were not yet on board with the divine plan, even though Abram was God's friend, he didn't seem to grasp what the program was, nor the timing needed to put it into effect.

Hagar found herself pregnant and got a little bit above herself; Sarai immediately spotted her change in attitude and blamed Abram. We can understand Sarai's annoyance, she had been married to Abram for many years and had no children to show for it, then here comes this Egyptian woman who probably only slept with Abram for a matter of weeks and quickly finds herself "with child." Sarai gives Hagar some serious grief, so that Hagar can see no way out but running away. She heads south along the "way to Shur," the same way she originally came with Abram and Sarai when she left her country, but this time there was no large caravan with access to food, drink, and help, she was on her own.

The "way to Shur" is about 150 miles long; Hagar would have been trying to remember where the water locations were and had made her way 50 miles south of Beersheba when she found one. She had probably travelled about 70 miles to that point. An angel of the LORD came looking for Hagar and found her by a water source. The angel may have had the appearance of a man, as often happened, but Hagar would have known that this was no ordinary man, because he addressed her by name and her position, not as Abram's wife but as Sarai's maid. Yet he spoke kindly and was concerned for her, asking what she was doing. Hagar told him she was "running away." It looks like Abram had been either talking to Yahweh, or praying to him about the situation because the messenger told her to go back and submit saying, "the LORD has heard of your misery." Her reward would be a son named Ishmael whose descendents would be too numerous to count. God spoke directly through the angel similar to the way he speaks through his prophets. Hagar replied by saying, "You are the God who sees me." On her hasty escape from Mamre where Abram and Sarai were living, she must have felt desolate as if no one cared that she was alone in the world, which would have been in contrast to her return journey to Mamre because she'd encountered someone from beyond this material world and was now filled with hope.

Abram was 86 years old when Ishmael was born; it had been 16 years since he first met Yahweh in Ur and 11 years since he'd left Haran. He seemed to like the location of Mamre and stayed there for the next few years; years in which Yahweh was quiet and was not seen by Abram. The new father had now got Ishmael to look after, teach, and play with, and that must have taken up Abram's attention, but he must have wondered where Yahweh was. In fact Abram was 99 years old when he next saw the LORD. Yahweh reminded Abram that the contract he'd made with him was still on course and that he'd greatly increase his numbers. Abram was overwhelmed to see Yahweh once again; it had been over 15 years since the last time they had spoken face to face, which was shortly after Lot had left. This time Yahweh introduces himself to Abram as God Almighty and tells him to walk before him and be blameless, in other words "trust me and don't try taking matters into your own hands." Adam had listened to Eve and now Abram had listened to Sarai—listening to God is what counts. Yahweh is being honest with Abram when he refers to himself as God Almighty, Abram and Yahweh are good friends but Abram ought to know exactly who Yahweh is. Abram falls facedown. God continues, "As for me, this is my covenant with you: You will be the father of many nations. No longer will you be called Abram; your name will be Abraham." The LORD, who enjoys making a point by poetic wordplay adds one letter to Abram's name and the old meaning of "exalted father" changes to "father of numerous people." The second half of Abram's name will now be *raham*, which in the Arabic language signifies "numerous."[1] God continues to explain that his half of the contract will be to make Abraham very fruitful and that kings and nations will proceed from him.

So that was God's part of the contract, then the LORD said, "As for you . . . You are to undergo circumcision, and it will be the sign of the covenant between me and you. For the generations to come every male among you who is eight days old must be circumcised," which was Abraham's part of the contract. Abraham stood up and acknowledged his part of the agreement. But the LORD had not yet finished, he continued, "As for Sarai your

1. Hottinger, *Smegma Oriental*, 88.

wife, you are no longer to call her Sarai; her name will be Sarah. I will bless her and will surely give you a son by her. I will bless her so that she will be the mother of nations; kings of peoples will come from her." Abraham didn't seem to realize that this contract he'd made with the LORD also included Sarai. She was from the close familial connection that had the seed implanted within it and God was watching over it. Sarai is now formally a part of the covenant, as she is to be the mother of the promised seed. Her name is therefore changed to Sarah, "princess"—an apt name for someone who is to be a matriarchal forbear of the King of kings.

This is news to Abraham who shows the relaxed friendship he has with Yahweh by falling down laughing as friends sometimes do in each other's company. He and Sarah are surely beyond the age of childbearing and childrearing, at least when compared to the general population. What will his employees think? Having a child at such an advanced age will be a wonder; it will astound people. Abraham could see the comic element involved. Once Abraham has recovered from his laughing fit he starts to reason with Yahweh. This is how Genesis puts it:

"'If only Ishmael might live under your blessing!' Then God said, 'Yes, but your wife Sarah will bear you a son, and you will call him Isaac. I will establish my covenant with him as an everlasting covenant for his descendants after him. And as for Ishmael, I have heard you: I will surely bless him; I will make him fruitful and will greatly increase his numbers. He will be the father of twelve rulers, and I will make him into a great nation. But my covenant I will establish with Isaac, whom Sarah will bear to you by this time next year.' When he had finished speaking with Abraham, God went up from him." Which means he ascended: allowing Abraham to see a little of what being God Almighty means.

The males of Abraham's household must have wondered what on earth was going on, because on that same day Abraham got to work on his side of the covenant, most likely announcing that the next few days would be a holiday for the men and the women would have to take up the slack. If any male didn't want to be a part of the contract between Abraham and God then he would have to leave Abraham's employ, that's the deal.

Abraham spent a few days recovering and telling Sarah what her new name was and what God had said would happen. On one of those convalescing days, probably just as he was starting to feel normal again, round about midday Abraham sat outside the entrance to his tent, looked over and saw three men standing nearby. He immediately recognized the LORD, but this time there were two other men with him. He may have met the two men before in Ur, because a similar mission was in operation to what had previously happened at Ur. Abraham gathers himself and hurries over to where they were and bows low before them. Then he speaks, probably thinking of his quickness to seal the covenant by getting circumcized, and says, "If I have found favor in your eyes, please stay for lunch." It was after all, lunchtime. The men agree and sit down under one of the trees, while Abraham heads back to the tent and probably says something like, "Sarah, Yahweh is here with two friends, can you make some nice lunch please? Serve that bread you make so well." Sarah gets to work, Abraham heads for the door and turning says, "Oh Sarai, I mean Sarah, please make haste." He then selects a choice tender calf and tells someone to prepare it. He then arranges for some water to be brought so his visitors can wash their feet, after which he brings out lunch along with some butter and milk. While they eat he stands close by in the shade of a tree.

It's interesting for us to note that Yahweh and the angels were happy to eat, as if once they had taken the form of a man their bodies could take on nutrients and benefit from them. They ate some carbohydrates for energy, protein for muscle growth, and a little fat. After Jesus was resurrected he too ate some food.

After lunch, sitting in the shade of the trees of Mamre the men ask where Sarah is. Yahweh and the two other men are now using Sarah's new name. "She's over there in the tent," Abraham replied. The LORD then said, "I promise I'll come back to you about this time next year, and your wife Sarah will have a son." Sarah is listening to this: Sarah, a long-liver, still had beauty and strength but she knew that her time of fertility had past, so with a laugh to herself she made light of the prospect. So Yahweh said to Abraham, "Why did Sarah laugh and say, 'Will I really have a child, now that I am old?' Is anything too exceptional for Yahweh to do? I will return to you at the appointed time next year, and Sarah will have a son." The tone of this suggests the response was less a rebuke and more of a reassuring plea. All the same Sarah is worried that she is being considered the weak link in the chain and feels constrained to make an appearance and reassure everyone that she didn't laugh. Yahweh knows better.

The men didn't stay too long after this because they had business to attend to. They started walking towards Sodom, and Abraham, still a little sore, walked with them to see them on their way. In these middle chapters of Genesis we get to hear quite a lot of the dialogue between Abraham and the

LORD. We may find ourselves wondering what they talked about at previous encounters with each other but here we find out how their conversation went. Yahweh said to his two companions, and of course Abraham could hear, "Shall I hide from Abraham what I am about to do?" Then he gave some reasoning why he should be frank and inform him about the plan for the current mission: "For I know him that he will direct his children and his household after him to keep the way of the LORD by doing what is right and just." This statement is similar to what any of us might say, "Yeah, I know Jim, he's a good guy, I'm sure I can trust him." Abraham received the Lord's endorsement in a similar way. We have already seen that Abraham is a fine teacher and instructor: when he needed to assemble the men of his household for a rescue mission they were trained and ready for it. Abraham took the role of instructing those around him and those who would come after him seriously. We are reading these words of what took place that day because of Abraham: he was from Mesopotamia, a people who were skilled in the art of writing, Abraham would pass on what he knew to his children, and they would value every word and pass it on to each successive generation all the way to us. Abraham is still instructing his children.

So the LORD explained to Abraham that, "The outcry against Sodom and Gomorrah is so great and their sin so grievous that I will go down and see if what they have done is as bad as the outcry that has reached me. If not, I will know." This is a similar statement to when the LORD first went down to see the tower and the city the men of southern Mesopotamia were building, which is where he first met Abram, and so now we see how it could have happened. Yahweh had been a part of Abraham's life for close to 30 years, they knew each other well. Yahweh lets Abraham know he wants to see how the people of Sodom will treat his two friends: will they welcome them or mistreat them? The cities of the plain were not far from the King's Highway and travellers would stop at the cities looking for accommodation. It was probably these travellers and their families that had been robbed, abused, and even murdered that had appealed to God in prayer, which is why the LORD mentioned the "outcry" that had reached him.

The quartet has been walking southeast which descends down towards the Dead Sea area. Tradition says Abraham walked as far as the village of Bani Na'im, which is about a walk of eight miles. This is where Yahweh and Abraham stopped, but the two angels continued on their way. Since the LORD had told Abraham his intentions for the day, and remembering what happened at Ur, he knew the LORD would take action if he deemed it necessary. So Abraham drew close to Yahweh as two men do when they are about to talk about a significant decision—a two-man conference. Yahweh listened as Abraham made his point:

> Will you actually destroy the righteous along with the wicked? Supposing there are fifty righteous ones within the city. Will you actually destroy it and not spare the place for the sake of the fifty righteous that are found there? Far be it from you to do such a thing—to kill the righteous along with the wicked, so that the righteous and the wicked are treated alike! The Judge of all the earth will do what is right, won't he? . . . Yahweh replied, "If I find fifty righteous people in the city of Sodom, I will spare the whole place for their sake."

Abraham continues to talk and Yahweh continues to listen, which tells us something about God's willingness to hear what we have to say. Yahweh showed no signs of impatience even though Abraham was taking some time to get where he was going. He listened to each point Abraham made, and gave an appropriate response to each question. Abraham whittled the numbers of righteous people down to ten; he must have thought it was a job well done because there must surely be ten righteous people there. Abraham had been trying to secure Lot's safety and feeling confident that Lot and his family would now be safe. Abraham made his way steadily back home and Yahweh went on his way.

It's a good walk to the plains from the village of Bani Na'im, the path descends and the strong angels would negotiate the walk at a good pace, but it wasn't until evening that the duo arrived at Sodom. Lot had been living there for about 18 years and was now an elder who sat at the city gates, which was customary. If Lot was round about the same age as Abraham he would by this point be in his late nineties. He was from the same strong stock as Abraham and was probably the oldest man in Sodom although he would not have looked it. It's possible that Lot noticed that the two men approaching the town were companions of Yahweh, they would have something about them that he'd seen before, or he may have possibly met them before in Ur. In the Gospel of Mark an angel is described as a young man, it's safe to assume that these two men also had a young appearance. Lot, who was old, gave the young men the same courteous greeting that Abraham had. Lot showed himself to be hospitable, caring, and righteous, so here was one righteous man, just nine to go to save Sodom. The two men politely refused Lot's offer of accommodation saying they would spend the night in the town square. They wanted to check the place out and see how the majority of the citizens treated them. But Lot insisted, which is an interesting scenario to think about because it means that it's possible for a man's resolve to prevail over an angel's point of view. Peter in the New Testament tells us that, "Even angels long to look into these things." Angels seem to have the same inquiring minds that we have and are able to be influenced.

The young men were eventually persuaded and accepted Lot's invitation and ate supper with him and his family. But Lot wasn't the only one who had spotted the young men because a rabble had assembled outside his house. In fact, these angels had made a big impression on the whole town. Word had quickly spread that there were some extremely good looking, handsome, and well proportioned young men visiting the town. The crowd was made up of both young and old who had become inflamed with lust and were shouting to Lot, "Where are the men who came to you tonight? Bring them out to us so that we can have sex with them." Lot went outside to appeal to them; he shut the door behind him. He'd seen this before and knew that they wouldn't be persuaded by reason. This was the "outcry" that had gone up to the Lord and it was why he was coming down to see it for himself. The men of Sodom were hell-bent on getting their way.

Lot tries to make a deal with the men, his two virgin daughters instead of the two men. This was Lot's way of trying to placate the men. It seems a ghastly deal, but we can see a little of what was going through Lot's mind. That his heavenly visitors should be abused was unthinkable, particularly as they were under the protection of his roof, so he took the drastic and warped step of offering his daughters to the lecherous men. The daughters were at least from earth and it would be a crime against human beings, but if the men of Sodom abused the angels it would be a crime against heaven. Lot's attempt to appease the men incited them even more. "Stand back!" was their menacing reply.

The two angels who were listening to all this behind the door quickly opened the door and pulled Lot back inside. Genesis tells us that the mob moved forward to break down the door. The Sodomites were then struck with blindness. That means darkness fell upon them so they could not see to find the door. Evening had already fallen and as we have said, the whole Dead Sea area lies between two tectonic plates that are pushing together. The area forms part of the Great Rift Valley, the deepest and most spectacular scar on the planet's surface. The two plates are moving in a general north-northeast direction, but the Arabian Plate is moving faster than the African

Plate. The grating together of the plates often causes seismic activity, which has been common throughout history right up to today. The deepest land trench on the globe lies at 1,300 feet below sea level, and had already started to billow some plumes of dust as the men of Sodom searched for the door to Lot's house. The dust darkened the area completely. It is at that point we know the men of Sodom had reached the point of no return. The plates were on the move and would soon engulf the area with burning bitumen in which the area was so rich. The men of Sodom "wearied" of finding the door to Lot's house and gave up.

The two angels knew now what was going to happen to the city: the men of Sodom had sealed its fate by their gross outrageous behavior. The angels walking into the town had been a test, they were even prepared to stay in the town square, but Lot knew it would be far too dangerous for them there. But even in the safety of Lot's house the two angels were still sought out by the town's people who wanted to abuse them. The two angels asked Lot if he had any other people in the town who belonged to him. "Yes," he replied, "I have two future sons-in-law." So, that's Lot and his wife, two daughters, and two men who were espoused to his daughters, that is still only six people, not yet ten. Sodom would not be spared.

Lot got a torch and made his way to where his daughters' boyfriends lived and told them that the two men who were staying with him have said that Sodom is about to be destroyed so flee for your lives. They couldn't believe it and thought it was some sort of joke.

When Lot got back home the two angels probably told him to get some sleep because he'd have to be up early and get moving. As dawn broke the angels told Lot to hurry and take his family and get to high ground. Lot lingered; after all, he was about to leave all his earthly goods. The previous evening Lot insisted that the angels could not stay in the public square, but now the tables were turned, the angels insisted he could not stay in Sodom. These were strong angels who couldn't easily be resisted, one angel grabbed Lot in one hand and his wife in the other, the second angel had a daughter in each hand and they dragged the family out of the town. It appears that the angels weren't about to let the Lord down, they were determined to do the task assigned to them, even if the earthbound humans were making it difficult for them.

The family was taken to relative safety but there was still some way to go. Lot and his family are told to continue to flee and not to stop anywhere in the plain, not to linger or look back, they are told to get to high ground.

It looks like the original trio of Yahweh and the two angels had regrouped and were now back together: Lot had originally called the two men "my lords" (*Adon*) when they entered the town, which is a term of respect that may be addressed to men, but now he calls one of them *Adonai*—the title reserved for God.

Lot asks if he can avoid the climb. Ezekiel tells us that a part of the sin of Sodom was being arrogant, overfed, and unconcerned. Perhaps a little of the ways of Sodom had infiltrated Lot's life, particularly the "overfed" part. Whatever the reason, he didn't want the long climb. The hills to the west of the Dead Sea rise less steeply than the hills on the east but the climb is still well over 1000 meters. Lot pleads his case, "Your servant has found favor in your eyes, and you have shown great kindness to me in sparing my life. But I can't flee to the mountains; this disaster will overtake me, and I'll die. Look, here is a town near enough to run to, and it is small. Let me flee to it—it is very small, isn't it? Then my life will be spared." Lot's power of persuasion worked once again: "Very well, I will grant this request too; I will not overthrow the town you speak of. But flee there quickly, because I cannot do anything until you reach it." Yahweh's friendship with Abraham was revealing itself. The LORD felt constrained to withhold sentence until Lot had reached safety. He took into account Abraham's intercession for Lot and Yahweh takes friendships seriously. Yahweh was a good and faithful friend to Abraham. We can see here a little of the importance of prayer. Even though ten righteous people had not been found, Yahweh was not about to let his friend Abraham down.

By the time Lot got to Zoar, which is the name of the town he escaped to, the sun had risen and the Lord carried out his plan. Friction from the movement of the plates set the tar ablaze and the violent earthquake sent plumes of debris into the air that rained back down upon the four cities of the plain. In December 2011 *National Geographic News* reported on the archaeological drilling taking place in the Dead Sea; core samples revealed sediment layers going back throughout history. Geologist Steven Goldstein and his team found that normally rhythmic layers had been disrupted by large earthquakes. Geophysicist Zvi Ben-Avraham reported that one seismically active time appears to have been about 4000 years ago, which is roughly the time of Sodom and Gomorrah. Ben-Avraham went on to say that during this period, according to the book of Genesis, God "rained fire and brimstone from heaven, and destroyed all."[2]

2. Lovett, "Bible Accounts," lines 51–52.

In the pool of melting asphalt and with the northern waters engulfing the plain, the cities sink. Lot's wife lingers behind her husband and looks back, which is contrary to the Lord's express command. She is caught in the sweeping tempest and becomes a pillar of salt, the spray of the salt-sulphurous rain seems to have suffocated her, and then encrusted her whole body. Josephus mentions that in his day the pillar was still there and that he had seen it. Other witnesses from antiquity, including Irenaeus and Tertullian, speak of it as being there too. Lot's concern that the thick dust storm caused by the earthquake and subsequent landslides from the hills on either side of the Dead Sea would overtake him became a reality for his wife, whose hesitation caused her demise.

High up on the western hills that same morning, Abraham was also up early and returned to Bani Na'im where he had last spoke with Yahweh. The village extends east to the mountains that overlook the Dead Sea and by the time Abraham got there he saw dense smoke rising from the plains below.

Lot didn't stay long in Zoar; they decided to climb higher and for a while they lived in a cave, in what was a sad state of affairs. Lot's daughters' boyfriends were gone and there was little prospect of finding anymore within the foreseeable future. They were under the impression that the devastation of the earthquake had killed everyone for many miles all around. Their plans of having a family had been dashed. They had wanted to become mothers, "as is the custom all over the world." So after a while the older daughter devised a plan: they got Lot to drink wine; grapes from that area are abundant, and as he lay in a daze she lay with him and conceived. When he awoke he didn't realize what had happened. When the younger daughter saw that the plan worked, she did it too. Lot had been prepared to sacrifice his daughters' virginity to the braying mob and now in a weird twist of reaping what you sow he finds he has taken their virginity himself. The older daughter's son was named Moab and he is the father of the Moabites. Moab sounds like the Hebrew words for "from father." The younger daughter's child was named Ben-Ammi which means "son of my people," and he became father of the Ammonites.

While all this was happening Abraham had to move southwest, most likely because the dust from the Dead Sea area was settling everywhere, making it hard for the animals to feed and uncomfortable for human life too. He went further south than Beersheba but not as far as Shur. There is a triangular depression extending from Beersheba to Gerar (near the west coast) and Kadesh in the southwest, the area is semi-arid and Abraham and his company moved throughout it finding grazing ground for his herds. As he moved closer to the western town of Gerar he came within reach of the king of that area, Abimelech. Once again fear took hold of Abraham and he asked Sarah to say she was his sister. Sarah was 89 years old but probably looked about 40 as her Adamic heritage dictated; she was still a stunning woman to behold. She soon found herself in the presence of King Abimelech who had serious designs on her. This turn of events is now cutting things close because Yahweh had told Abraham that in about a year from when they last met, Sarah would be giving birth to a son. God had to step in pretty quickly here, and before Abimelech had had a chance to get close to Sarah the Lord came to him in a dream with words that could have come straight from a movie:

> "You are a dead man, for the woman you have taken is already married!" Shocked and fearful Abimelech pleads his case, "Didn't Abraham tell me, 'She is my sister?' And she herself said, 'Yes, he is my brother.' I acted in innocence! My hands are clean."

God tells Abimelech to return Sarah to Abraham, who is a prophet and will pray for him, and also says, "Yes, I know you are innocent. That's why I did not let you touch her." How God stopped Abimelech sleeping with Sarah we don't know, the situation may have been similar to when Esther found herself in King Xerxes's harem, where she had to undergo twelve months of treatments before she was considered suitable enough to sleep with the king. Abimelech probably didn't have that long a time period to wait but he may have had some sort of process in place. Suffice to say that God had his ways of keeping them apart. Abimelech told all his officials about his dream and they were greatly concerned, they seemed to realize something was wrong because no one in the king's household had got pregnant since Sarah had been among them. This gives us another opportunity to see how God speaks and deals with ordinary men. God is able to speak to all men and they are able to hear him, though not all obey and when that happens they drift away from the truth and sometimes drift a long way from it.

Abimelech and his officials called in Abraham and Abimelech gave him a serious dressing down, "What have you done to us?" he demanded. "What crime have I committed that deserves treatment like this, making me and my kingdom guilty of this great sin? No one should ever do what you have done! Whatever possessed you to do such a thing?"

Abraham replied, "I thought, 'This is a godless place. They will want my wife and will kill me to get her.' And she really is my sister, for we both have the same father, but different mothers."

Abraham's family ties were very close indeed; Sarah was his half-sister. This was not in keeping with the law that would later be issued by Moses, but we are talking about a special family where the original parents shared the same genes.

Abimelech showed himself honorable and gave Abraham and Sarah sheep, cattle, and male and female slaves, and then said, "My land is before you; live wherever you like." Then he said to Sarah, "I am giving your brother a thousand shekels of silver. This is to cover any offense against you." Abimelech was open and humble before God, Abraham, and Sarah. Then Abraham prayed for Abimelech and God heard the prayer because soon the ladies of Abimelech's community were getting pregnant again.

A lot had happened in the three months since Yahweh made the covenant of circumcision with Abraham; three months had passed by and Abraham and Sarah were back together, and very pleased to see one another. Nine months later a son was born to the couple.

God said he would return and Sarah would have a son. We don't read in Genesis that Yahweh visited in a physical way this time. Abraham was learning the extent of God's capabilities, he didn't need to turn up as a man to keep his promise, God can visit us anywhere anytime because he is Spirit. Sarah said "I have born him a son in his old age." Abraham was 100 years old. This shows us that Sarah was now comparing herself and Abraham to the general populace regarding their age. Actually Abraham would go on to live another 75 years, he had actually lived 57.2 percent of his overall life span when Isaac was born. He had much to say to his son Isaac and God granted him long life to do it. God had already pointed out that Abraham had been chosen to direct his children and he now had 75 years in which to do it.

CHAPTER 16

Adopting a Baby

MORE TROUBLE ENSUED BETWEEN Sarah and Hagar. Ishmael was about 15 years old now and sibling rivalry is not unusual in any family, but Sarah couldn't cope with it and demanded that the "slave woman and her son" be thrown out. Abraham was greatly worried about this but God spoke to him:

> Don't feel badly about the boy and your maid. . . . be assured that I'll also develop a great nation from him—he's your son too. (Gen 21:12–13 msg)

Abraham was also told that it was Isaac who was carrying the "seed." Poor Hagar once again found herself on the desert road, this time along with her son. By the time their skin of water had run out they were both exhausted, Hagar sat the boy under a bush and went a hundred meters or so because she couldn't bear to watch him die. She sat down and sobbed. Once again an angel spoke to her and told her not to be afraid. Just then she saw a well of water that somehow she'd missed and was able to give Ishmael a drink, so the crisis was averted. God was with Ishmael and he became a skillful archer and he married an Egyptian woman.

Looking back, if we think of God breathing into Adam and then making Eve from his stem cells, the couple would be the main trunk of what God had invested; the benefits of that investment were felt throughout their family. As time went on and parts of the family branched off and married generic humans the effects were minimized until they weren't felt at all.

We know the earth has a long history because the evidence can been seen in many ways. For instance we mentioned the core drilling at the Dead

Sea that *National Geographic News* reported on, when they drilled down further than the 4000-year mark they noticed that the Dead Sea area had been having earthquakes right back to 200,000 years ago. And before that the whole area was under water. Sediment composed of the shells of tiny sea animals that slowly sunk to the sea floor were compressed over many years to form the brilliant white limestone that Solomon would one day quarry to build the Temple in Jerusalem.

Humans also have a long history on earth. We said that Jericho is one of the oldest city's in the world, and it's been a recognizable city since 7000 BC, but there is evidence of a smaller settlement there dating back to 8000 BC. Adam came on the scene some time before 4000 BC. (Before 5000 BC according to the Septuagint.) God made us all from the ground, none of us are any better than each other, we are all equal. Adam received some benefits from being the seed-bearer, but it didn't make him a better person with higher morals or even strength to overcome sin, in fact it didn't take him too long to break the command that God had given him. His posterity also struggled with doing what was right, as we all do. It looks like Sarah held a grudge against Hagar, and Abraham was quick to utilize deceit when it suited him.

We may wonder how God came to choose Adam in the first place, what made him different to anyone else that God had made? We know there is some concealment involved, but as the world has moved forward with advances in scientific knowledge, the second half of the proverb we began with—"It's the glory of kings to search them out"—has been true for our times more than any other generation in history. Men have searched out truth geologically, archaeologically, and scientifically, and we all receive the benefit of their hard work. This helps us to understand the scriptures a little better, God doesn't always give us a complete picture the way we would like it in a textbook but he does give us enough information for it to all make sense. God's aim is usually straight to the heart, he appeals to our inner-self, he sings to our soul, he beckons us to follow, and textbook language gets in the way of that cry. He does want us to reason but the love of God must reach us first, because God is love.

We get what look like hints of how Adam was chosen in other parts of the Bible. Firstly, let's say that God could have made Adam fast as a direct new creation, even though there were other people around, God could have made Adam that way. However, apart from the fact that God usually operates within the laws he has created, Adam needed to be a part of the human race that already existed because it was that race of people that Jesus wanted to save. God the Son took on human form and we know that human beings have been on the planet before Adam, so therefore it looks like Adam needed to be one of them, not a new creation that was very similar to them, but actually one of them. A human who had the same biological, physiological, and spiritual ancestry they have. He needed to proceed from human stock that humans may proceed into what God intends us to be.

Genesis informs us that the timeframe for Adam, Eve, and their children is based in the Neolithic period of human development, where we read of cities, agriculture, tilling the ground, keeping livestock, irrigation, and farming. It's too late to be included in the Paleolithic period; people had got well past the hunter-gatherer stage. Around 5500 BC a distinctive style of impressive pottery—known as halaf—spread across the whole of northern Mesopotamia. The high quality of the firing means that many examples have survived. Adam had stepped into a recognizable civilization.

Science helps us understand the scriptures; the men who follow the proverb we started out with—"It's the glory of kings to search them out"— help us understand how we should view the Bible. Their "searching out" has helped us understand that the sun doesn't move around the earth, so we now understand how to interpret the Bible in matters relating to the sun. Science has also explained that humans have been on the planet much longer than 6000 years, so that also helps us grasp what the Bible teaches us.

Adam and all humans are made from the dust of the earth. There's another important way we can view this fact, apart from thinking that many years ago God formed life from inorganic matter. There's something we ought to consider: we are all made from the earth, because what is now part of our body was just a few short weeks ago inanimate earth, soil, or dirt. Let say we buy a radish from the supermarket, that radish has been freshly picked, it ended up on the supermarket shelf just a matter of days after it was uprooted from the earth. While the radish was growing in the ground its roots reached down into the soil and absorbed lifeless dirt, transforming it into a part of the succulent red radish that looks appetizing on our dinner plate. We eat the radish and it becomes a part of our body. So what was earth just a few days ago is now a part of a human being. Everything we eat was soil not too long ago. Even if we eat meat, let's say beef, the cattle we eat were eating grass not too long ago, and we eat the beef; so what was grass, was formerly earth, and is now a part of a human being. Everything we eat was soil just a few months ago, so we are all made from the earth, and that's recently, not thousands of years ago. Every cell in our body was earth. When a human being dies we go back to being dirt. Dust to dust. Every human being was earth not too long ago. Adam was made from the earth, as we all are.

Other scriptures in the Bible may throw some light on how Adam was chosen. Firstly, it will help us to know that in ancient Mesopotamia adoption was an official practice that took place; there were a number of ways a child could be adopted. We have clay tablets that document adoptions. One route to adopt a child involved a newborn that had been abandoned from birth, what was known as "to the dog" while still "in (its) water and blood."[1] In one tablet that's been found a woman has abandoned her newborn son, and this is expressed as "throwing him into the dog's mouth" whereby she legally forgoes all her rights to that child. Another tablet has been translated as, "If a man an infant out of his amniotic fluid for sonship has taken and has brought him up, that adopted child shall not be (re) claimed."[2] This suggests that the parents abandoned the infant, and he was quickly adopted while amniotic fluid was still on him. If the adopter has raised the infant, the adopted child could not be reclaimed by anyone, including the child's natural parents. This is an interesting view of life in Mesopotamia, it doesn't make the people of Mesopotamia less civilized than we are, because babies are sometimes abandoned in the modern world too, it's not a good thing, but it sometimes happens. Mesopotamians showed themselves to be civilized by having documentation for someone who had found an abandoned baby and adopted the child.

In Ezekiel 16 we read:

> Your ancestry and birth were in the land of the Canaanites; your father was an Amorite and your mother a Hittite. On the day you were born your cord was not cut, nor were you washed with water to make you clean, nor were you rubbed with salt or wrapped in cloths. No one looked on you with pity or had compassion enough to do any of these things for you. Rather, you were thrown out into the open field, for on the day you were born you were despised. Then I passed by and saw you kicking about in your blood, and as you lay there in your blood I said to you, "Live!"

In this chapter Ezekiel is told to confront Jerusalem. As we read though the chapter we realize that God is speaking in an allegorical way about their

1. Stol, "Private Life," 491, parentheses in original.
2. Yaron, "Varia on Adoption," 173, parentheses in original.

ancestry and history and telling the people to look how far away they have moved from their beginnings. It seems at that time Jerusalem is the focal point for the Israeli nation, some of which is already in captivity, including Ezekiel himself. The allegory continues and mentions that God adorned Jerusalem with jewelry: putting bracelets on her arms and a ring in her nose. We are reminded of how the Israelites first started to become a nation. Rebekah was given two gold bracelets weighing ten shekels and a gold nose ring weighing a beka. Ezekiel laments at how far the nation has fallen. But it is the first part of Ezekiel's message that may be of interest to us. He starts off talking about their ancestry saying, "your father was an Amorite and your mother was a Hittite." That sounds a little odd because weren't Abraham and Sarah father and mother to the nation of Israel? And they were from Ur. The Hittites crop up in Canaan when the Israelites first start to take the land of Canaan for themselves. They had descended from Ham, Noah's son. But there is a second people group also named the Hittites who were a major empire with a capital city called Hattusha who descended from the early settlers in Anatolia now part of Turkey. The Amorites were nomadic people and were well known to the Mesopotamians and early Canaanites.

Also, when Moses wrote his song in Deuteronomy there's a stanza which says, "Remember the days of old; consider the generations long past . . . In a desert land he found him, in a barren and howling waste. He shielded him and cared for him; he guarded him as the apple of his eye . . . The LORD alone led him; no foreign god was with him. He made him ride on the heights of the land and fed him with the fruit of the fields."

Isaiah begins his prophecy with, "Hear me, you heavens! Listen, earth! For the LORD has spoken: 'I reared children and brought them up, but they have rebelled against me.'"

When these scriptures ask us to look back, we may wonder just how far back are we talking about? Did Yahweh really find an abandoned baby kicking about in its blood and amniotic fluid with its cord uncut? If that happened then Yahweh spent a lot of time with Adam raising him as his own son. He breathed into him, investing something of himself within Adam. Yahweh would have spent time on earth raising a child just like we do. He would have taught the child, fed him, and made a home for them to dwell in. He arranged for irrigation ditches to be dug from the Euphrates and planted a garden and taught Adam about looking after the fruit trees. Adam got to know the animals in the area and made up names for all of them. Yahweh would bring an animal along and say, "What do you think of this one?" They may have laughed as Adam came up with a name for each animal that his father Yahweh brought to him, just like any parent would have fun while teaching their children. Adam was very young while all this was happening. Every now and again Adam might see a human being, but he knew he was different; they didn't have Yahweh rearing them. Yahweh taught Adam about love, sincerity, humility, and having an open heart, and how to live without guile, there would be no better father in the world to be raised by. Adam received some of the "life" that Yahweh had. When Ezekiel tells us the story about the baby being found, the word spoken to the baby was "Live!" He gave Adam "life," he received the "living" tag, and Adam could have gone on to receive the fullness of that life, the completion was within his grasp. He was an ordinary man, *ish* in the Hebrew language, but his adoption as a son of Yahweh meant he was chosen for a special task, it changed his being.

Jesus also tells us to look back to the beginning of the human race in Matthew 19:4–5. The first scripture he draws our attention to is from Genesis chapter 1 saying, "at the beginning the Creator 'made them male and female.'" Jesus reminds us that the creator set the established order of male and female, which equates to father and mother; each pair has offspring who in turn become fathers and mothers themselves.

Then Jesus moves several verses further forward into Genesis chapter 2 and reminds us what the text declares just after Eve has been created. "For this reason a man will leave his father and mother and be united to his wife, and the two will become one flesh." Why does the text of Genesis use Adam as an example relating to people leaving their father and mother if Adam didn't have a father and mother? We can't say that God begot Adam, because he didn't—God only has one begotten son. We can say God created Adam, in the same way that God is the creator of us all, but we can't say that God physically fathered Adam.

We may say God was Adam's father by adoption. If, as some people say, Adam was the first man created, then drawing a parallel about leaving your father and mother doesn't fit well if Adam never had a father and mother to leave. But if Adam was adopted by Yahweh, that means he had a natural biological father and mother that he left, and then the parallel would fit.

Furthermore, if God found a baby that had been abandoned by his parents and adopted the child, the place where he found the baby was a different location to where Adam was raised, because it looks like a journey took place. Adam existed before he was placed in the garden: "Then the LORD God planted a garden in Eden in the east, and there he placed the man he had made" (Gen 2:8 nlt). Ezekiel's story of the abandoned baby tells us that the part of the Fertile Crescent where the child was found was Canaan; we know the garden was in southern Mesopotamia, so that could be why the text of Genesis informs us that Adam was *placed* in the garden rather than originating from that area. And to make sure we understand that Adam was taken to the garden rather than beginning his life there, Genesis chapter 2 states the fact one more time in verse 15: "The LORD God took the man and put him in the garden of Eden." This verse clearly says Yahweh "took" the man, which implies that a journey took place.

If that's how Adam came to be located in southern Mesopotamia then when Yahweh spoke to Abram in southern Mesopotamia and told him to go to Canaan, Abram would have taken the return journey back to Canaan from where Yahweh and Adam had first travelled.

Adam needed someone near his own age, not for sex because he's not yet at that stage in his development. Other humans were different to him, they had been brought up knowing the ways of the world, they knew how to make insincerity look like sincerity, they didn't have the scope of virtuous learning that had been given to Adam by Yahweh, they didn't have the strength of body that Adam had, they didn't have the length of years. So God anaesthetized Adam and from his stem cells made a female companion who would be suitable, because there were no others suitable. It's interesting to note that when Genesis chapter 2 says, "whatever the man called each living creature, that was its name," the word for "creature" is *nephesh*, which can be also used of humans. Adam may have looked at other humans and had names for each of them, but none were found suitable for him to partner with. Genesis 2:20 says, "No suitable helper was found," which suggests there was some searching done. The picture of Eden is further enhanced when we read that God questioned Adam about the fruit: Adam said to the LORD God, "The woman you put here with me—she gave me some fruit from the tree and I ate it." Adam's replay can be viewed as a statement of defiance, in which he tries to wriggle off the hook—"The woman you put here with me." But what Adam's statement can also reveal is that there were in fact other females around, so he qualified which female he was talking about—"The woman you put here with me."

The female that God made for Adam was younger but not too much younger. Their natural fertility cycle would not kick in for sometime, they were innocent. In fact they wouldn't become parents for many years; length of days probably meant length of childhood and adolescence too. The female proved to be a good helper and companion for Adam, she had all the same physical and mental characteristics that he had. She had powerful strength, physical beauty that surpassed that of regular women, and she had the "life." She was too young to conceive at this stage, for how many years this carried on we don't know, but at some point one of the angels whose nature was being corrupted by selfish ambition, decided to break the stillness and approached the female. Later in Genesis some of the angels who appeared as men actually took wives and inseminated their own DNA into them and a hybrid offspring resulted that was never part of God's intention for creation. But it was part of the serpent's plan to destroy the seed. If Eve had been of age the serpent could have followed the path that the later angels took and inseminated the woman himself, but she was too young and God took away his ability to appear as a man soon after, so that possibility was providentially never an option.

There may not have been anything particularly special about the tree of the knowledge of good and evil apart from the fact that God had told Adam not to eat from it. If God said, "don't eat from this tree," then that's fair enough, Adam didn't need to know why, because he trusted his father. Adam told Eve what God had said to him about the tree and she accepted it without question. That is, until the serpent came along. Once she had listened to the serpent and he had put it into her mind that Yahweh didn't want them to know about all the options available to them, options of evil as well as good, she listened to the serpent and took his advice. The LORD God's word didn't have to be obeyed and they ate the fruit to prove it. This gave both Adam and Eve a fundamental shift in their psyche. Up to that point God had looked out for them, protected them from moral corruption, and made sure their hearts were soft. But now things had changed.

The tree itself may have been an ordinary date palm tree. In Mesopotamia a repeated theme on the cylinder seals is one of a date palm tree with a man and woman on either side of it with a serpent next to them. The date palm tree is thought to have been cultivated around the area of southern Iraq, so the garden of Eden may have played its part in its cultivation.[3] What counted was Adam and Eve were now growing wise in their own eyes, and along with that knowledge came pride, shame, and all the other moral maladies that come along with disobeying our heavenly father.

3. Morton, "Date," 5–11.

Adam made some clothes, he may have seen them worn by other humans, but not thought much about them, he didn't need them before. He now had an urge to clothe himself, he was different to the other humans, he hadn't cared about it before; he didn't have a competitive spirit within him, he didn't need to keep up with the Jones's. But now he wondered, *What will people think?* He didn't want Yahweh to see him with his new clothes so he hid. He was starting to learn how sin worked: if in a tricky situation, hide. Yahweh realized that this rebelliousness had come from somewhere and asked, "Have you eaten from the tree I told you not to eat from?" Adam found another use for his newly found knowledge of evil, and replied by saying, "You know the woman that you put with me? Well. . . . " We can see the teenage rebellion starting to kick in. And all this learned from listening to the serpent. How quickly we learn the ways of the world.

Yahweh decided to make some nicely fitted clothes for Adam and possibly some ornate and nicely styled clothes for Eve, after all they were getting close to the time when they would reach puberty. In Ezekiel's story when the baby who had been found grew up, God said, "Later I passed by, and when I looked at you and saw that you were old enough for love, I spread the corner of my garment over you and covered your naked body . . . I clothed you."

Ezekiel's allegory isn't a direct link to the story of exactly what happened in the garden of Eden, but we may have a reflection or a shadow of how events occurred. One of the main objectives of God first investing in Adam was the seed that he wanted to look after. If we look at what God was doing from beginning to end it helps us see a little clearer. Looking at it from a bird's eye view and cutting out all the intervening generations, first with Adam and Eve and later with Mary and Jesus, we see that:

> God placed a seed in a man (Adam); then a woman (Eve) proceeded from the man. God fertilized the seed in a woman (Mary) and a man (Jesus) proceeded from the woman.

Or we could put it this way:

> A woman came from a man without the aid of a woman, then a man came from a woman without the aid of a man.

God was the author and finisher. Paul in the New Testament spoke about this in a way that is not always easy to grasp on first reading. He uses some phrases that may seem hard to understand; let's remember he was caught up to heaven and saw things that were hard for him to put into earthly terms.

He said, "The man is not of the woman; but the woman of the man. Neither was the man created for the woman; but the woman for the man . . . For as the woman is of the man, even so is the man also by the woman" (1 Cor 11:8–12). There are a number of ways we can view these verses, but if we remember that Christ was a man born of a woman then he gets included into the picture—"even so is the man also by the woman." The man Christ Jesus was born of a woman: Mary.

When the seed that would lead to Christ's birth was first planted it was put into a man, and a woman came from the man, when the seed was ready to burst out and grow into maturity, the man Christ Jesus was born of a woman. The women of Adam's line had power and beauty, Mary was from that line, and when she gave birth to Christ the power was released into the world. The power and beauty that the women from Adam's line had was only there as a symbol of the real power and beauty that lay within them, and was to come into the world! For it is Christ who is fairer than ten thousand, it is his beauty that David wanted to gaze upon all the days of his life; it is Jesus who is the rose of Sharon, a lily of the valley.

Paul would sometimes grasp upon a local custom to explain a spiritual point. When he was in Athens he used the statues of gods, and he quoted their own poets. Paul was always ready to seize an opportunity. When talking to the Corinthians he knew that their married women tended to cover their heads in public. In *Sayings of Spartans* (written in the first century AD), we read the humorous statement: "When someone inquired why they took their girls into public places unveiled, but their married women veiled, he said, 'Because the girls have to find husbands, and the married women have to keep to those who have them!'"[4] Paul is clever the way he uses the word "head" because it has two meanings, our physical head and also someone who is over us in authority. Previously in 1 Corinthians 11 Paul has been using head coverings in public prayers to make the point saying, "I want you to realize that the head of every man is Christ, and the head of the woman is man, and the head of Christ is God. Every man who prays or prophesies with his head covered dishonors his head. But every woman who prays or prophesies with her head uncovered dishonors her head." Paul goes on to say, "Nevertheless, in the Lord woman is not independent of man, nor is man independent of woman." The Lord was born of a woman, he was born a man, so he is the head of the woman. "For this cause ought the woman to have power on her head on account of the

4. Plutarch, "Sayings of Spartans," 393. Plutarch was a Greek author (AD 46–120).

angels." Christ is the power and he is the head as the account of the angels revealed. An angel visited Mary and told her that the power of the Most High would overshadow her and the holy one to be born would be called the Son of God. After Mary gave birth the angels endorsed the birth to the shepherds by giving them a sign to look for. When the shepherds searched they found Mary and the baby.

Paul wasn't giving our freedom in Christ away when he used the custom in Corinth of women covering their heads when praying, but he saw an opportunity to explain something deeper. "Neither was the man created for the woman; but the woman for the man." Again we see a double meaning, Adam had a woman as a wife but Christ had a woman as a mother, either way the woman was there for the man. Which man, Adam or Christ? The answer is both. The man Adam wasn't created for the woman, and Christ wasn't created at all, but the woman Eve, that came from Adam, and Mary that came further down the line, both were created as a means for the man Christ Jesus to be born. They were created for the man. Peter told us Paul's writings contained some hard things to understand, and Paul has a way of enclosing a deep message within everyday customs. Paul started this discourse by saying:

> I want you to realize that the head of every man is Christ, and the
> head of the woman is man, and the head of Christ is God.

Let's look at this for a moment in regard to someone's physical head. If we look at the head of a man we see Christ, because Christ became a man: Christ represents all men, he is the second Adam, just as the first Adam represented us all, so too the second Adam became one of us and "tasted death for every man."

If we look at the head of the woman (i.e., Eve's head), Paul says "the woman" singular, not "every woman." Looking at Eve's head we see Adam because Eve proceeded from Adam and was covered by being in Adam before she was made. (And she probably did actually bear his resemblance because they had the same genes, just like twins often look like each other.)

And the head of Christ is God because when we look at the head of Jesus we see God. "Philip said to Him, 'Lord, show us the Father, and it is enough for us.'" Jesus said to him, "Have I been with you such a long time, and yet you have not come to know me, Philip? He who has seen me has seen the Father; how can you say, 'Show us the Father'?"

So in the line to Christ God started the process in Adam, the woman was also in Adam to begin with, then she became an individual, which led to Christ. So Paul explains that when a Greek woman covers her head it can be thought of as Eve being covered by Adam. But when a man prays without covering his head it signifies Adam's direct link to Yahweh, who first breathed directly into him.

If some people struggle with the thought that God made Eve from Adam then they will also struggle with the fact that Mary had the seed inside her fertilized without the aid of a man. God was there at the start of the process using his power and he was also there at the end of the process when Christ's conception took place, again using his power.

CHAPTER 17

Serious Drama

> Sarah saw that the son whom Hagar the Egyptian had borne to Abraham was mocking, and she said to Abraham, "Get rid of that slave woman and her son" . . . Early the next morning Abraham took some food and a skin of water and gave them to Hagar . . . then sent her off with the boy. Gen 21:9–14

ABRAHAM HAD BEEN GREATLY distressed about what had happened to Ishmael and his mother Hagar. Mother and son lived a little further southeast than Abraham in the desert of Paran, where Ishmael quickly learned how to use his skill as a hunter. Abraham was still in the south of Canaan not too far from King Abimelech on the west and the village of Beersheba to the east. After the move down south from Mamre near Hebron, which took place after the earthquake and was a move of necessity, Abraham and Sarah stayed in their southern location, raising Isaac and providing work for the many people they employed. They moved their flocks between Gerar and Beersheba on a west to east latitude. Abimelech seemed like a fair man to have as a neighbor, the two men had a mutual respect for each other and made a deal or two. Apart from Abraham's heartache over Ishmael, life was good and settled. But things were about to change.

Yahweh hadn't been seen by Abraham since the circumstances surrounding Isaac's birth, which was quite some time ago. God had spoken to Abraham concerning Hagar but not in the form of a visit. The last time Abraham had actually seen Yahweh was when they sat beneath the shade of trees in Mamre, so Abraham in an effort to reach out to Yahweh and perhaps solicit a visit, planted a tamarisk tree in Beersheba and called upon the name of Yahweh. We don't read that Yahweh turned up, at least not as a man. There isn't a way of holding God's arm behind his back so that we can make him do what we want him to do. He is his own person and answers to no man, he does what pleases him.

Sometime later God did speak to Abraham in the form of a voice; Abraham immediately said, "Here I am." He had been waiting for this for a long time and although it wasn't Yahweh in the form of a man, he knew Yahweh's voice. One of the features of Genesis is its ability to tell the main story through another story; there are many instances of preachers who use scenarios within Genesis to preach the gospel of Christ. Joseph is a common theme and also Abraham himself when he instructs his servant to get a wife for his son. Dramas unfold within the Genesis text and we realize that we are actually seeing a parallel to the larger story of God sacrificing his Son. Abraham now knew Yahweh well enough to trust him implicitly. Did he know God's penchant for drama and acting and putting on a play for people to watch? Perhaps he did, the story in the garden of Eden had been a scenario that reverberated with everyone alive.

Later in the Bible God would ask Ezekiel to act out some bizarre scenes for his audience to watch and Abraham was about to take part in a play where he would be one of the main characters. God said to him:

> Take your son, your only son, whom you love, Isaac, and go to the region of Moriah. Sacrifice him there as a burnt offering on a mountain I will show you.

What did God mean take your only son? Abraham had another son, Ishmael; Isaac wasn't his only son. But this was all a part of the drama that was unfolding, this was the script, Abraham was playing the part of God, and God only has one begotten son. Adam was created along with us all, he wasn't begotten, he became God's son through adoption, but Jesus was actually fathered by God with Mary as the mother. Abraham didn't know it was a play being acted out or at least he wasn't sure what was going on, but we know he trusted God enough to raise Isaac back from the dead, and knew that God had the power to do that. This was a real test of character for Abraham. He obeyed all the orders given to him.

Abraham, Isaac, and two servants set out early the next morning. This directive was issued to Abraham alone, Sarah would still be in bed and by the time she was ready for the day, the quartet may have been on their way. As far as people knew they were going on a trip to build an altar and sacrifice to God somewhere close to where Melchizedek lived. Building altars had been a family tradition since Adam so it wasn't a strange thing for them to do, but Sarah, if she knew anything about it at all, may have wondered, "Why now?"

The region of Moriah is about 60 miles from Gerar. Abraham knew the region well, he'd moved along the north-south ridge pathway of the Judean hills several times before. He would pass his old town of Mamre and then head further north to where he'd met Melchizedek. They camped overnight twice on the journey. During the second night God must have given Abraham the final instructions of exactly which mountain to head for because on the third day they reached the area of Moriah and Abraham knew where to go. He'd also been told to let Isaac carry the wood—which ties in with Jesus carrying his wooden cross, which would happen in the same area just over 1800 years later. This is the script and Abraham followed it.

The two servants had stayed at the campsite; Abraham and Isaac were by themselves and walked to the exact location. It's sometimes thought that Isaac was a willing party to this unfolding drama, but I think Isaac would have reacted the same as we all would if we knew someone was going to stab us: we would run for all we were worth. Abraham had kept what was about to take place very quiet; he even had a chance to tell Isaac because his son asked where the animal was. Abraham gave the cryptic reply that God would provide himself a lamb. The fact that Genesis mentions that Isaac was bound before he was placed on the altar lets us know that Isaac probably didn't go willingly; otherwise he would have meekly lain down on the altar without the need of being bound. Abraham was still a strong man from Adam's extraction and Isaac was a young man, maybe a teenager. Abraham would overpower him and bind him, then place him on the altar. There may have been quite a scuffle with Isaac screaming out, dust and dirt being flung into the air. But Abraham prevailed and Isaac was placed on the wood that was on top of the altar. Abraham felt around his waistband for the knife and got hold of it to get the job done.

Suddenly a voice from heaven called Abraham's name twice, just in case he didn't hear it the first time because maybe Isaac was crying. The voice was loud; the same Hebrew word is used for when a proclamation is made. Abraham stopped in his tracks and said, "Here I am." He was then told not to lay a hand on the boy; he had proved his willingness to obey God and not withheld his only son. We are immediately reminded of the most famous verse in the New Testament: "For God so loved the world, that he gave his only begotten Son, that whosoever believeth in him should not perish, but have everlasting life" (John 3:16). This was the story that was being told. It must have been hard for Isaac to endure, as it was hard for Jesus to endure, who prayed if it be possible for the cup to pass from him. Even on the cross Jesus shouted, "My God, my God why have you forsaken me?" Isaac must have been uttering similar phrases. Abraham then spotted a ram caught in a thicket and went over and carried the ram to the altar, released Isaac, and sacrificed the ram instead. On the way to the mountain Abraham had told Isaac that God would provide a lamb himself. Now they had a ram, so this wasn't the lamb that God would provide. That lamb would come much later. A messenger named John heralded the entrance of that lamb when he said, "Behold, the Lamb of God who takes away the sin of the world!"

The voice from heaven spoke to Abraham again, telling him that through his seed all the nations on the earth would be blessed. Abraham made his way back to the two men who were waiting. Previously Abraham had told the two servants that he and the boy would go and worship and then come back to them. Yet we don't read that Isaac was with him on the return journey to the servants, the text tells us that "Abraham" made his way to the servants. It's understandable; Isaac was shook up, probably wondering what his dad was going to do next. He hadn't realized that it was a prophetic story and that he was playing the part of Christ, the sacrificial lamb. And perhaps the play had not finished yet because after his death on the cross Jesus went elsewhere, so perhaps Isaac's absence is indicative of Christ's sojourn in between his death and resurrection.

We don't know how Sarah took the news of Isaac's close call, but we do know she was living at Hebron when she died and Abraham was living in Beersheba, which is 20 miles to the south. Sarah had moved back to the area where they used to reside at Mamre, Hebron. That may tell us all we need to know. The road had not always been smooth for them as a couple, we don't know if Sarah minded being sent to possibly sleep with other men twice. Abraham did in fact sleep with Hagar and the result of that was hard for Sarah to bear. The road for married couples is not always smooth.

Beersheba is not too far away from where Ishmael resided so perhaps Abraham got to see him from time to time. We know that Isaac spent time down south particularly at Beer Lahai Roi, which was where Hagar met the angel when she first ran away. Isaac also would get to see his brother and compare notes and the two of them got to know each other.

Sarah was 127 years old when she died, a long age, but not as long as others in the line of Adam. Abraham went to Hebron and mourned when Sarah died. He also made some funeral arrangements and bought a cave from the local Hittites. The Hittites were aware that Abraham was a prince and made a bit of a show of offering him the opportunity of burying his dead wife in any of their picturesque tombs. But there was something that had kept Abraham's family close and separate from the surrounding tribes and nations in life, and so it would be in death. Abraham knew of a cave in Mamre that was ideally suited for a family tomb. Ephron, the tomb's owner, heard his name mentioned and saw an opportunity to sell the field as well as the cave, and mentions that he is willing to freely give the cave and the field in which the cave sits. Abraham replies saying he is willing to buy the field too, how much is it? Abraham is told that the land is worth 400 shekels, "but" adds Ephron, "what is that between me and you? Please bury your dead." Evidently once the price has been mentioned then that's the deal unless you want to barter. Abraham was prepared to pay it; the interchange between Abraham and the Hittites in Genesis chapter 23 is an interesting window to look through to see how business was conducted at that time. There was a high degree of civility but it seems there was also some affectation. Abraham laid Sarah in the cave, which was called Machpelah. The Hittites had legally transferred it over to Abraham.

Isaac had to come to terms with the scare he'd had at the hands of Abraham and the reason it happened, he was a contemplative man and I'm sure it wouldn't take him long to get things back on track with his father. Abraham would have told him that he shouldn't get married to a local girl; Yahweh had specifically said that Isaac was the seed-bearer and Abraham gave the job of finding a wife for Isaac to his trusted servant. But this was too important to over-emphasize so he made the servant take an oath promising he would only get a wife from Abraham's relatives.

Abraham was about 140 years old and Isaac was 40, Sarah had been dead around 3 years. So Abraham thought the time was right to get on with the job of propagating the seed that Yahweh had spoken about so often to him. He sent his conscientious servant back across the Euphrates River to his brother Nahor's town. Abraham had heard that his brother Nahor and his wife Milcah had had eight sons, plus another four through a concubine. We know that Abraham's father Terah had at least two wives, and Abraham and his two brothers could have been from the same mother. However Sarah was also a child of Terah, and if Terah married (or had a concubine) who was a short-liver or mixed heritage, that may account for Sarah's shortened years compared to Abraham's 175. Ishmael lived to be 137, not as long as his brother, but his mother was an Egyptian with a regular life span. It was his father Abraham's connection to Adam that gave him his long life. Ishmael's mother would have died at a normal age, because Abraham got married again just after Isaac got married. So if Hagar was in her early twenties when she gave birth to Ishmael she would have been about 75 years old had she been living by the time Abraham got married again. Seventy-five is a good life span for generic humans in that day and age, so she was probably dead, or we would have heard something of her because Abraham had no need to be separated from Hagar now that Sarah was no longer living. Abraham was an honorable man and would have settled back down with Hagar if she was alive.

Abraham's servant followed the route Abraham gave him to the town where Nahor lived in northwest Mesopotamia. Abraham had waited a long time to have children so his brother's family would now be well into their second generation. It would not be his brother's children that Isaac would need to marry but his brother's grandchildren. The servant took a caravan of ten camels laden with goods. The journey was over 450 miles and would have to be taken steadily over a three- to four-week period. Abraham knew precise directions for the journey and would have given his servant instructions or a map.

When he approached the vicinity of Haran, the servant and his camels would have had some climbing to do, on arrival they would be thirsty and hot. The servant prayed for the LORD God to make his long journey successful. He knew what he was looking for. He would watch for a girl from Abraham's family who would have the characteristic traits of the females that came from Adam's descent: beauty and strength were two of the main features. So he devised a test; he needed a girl who would be strong enough to pull up enough water for ten camels because camels drink a lot of water. A gallon of water weighs about ten pounds. One thirsty camel can drink over 30 imperial gallons (36 gallons). He prayed for a girl who would come along at water-drawing time who would be the right girl for Isaac. Nahor's granddaughter Rebekah came to draw water at that exact time, and she was "very beautiful," so that was one trait ticked. The servant asked her for a drink, which she willing gave calling the servant "lord," she then offered to draw water for his camels. Genesis puts it like this: "Now when she had finished giving him a drink, she said, 'I will draw also for your camels until they have finished drinking.' So she quickly emptied her jar into the trough, and ran back to the well to draw, and she drew for all his camels." She not only had strength, stamina, and speed she was also courteous, humble, and willing to take part in acts of random kindness to complete strangers. These were the marks that befitted someone in the line to Christ, because he was humble and lowly of heart, also willing to show kindness to strangers.

People have suggested that Abraham's servant was Eliezer, the man Abraham had mentioned to Yahweh 41 years before as being the heir of his estate. But the name of the servant in this story is never mentioned so it could be Eliezer, or perhaps Eliezer's son.

Some also point out that the story of finding a bride for Isaac is similar to the overall story of the Bible, whereby Abraham represents God the Father, Isaac represents God the Son, and the servant represents the Holy Spirit. It's another drama sketch that unfolds. The Holy Spirit magnifies Jesus, and does not speak his own words but only those he hears from the Father, like the servant in the story who remains nameless but is intent on doing the work he's been sent to do. Rebekah is the bride, and there are a number of allusions to the bride of Christ in the New Testament. The doctrine of the Holy Trinity begins in Genesis and is expanded on throughout the rest of the scriptures. God—Father, Spirit, and Son—spent time on earth, earth is part of God's work, and he's intensely interested in it. We first read of the Holy Spirit in the first few words of Genesis when the Spirit of God hovered over the waters. Then Yahweh spends time on earth and walks around and makes himself known. He teaches Adam all he needs to know, spending time with him and providing for him as a good father does for his son. Then God the Son was born into the human race as one of us: brother, friend, and teacher. He came to save us from ourselves, from the sins that swamp us, to take us higher into that land where he resides, the land that the garden of Eden was a symbol of. As God prepared the garden for Adam, Jesus has now gone to prepare a place for us. Laying out the garden for Adam would have taken quite some time, as gardens take time to plan, landscape, and irrigate. Then the trees need to grow until they are ready to bear fruit. Preparation of another sort is now underway, we read about the river feeding the trees in the last book of the Bible.

God has come into the human race that we may be in him. Jesus prayed, "Father, just as you are in me and I am in you. May they also be in us." To those who receive him Christ enables us to "participate in the divine nature, having escaped the corruption in the world caused by evil desires" (2 Pet 1:4).

The cross of Christ is central to the story of the Bible and we start to pick up on that theme in Genesis. Abel's blood was spilt onto the ground and Cain was driven from the land that opened its mouth to receive his brother's blood. Moses had warned that the Israelites risked being scattered among the nations if they followed other gods. Jesus warned the Pharisees and teachers of the law that their house would be left desolate, he wanted to gather them as a hen gathers her chicks but they were not willing. He told his disciples that the temple would be demolished, and they asked, "When will this happen?" Jesus answered, "This generation shall not pass away," and less than 40 years later, in AD 70, the Romans destroyed the temple, removing the main altar where the Pharisees and teachers of the law practiced their religion. Josephus reports that the Romans took 97,000 prisoners. The altar had been one of the main links with Yahweh all the way back to Adam. But in 70 AD the altar was destroyed and has not been reinstated. Christians believe that Jesus was offered on the real altar and that all previous altars were a shadow of the sacrifice that Christ made. Christ's death was the point of all the previous altars, and Isaac played his part in the portrayal of that story. It was unpleasant for Isaac as he was bound and laid upon an altar, but I'm sure that as he looks back he's grateful for the part he had to play in the unfolding drama that would lead up to the salvation of the world.

And now in the narrative that unfolds in Genesis, Isaac is about to receive the beautiful and strong woman that God has selected for him. The servant detects some resistance from Rebekah's brother Laban, who may have seemed a touch too interested in the gold bracelets and gold nose ring that Rebekah had suddenly acquired as a gift from Abraham's servant. Both Laban and his father Bethuel tried to detain Abraham's man "ten days or so," where we get the feeling the "so" could easily turn into another ten days and so on. Abraham's servant is resolute, "Do not detain me!" he cries out. They call the girl and let her decide: "I will go," she says. So the long journey back to southern Canaan begins, they arrive weeks later towards the end of the day, and that particular evening Isaac has decided to go out and meditate in the fields. The timing for the servant's arrival in Rebekah's hometown was perfect and the timing when Rebekah was to meet Isaac was again precise. The servant must have been enjoying the way God's providence was working; he would speak of it with awe for many years to come. When the servant first queried Abraham about the logistics of such an undertaking asking, "Suppose the woman does not follow me?" Abraham answered, "The LORD, before whom I have walked, will send his angel with you to make your journey successful, and you will take a wife for my son from my relatives." The angel was still attending to his work as the servant and Rebekah approached Isaac.

Isaac looks up and sees the camels approaching; Rebekah looks up and sees Isaac. The Genesis text captures the romance magnificently; it was love at first sight. "She became his wife and he loved her." Rebekah was Isaac's cousin's daughter, the close familial bonds remained: this was offspring straight from Shem on both sides. Isaac was ten steps removed from Shem, the years of their lives had been shortened, the Lord had said that his Spirit wouldn't always strive with man (Adam) and then mentioned that the years they lived would be cut, but he didn't say anything about the beauty and strength. The years may have been cut shorter but the fairness of the females and the strength of the genetic line continued.

Abraham had gone to some effort to obtain the correct wife for Isaac, he knew there was a reason that his family line had been chosen to carry an important seed. However, that job was now done and Abraham didn't need to go to any length to secure a wife for himself. The promised seed was now being carried by Isaac, which meant Abraham was free to marry whomever he wanted, even a local girl. His new wife was called Keturah, and Abraham, though over 140 years old, was still strong and had no problem fathering more children and raising them. He was now living up to his name. Keturah would have been of childbearing age, and most likely short-lived so by the time Abraham died she would be about 60 years old, with six male children to look after her in her old age, and probably some daughters too. Abraham and Keturah's sons included Midian whose family became traders. Jethro was a priest of Midian and Moses married Jethro's daughter Zipporah.

As Abraham settles down with his new wife the time is right for Isaac to get to know Yahweh for himself. The Lord has his ways of encouraging people to call on him and Isaac noticed Rebekah was not bearing children after some 19 years of trying, so it was time to call on Yahweh. The LORD answered Isaac's prayer and Rebekah became pregnant. Later, Rebekah herself needed to inquire of Yahweh because she was having a turbulent pregnancy, which felt like the babies were jostling each other in her womb, so she went to inquire of Yahweh. There were places Rebekah could go to inquire, places she'd been told Yahweh or his angels had visited, in fact she was living near one of them: Beer Lahai Roi. The Lord did not disappoint her and explained that two nations were in her womb represented by twins, and, she was told, the older would serve the younger. Through the drama of Rebekah's pregnancy the Lord again highlights a little more information regarding the special offspring that would one day be born. There would be some struggling involved and some serving. When the twins were born the younger boy was named Jacob, who would be the next bearer of the seed of "life," and father of the twelve tribes of Israel. But the firstborn was Esau who would be the father of the Edomites. Herod the Great was an Edomite, he reigned in Judea at the time Jesus was born and tried to kill the baby Jesus, so the struggling babies in Rebekah's womb were also taking part in a piece of theater that would prove to be a true picture of reality many years later. And though Herod was called great, and was a king, Jesus would be named King of kings and at his name every knee should bow, in heaven and on earth and under the earth: the older will serve the younger.

Abraham would be able to see his grandchildren, Esau and his twin brother Jacob, and spend 15 years with them. Abraham finally died at a good old age. His sons, Ishmael and Isaac took care of the funeral arrangements and together took the body of their father back up north to Cave Machpelah, to be laid alongside Sarah.

Esau and Jacob were different in character, Esau was a skillful hunter but Jacob was a quiet contemplative man much like his father. Jacob stayed around the camp; his mother had a special closeness to him. Isaac thought a lot of his son Esau. One day Esau had been out running and chasing deer without success and came home famished and in need of some carbohydrates. Jacob used the opportunity to get the privileged rights that belonged to Esau. He'd been baking bread and making lentil soup, Esau asked for some, Jacob wanted to trade for it, Esau made a joke about it, but Jacob was serious and made Esau take an oath allowing Jacob to have his birthright before the food came his way.

There was a shortage of food at this particular time and Yahweh had been to see Isaac to talk to him about it, and told him not to go to Egypt to get food but to stay in the land that had been promised to his family. Yahweh also told Isaac that his seed would bless all the nations of the earth. Isaac and his family generally kept to themselves, as Abraham did too. Some critics point out that Abraham doesn't seem to be named in documentation from that era, but that's exactly what we would expect. Abraham purposely kept himself and his family separate; he only lifted his head above the parapet when it was absolutely necessary, such as when Lot was taken captive or when there was a shortage of food. He didn't camp in the towns but outside them, he kept his family's profile low.

Isaac followed suit, but because of the famine he moved his tents 40 miles northwest to Gerar where there was grazing land for his animals that could also be utilized for crops, plus there would be traders passing through who brought food from Egypt and elsewhere. Isaac did not trust city dwellers or their king, and thought they may kill him and take his beautiful wife, because even though she was the mother of two children and must have been around 55 years old, she was from Adam's lineage and retained her strength and beauty as well as some longer years than the average population. So the tip he picked up from his father was to let the townsfolk be under the misapprehension that Rebekah was his sister and he would then be treated well because of her, which is what he did. Soon the misnomer became common knowledge and I'm sure that suitors were appearing on Isaac's doorstep asking if they may court, or give a gift to, his sister. Isaac's deception may not have been as risky as his father's. Rebekah always seems to have been fairly close to Isaac throughout this deception and if there was a threat of Rebekah being taken into someone's household, Isaac and his family would probably have backed away fast and got out of that area. But while he was being treated well on Rebekah's behalf he courted the people of Gerar to his own advantage, there may have even been trips to the local marketplace to see all the wares for sale, when really Isaac was showing off his own wares. All went well, until his cover was blown.

Abimelech (most likely not the same person who took in Sarah, since Abimelech seems to be a name for Philistine kings just like Pharaoh is the name for Egyptian kings) saw Isaac and Rebekah caressing each other. Abimelech had not touched or even called Rebekah in, he'd probably had his suspicions from being told a similar story from his predecessor about a Hebrew with a stunning woman who pretended to be his sister. Abimelech was on the lookout and his waiting game paid off when he saw Isaac and Rebekah caressing. He hauled Isaac in, and Isaac found that the leader of Gerar had a lot more moral fiber than he'd credited him with. Abimelech didn't want any guilt on him or his town, he'd heard that Yahweh was capable of closing the wombs of females and appearing to kings in dreams telling them they were as good as dead. No wonder Abimelech kept his distance from Rebekah. But what frightened Abimelech about Isaac's deception was the fact that one of his men could have slept with Rebekah without anyone knowing about it except Rebekah, the man in question, and Yahweh. And Abimelech, to his credit, did fear God. There was no need for the Lord to speak to him in a dream or any other way because he'd spoken to his predecessor, who could well have been his father, and his father had passed on the knowledge. Abimelech issued a decree saying, "Anyone who molests this man or his wife shall surely be put to death."

Isaac's husbandry skills paid off, particularly with the blessing of God upon him. Living in Gerar was working out well for him. That is until the local inhabitants noticed how fantastically rich he was becoming, and how they were going to get crowded out, so they made it harder for Isaac by filling up some of the wells of water he used, wells his own father Abraham's workmen had dug. It didn't take long for Abimelech to act; he told Isaac that the time for him to move on had come. Isaac didn't go too far though, moving to the valley of Gerar about 5 miles away. Isaac told his men to start digging for water and they found some, but more disputes ensued with local people. Eventually Isaac decided to move the family 20 miles east to Beersheba, where his father had lived in his later years. The move turned out to be a good one because the very night he arrived there Yahweh was waiting for him. Isaac built an altar, something that always resonated with Yahweh. At the same time, Isaac's men began to dig for water at Beersheba. A relationship between Isaac and Yahweh was now beginning to grow, Abraham would have told Isaac about all the times Yahweh walked and spoke with him, from the very first time back in Ur, and now Isaac was becoming a genuine friend of Yahweh too.

The times we live in are a different era to the days of the patriarchs; God is with us by his Spirit, who came among us on the Day of Pentecost. God has always been willing to meet with us and has never been far from any one of us. Before the coming of the Holy Spirit, God was among us through his Son, and before Jesus was born he made himself known as Yahweh, walking, sitting, and eating with men. He didn't always appear as a man, he sometimes spoke in dreams or sent an angel, or occasionally just used his voice, and he also spoke through people. It seems that Father, Son, and Spirit have all reached out to us and made themselves known in corporeal form.

> Yahweh walked and ate with men, so too did Jesus, and the Holy Spirit descended on Jesus in bodily form like a dove. (Luke 3:22)

If a person who is in authority befriends us there is a temptation for us to become a little too familiar with them. The familiarity can cause some people to take liberties that they wouldn't normally take. A few people may even treat a person in authority with contempt, because of the familiarity. Jesus had a similar problem: "Then they scoffed, 'He's just the carpenter's son, and we know Mary, his mother, and his brothers—James, Joseph, Simon, and Judas. All his sisters live right here among us. Where did he learn all these things?' And they were deeply offended and refused to believe in him" (Matt 13:55–57). That may be the reason why Yahweh didn't visit too often and chose who he appeared to carefully. Paul in Philippians 3:10 cried out, "That I may know him." To know God is an exciting prospect, it is one that is available to us all and those who trust him sometimes get a special revelation. But the trust must come first, colors must be nailed to the mast before the ship sails—"Blessed are those who have not seen and yet have believed."

Isaac told his household that he'd had a visit from Yahweh. News of the visit spread around the local area and may have got as far as Gerar because to Isaac's surprise, Abimelech with some of his men, including Phicol (the name they had for their prime minister) made the 20-mile journey to pay him a visit. Isaac inquires about the reason for the visit, didn't they tell him to get out and leave Gerar? Abimelech replies by saying, "We saw plainly that Yahweh was with you; so we said there ought to be a sworn agreement between us. Do us no harm, as we did you no harm when you were among us, now you are blessed by Yahweh." Isaac was agreeable and prepared a sumptuous dinner for everyone. The next morning they each took an oath, and Abimelech went on his way and left Isaac in peace. That same morning Isaac's workmen struck water. Yahweh was living up to the name the Mesopotamian's had for him: "lord of the sweet waters that flow under the earth."[1]

The peace didn't last too long. Esau was now 40 years old and he took two wives, named Judith and Basemath, both of them Hittites, and much grief ensued for Rebekah and Isaac because of their daughters-in-law.

---

1. Encyclopaedia Britannica Online, s.v., "Eridu," accessed June 19, 2014, http://www.britannica.com/EBchecked/topic/191402/Eridu.

Chapter 18

Corresponding Celestial Counterpart

Whatever you bind on earth will be bound in heaven. (Matt 18:18)

ISAAC'S EYES BEGAN TO grow weak, it's true he was getting old; we can work out that he was about 130 years old, but he would still live another 50 years. Esau and Jacob were about 70 years old. Isaac having a bodily weakness does seem a little unusual; Isaac came from strong stock and physical faults had not been one of its features, now he is almost blind. There are probably two reasons for this, and one of them we can look at now. Esau had been born first and had the rights to his father's blessing, but Jacob was carrying the seed that would lead to Christ. Esau had married Hittite women and ruled himself out, plus many years before he took an oath to give the blessing of the firstborn to his twin brother Jacob. It was so long ago now that he may have forgotten all about it. Isaac either didn't know about the oath or didn't care, to him Esau was the firstborn and that was that. He called Esau to him, Isaac was feeling a bit low and thought his death might not be far away so it was an opportune time to give Esau his blessing. Isaac may have been nearly blind but he still had a good appetite and some strong teeth that could rip into some wild game that Esau caught from time to time. He told Esau to take his bow and hunt some fallow deer, prepare it, and bring it to him so he could eat it and Isaac would then give him the blessing.

Esau had always been passionate about the world around him; he loved the outdoor life, and had an impulsive nature. Jacob was a quiet man, a thinker, and someone who valued the blessing that could be passed on from a father in Adam's line to a son in the same line. This was not the "well

137

wishing" of a father to a son; something tangible was about to be passed on. A quality that could not be seen but was coupled with heaven, and Jacob earnestly desired it, and was prepared to go to some lengths to get it. Rebekah helped her favorite son, firstly by tipping him off that the blessing was about to be administered, and secondly, furnishing him with a plan of deceit that would secure the blessing for himself. Isaac wanted venison but Rebekah thought she would be able to cook something very similar from choice goat kids. She knew how Isaac liked his food and quickly got to work, probably employing the help of Deborah, her nurse and confidante. And because Esau had more body hair than Jacob she cut out hand and finger shapes from the thin underbelly parts of the goat that most resembled human hair and stuck them on the back of Jacob's hands, she also wrapped some around his neck. Rebekah had made some bread too, some of the flour could be used as paste to attach the goatskin to Jacob. The result wasn't great to look at but would be enough to deceive a blind man. Finally she dressed Jacob in some of Esau's clothes.

The deception worked well enough, although Isaac had some misgivings, it was the smell of Esau's clothes that did it. Jacob found himself telling a number of untruths to get the deal done. A chain of events was set in motion, and Jacob would reap what he had sown. When Isaac asked Jacob how he was able to catch the game so fast, Jacob replied by saying, "The LORD your God gave me success," which was a lie but it's interesting to note that Jacob called the LORD God his father's God and not his own God. He was saying what he thought his father wanted to hear, but also reveals that Jacob had not got to know Yahweh yet.

Scarcely had Jacob left his father's tent than Esau came back and Isaac realized what had happened. He shook in his shoes as he too realized that Jacob had received something that could not be taken back. Something had been passed on from father to son. It is at this point we begin to see there is something extra making its way through the generations of Adam's lineage. We find that there is something more than a certain code of DNA, yes there were genetics involved, but there was something more: an essence not from this world, something immaterial from another dimension, a quality that came from God breathing into Adam—a spiritual counterpart that transformed someone in Adam's lineage into "the seed-bearer." Without the divine counterpart the DNA may have had some excellent features but would not admit the human involved into the special line to Christ. Isaac, trembling violently, stated to Esau, "I blessed him—and indeed he will be blessed" (Gen 27:33).

While Isaac was delivering his blessing to Jacob we see the repercussions of it reach far into the future, to the Son of God who would be born, and people would bow down to him and nations would serve him as stated in the blessing Jacob received. He would be Lord over his brothers, there was obviously something prophetic about this blessing because Jacob only had one brother. When the nations embraced and worshipped Christ, this prophecy came true. Even as a young child, wise men came from the east and "fell to the ground and worshipped him."

Esau cried out to his father, who replied by saying, "What can I possibly do for you my son?" Esau managed to illicit a lesser blessing of a sort from his father but he began to feel hatred for Jacob and held a grudge. We've seen this scenario before with Cain and Abel, and so had Jacob, he knew he had to get out of there.

The blessing had been passed to Jacob so he would be well looked after wherever he went. Now that he was the seed-bearer he needed to add someone who's quite important to the process: a female. Providentially, as soon as Jacob receives his father's blessing his desire for a mate kicks in. He had seemed quite happy up to this point living a quiet life among the tents, but now that he is the seed-bearer he is on the move. Esau's grudge against Jacob was becoming common knowledge. Isaac and Rebekah decided it was time to get Jacob back to Mesopotamia where the correct partner for a male seed-bearer could be found. Isaac's failing eyesight had a part to play in the process. Isaac wanted Esau to take his rightful place in the line from Adam; and we can see divine providence at work using men's freewill like pieces on a chess board. God has his ways of getting his objectives completed: "The king's heart is a stream of water in the hand of the LORD; he turns it wherever he will" (Prov 21:1).

So Jacob begins the long journey north. He has lived in southern Canaan for 70 years and now he's on the move. Isaac knows that God is with his son and won't be concerned for his safety, too much is at stake for Jacob to come to harm, there will be angels watching. The family had talked about the exact route to follow and Jacob knew he had to take the ridge route north along what would later be called the Judean hills past Hebron and Salem (Jerusalem), the route his grandfather had taken so many times. Then he would need to turn sharp right at Shechem and descend to the ford at the Jordan River, cross over into the valley of the river Jabbok and head northeast towards Damascus where he could pick up the King's Highway which would take him to the Euphrates River. Then once across the river he still had some way to go to the area where the town of Haran lies.

The first two or three days Jacob made good progress on his journey from Beersheba, he was about ten miles north of Salem when he decided to bed down for the night. He wrapped some cloth and padding around a flat smooth stone and used it as a pillow. When he fell asleep he dreamt of a stairway to heaven, Yahweh stood at the top of it and angels were using it to climb up and down. Yahweh introduced himself to Jacob. Isaac also had an encounter with Yahweh at Beersheba but it happened at night and sounds as though it was a visit to Isaac alone. The dream was the first time Jacob had seen Yahweh, and although it wasn't an appearance on the earth but in a dream, it still counted.

Only a short time ago Jacob had received something from his father, something spiritual. The seed planted in Adam was something physical and yet it was administered by God's breath from which we understand there was something of spirit about it too, a coupling of flesh and spirit. Both were passed on from generation to generation, many people were recipients of the DNA or part of the DNA that would become the Christ child, but only one person at a time received the spiritual counterpart attached to the DNA. And it was the accompanying birthright that counted. The Father breathed into Adam, the Holy Spirit overshadowed Mary, and the Son took up residence in the body that was prepared for him, "For in him dwelleth all the fullness of the Godhead bodily." This wasn't simply a physical seed that was being passed down through the generations, it was greater than that, and Jacob was now beginning to realize the import of the prize that he so earnestly desired. It was the generations of heaven and earth, it was the connection with which heaven touches earth, and right now Jacob realizes that the connecting ladder comes from heaven to right where his head is laid. He is now in receipt of the seed that will grow into the means through which the world is able to climb to higher ground. He'd only been in possession of it a matter of days and already he was receiving instructions from beyond this universe about the seed he was now carrying.

We may wonder why the process started with Adam. Why couldn't God place the seed directly into Mary and bypass all the previous generations? Alternatively why couldn't Eve have given birth to Christ and then 4000 years of the seed being in the ground could have been avoided? When a seed is planted it can lie in the ground waiting for the conditions to be just right for it to germinate. Galatians 4:4 tells us that, "When the time had fully come God sent his son." There was a perfect time for Jesus to be born. But up to that point God was still with us, implanting something of himself within the human race; after all, we are made in his image so what better receptacle could there be? From Adam to Mary any one of those people could have taken the human race higher, but each one in their own way failed. They all fell short of the mark, and many of the shortcomings are written down for us to see. But there was finally one man who would not fall short; he would be able to raise the sons of earth. And just as the Ark of the Covenant was carried around by the Israelites as a sign of God's presence with them, the seed was also carried by those chosen to bear it. The Ark of the Covenant had to be carried, it couldn't be wheeled around on a cart, it had to be borne by men. The Ark was passed from generation to generation until the true Ark of God was revealed. The Ark of the Covenant contained the law, manna, and Aaron's rod that budded, which endorsed Aaron's call to the priesthood. Jesus had the law in his heart, he was the bread from heaven and he was the chosen priest.

When a relay is taking place there is an objective of getting a baton from one person to the next over a certain distance. God chose Adam to begin the relay, there was much that would be accomplished along the way. In the opening Olympic relay a flaming torch has been carried from one person to the next for several months; the flame brings light to each town it passes through. In a similar way the seed that was carried from Adam to Mary brought a lot of light along the way. Much was accomplished, the law was given, the Israelites were established, the prophets told us what we needed to hear, the Old Testament scriptures were written, and the principle of the altar was laid down, and it all centered around the "breath of life" that had been placed in Adam's line. God was close to what he had breathed into Adam's family.

James in the New Testament says, "Do you think Scripture says without reason that he jealously longs for the spirit he has caused to dwell in us?" (Jas 4:5). Some commentators struggle to find what scripture James is talking about, but if James isn't talking about one particular verse he could be referring to the breath God caused to live in Adam and all the way through to Christ. God jealously guarded that "breath of life." It could have spread through to the whole human race, but Cain killed his brother, and Adam's seed went from bad to worse until by the time of the Flood there was only one man who found favor in the eyes of the Lord: Noah. God gave us all a chance, but it came to the point where God said, "My Spirit shall not strive with man forever." Part of the learning process is the lesson that we cannot save ourselves, salvation is by God's grace and there's nothing we can do to secure it for ourselves. Man was made from the earth, from the dust or topsoil, that's where seeds are planted. Mankind was the earth and the seed from heaven was planted in one particular man: Adam, the generations (*toledoth*) of heaven and earth were in a position to start to produce life. Adam failed to capitalize on the opportunity but the second Adam did not.

God planted a garden in southern Mesopotamia, formerly it was a dry barren place but God brought water to the area and it blossomed. He also planted a seed in the dry heart of man, where it remained a seed. Adam failed to use its strength and gave in to the woman's offer. Cain failed to master the sin crouching at his door. They used the physical benefits of carrying the seed—long-life, physical strength, and beauty—but none of the spiritual qualities. But over 4000 years later and a chain of 76 generations (including God as the first and Jesus as the last) a man was born who displayed all the spiritual qualities of beauty, strength, and eternal life that were needed to lift men to heaven. Cain used the carnal benefits for selfish gain, but the physical qualities were there to mirror the spiritual qualities. God teaches us about spirituality by using the physical world around us. God uses drama, theater with a storyline, that always has a valuable lesson. That's why Jesus would point to the world around us when he taught in parables. Adam exhibited physically what Jesus exhibited spiritually. The physical qualities of Adam could have turned into spiritual qualities, and he could have eaten of the tree of life and lived forever. The spiritual qualities of Jesus turned into physical qualities, hence he rose from the dead and now lives forever.

CHAPTER 19

Jacob Sets Up a Stone and Removes One

IN THE DREAM, YAHWEH told Jacob that his seed would bless all peoples on the earth. Jacob woke up, alarmed and afraid, and exclaimed,

> Surely the LORD is in this place, and I was not aware of it. . . . How awesome is this place! This is none other than the house of God; this is the gate of heaven. (Gen 28:16–17)

Jacob's grandfather Abraham had stayed in that same area and erected an altar to the LORD. Now Jacob took the stone he'd rested his head upon and set it up as a pillar before pouring some oil on it. This was all new to Jacob; he had much to learn about God and his character. Jacob means "one who grasps the heel," figuratively that means he's a supplanter or deceiver, Jacob was born grasping Esau's heel and when Esau realized Jacob had taken his birthright blessing from his father Isaac, he lamented, "Isn't he rightly named Jacob?"

Jacob set the stone up as a shrine. We know that God wasn't so much interested in shrines as in altars, because altars had an important part to play in the unfolding story of his Son's sacrifice. Then Jacob makes a speech as he stands before the shrine, and the feel of his talk has the ring of a business deal about it: "If God will be with me and will watch over me on this journey I am taking and will give me food to eat and clothes to wear so that I return safely to my father's household, then the LORD will be my God and this stone that I have set up as a pillar will be God's house, and of all that you give me I will give you a tenth." And so Jacob took his first faltering steps towards God, and of course God was gracious to him, but how enthralled God was with the thought of a little stone pillar being his home we can only guess.

Once Jacob got to Damascus he probably attached himself to a group of traders heading north who often made the journey along the King's Highway to a safe crossing point on the Euphrates River and then on into Mesopotamia. We can get a very useful idea of the route by looking at a modern Internet map: from Damascus (in present-day Syria) head northwest to Palmyra then pick up the M20 all the way to Deir ez-Zur. Just below Deir the Euphrates River opens out into a plain and splits into two channels where the river can be forded. The site is one of great antiquity and there are numerous ancient mounds. The Romans and Greeks called it Thapsacus; the Hebrew name used in the Bible looks like it is Tiphsah. These days we use bridges to cross rivers, in antiquity fords were made passable by breaking up the flow of the water into a number of shallow channels. Jacob's journey from Damascus to the Euphrates ford would have been about 280 miles. Once across the Euphrates he would then follow the Euphrates on its north bank heading northwest for about 90 miles until he came to the Balikh River which would take him 60 miles north to the region of Haran, the source for the Balikh River is a little south of Haran. The journey was arduous with a climb at the end of it. As Jacob arrived in the general area he saw three flocks of sheep, which let him know he was moving in the right direction. Numerous wells that are now dry have been found in the old city of Haran suggesting that the water table may have been higher in the past. Jacob headed for one of these wells and spoke to the shepherds that had assembled there, greeting them with, "My brothers, where are you from?" They said, "We are from Haran." He then asked much the same questions we would ask when we find out someone is from the same town as one of our relatives: "Do you know Laban, Nahor's grandson?"

"Yes, we know him," they answered.

"Is he well?"

"Yes, he is," they said, "and here comes his daughter Rachel with the sheep."

The prevailing custom was that male shepherds always watered their flocks before the women and girls. We see the same scenario with Jethro's daughters and Moses in Exodus 2:16, as well as reports from witnesses to the area of northern Mesopotamia.[1] The well that Jacob now finds himself at had a large stone over its mouth because the plains of Haran could be

1. Thomson, *Land and the Book*, 400.

dusty and the stone would protect the water from the sand and dust. The stone would also take several men to move so the water couldn't be easily stolen.

The male shepherds probably had larger flocks than the girls, so as Rachel approached with her few sheep Jacob wanted to get the process of watering the sheep over and done with so he could finally finish his long journey and get to his uncle Laban's house. He knew that the male shepherds had to water their flocks first so he asked the local shepherds to water their sheep and get the sheep back to pasture. The men who may well have been young men replied that they couldn't water their sheep yet because all the flocks had not yet gathered, and also the stone over the mouth of the well had not yet been moved. There may have been men appointed for the job of actually moving the stone, strong men from the local community who went round each well one by one moving and replacing the stones.

Jacob took the matter into his own hands: using the special strength he had from being a part of Adam's line, and which seemed to kick in with greater momentum since the birthright was put into his possession, he moved the stone by himself. He made sure his uncle's sheep were watered; a leather bucket was lowered into the well and the water was then poured into a receptacle from which the sheep could drink. This courtesy was a return of the favor that Rebekah had shown to Abraham's servant. While the sheep were drinking Jacob kissed Rachel and wept loudly, he probably didn't want to do all this in front of the local shepherds and that's another reason he wanted them to get on with watering their flocks, but he could no longer contain himself. He explained to Rachel who he was, and seeing all that Jacob had said and done, she ran off, back to her father Laban to tell him the news. Laban himself hurried out to meet Jacob, who by this time may have been trying to make his way into the town while struggling to keep the sheep beside him. Laban embraced Jacob and kissed him and welcomed him into his home. Jacob told Laban the news from Isaac and Rebekah's household. Then Laban said to him, "Surely you are my bone and my flesh." Laban was picking up on what Adam said about Eve when she was first created from his side. It may have been a family motto and only those in Adam's unadulterated line could say it, because Eve really was pulled from Adam's flesh and bone.

CHAPTER 20

Eye Problems

JACOB STAYED WITH LABAN and his family; he worked hard and helped wherever he could, he got to know Rachel too and began to fall in love. After a month Laban approached Jacob and said,

> What shall we do about your wages? Just because we are close relatives doesn't mean I shouldn't pay you for the work you do. (Gen 29:15)

Jacob was quick to suggest 7 years of work for his daughter Rachel. Laban agreed. It is at this point in the text that Genesis mentions that Laban has another daughter named Leah and "Leah had weak eyes." And that's it. All we know about Leah at this point is her eye weakness. Isaac had almost lost his eyesight, and now another family member is suffering from some sort of eye weakness. Normally the line from Adam was strong, robust, and healthy, but Genesis wants us to know that there was one area where the normal state of affairs was not upheld. This weakness could have been genetic or there may have been another reason for it. If it was genetic it must have come from Terah's line because Isaac came from Terah and so did Leah. Eye weakness wasn't something that Abraham developed, it was earlier than that, because Leah wasn't from Abraham or Sarah. Terah is the common link between the two people we know had something wrong with their eyes. Genesis wants us to note that it's there. It's a small break with the normal healthy nature of Adam's posterity and it is most likely there for a reason.

Jacob was truly in love, he'd never felt like this before. Esau had got married years before but Jacob had shown no interest in women, until now.

Jacob was so much in love that the 7 years seemed like a few days to him. When the wedding came, Laban put on a big feast. We know that Laban had an eager eye for business when he showed interest in the gold and jewelry that his sister Rebekah had been given by Abraham's servant. Laban now saw a way of getting another 7 years work out of Jacob, who was strong and ready to work hard. Jacob had been feasting with the other guests and there was probably some fine wine consumed and Jacob may have been feeling slightly the worse for drink. Leah was veiled and, under Laban's direction, made to look like her sister and probably given instructions to keep quiet until the union had been made.

Rachel would have been taken, by some ruse or perhaps forcibly, somewhere else but certainly not close by in case her screams could be heard. Laban gave Leah to Jacob when it was night, and in the dark tent he consummated the union, only later did he realize his bride was Leah and not Rachel. The next morning Jacob went straight to Laban demanding an answer to why he had been deceived. Laban gave him his answer: the local custom, conveniently for Laban, was always to give the older daughter in marriage first. That was Laban's answer, but there are another two answers to the question. Firstly, Jacob was reaping what he had sown—he had formerly veiled himself with goat skin and deceived his father Isaac, and now he himself was deceived by someone wearing a veil. Those who deceive others are themselves deceived. Secondly, Leah was the chosen route through which the Christ would come, not Rachel. Jacob would not have married Leah if Laban hadn't seized the opportunity. Laban told Jacob to see out the bridal week, he would then give Rachel to Jacob too, in return for another 7 years of work. Rachel became his wife at the end of the seven days and he consummated that union as well. Jacob was disgruntled, but he now had Rachel so things weren't too bad.

If Moses was the one who compiled most of the text of Genesis we can say that he got the next bit of light straight from his time spent with God, either on the mountain or in the tent of meeting. We are told that Yahweh was not pleased with Jacob's attitude to Leah, and as a result the Lord saw to it that she became pregnant very quickly indeed, perhaps from that first honeymoon week. She gave birth to Reuben and offered this explanation for his name: "It is because Yahweh has seen my misery. Surely my husband will love me now." Jacob was probably not spending much time at night with Leah at all; it was Rachel who had captured his heart. However, when he realized how Reuben got his name and particularly hearing the name of

Yahweh invoked, his attitude changed a little. Yahweh was not a name he would hear much of in Haran. Four generations before, Terah had moved away from the God that Adam and Noah knew, and was taken by the idols in Ur and Haran. Rachel herself valued the household gods, but now Leah was harkening back to the time her family knew God, her appeal was to Yahweh, not to the moon god Sin, or any other Mesopotamian deity. Yahweh's name rang true with Jacob and he remembered his dream and the deal he had announced to Yahweh. He decided to spend a little more time with Leah and his newborn son Reuben.

When the Apostle Paul first saw the Lord, he suddenly found himself blind for three days, then Ananias prayed for him and something like scales fell from his eyes, resulting in his sight being restored. However, we get the impression that his eyesight was always a bit of a problem to him after that first occasion. When he wrote his letters he normally dictated them, Tertius wrote the book of Romans under Paul's dictation. When he wrote the Letter to the Galatians, towards the end of the letter Paul wrote some of it himself saying, "Notice what large letters I use as I write these closing words in my own handwriting." We know that Paul had a thorn in the flesh and had prayed for it to go but God wanted it in Paul's life. Poor eyesight for Paul would always be a reminder of what God had done for him. When he thought he could see, he was blind, and when his eyesight was taken from him, that's when he truly began to see. Paul spoke about the visions and revelations he had seen. It was because of what he saw in heaven that he was given a thorn in the flesh to stop him from becoming conceited. He could see into heaven but "seeing" on earth would not be so easy.

Seeing into the spiritual world could have physical repercussions: Daniel had a vision and after it he lay exhausted and sick in bed for several days. Moses spoke with Yahweh on Mount Sinai, and when Moses went down the mountain and back to the people his face was radiant and he didn't even know it. Aaron and the Israelites were afraid to come close to him, but he reassured them and they came close enough to hear the commands that the LORD had given him. After they had finished hearing the words of the LORD from Moses, he covered his face with a veil. He removed the veil whenever he spoke to the LORD, and he removed it whenever he spoke to the people. Moses may have done this because the veil was the equivalent of sunglasses. He wanted to see the LORD and he wanted to speak to the people properly but the rest of the time he put on his veil. He didn't want any unnecessary light hitting his eyes when he could protect them. In

Genesis chapter 26 Isaac moved to Beersheba from the valley of Gerar, and that evening Yahweh appeared to him. The first verse of the next chapter tells us that Isaac's eyes were weak. We know that it was partly Isaac's failing eyesight that secured the blessing for Jacob. If Yahweh had let just a tiny amount of his glory be seen, Isaac's eyes could have been affected by it. Moses asked Yahweh to show him his glory; Moses wouldn't have been able to withstand the full force of Yahweh's glory, so he stood in a cleft in a nearby rock and Yahweh covered Moses with his hand so that Moses's eyes would not see his face shining in its glory. As Yahweh moved his hand away Moses was able to see Yahweh's back, still glorious but not overpowering.

For some reason Leah was reaching out to Yahweh, Rachel was close to her father's household gods, and Laban also loved those gods and wanted them close. Leah was the chosen vessel through which the Messiah would be born and her weak eyes and her appeal to Yahweh may be a clue that she had had an encounter with Yahweh at some point in her earlier life.

Yahweh didn't always show his glory to those he met, similar to Jesus, who walked around without a number of people realizing who he was. But he did say to his disciples, "I tell you truly, there are some standing here who will not taste death until they see the kingdom of God." After six days Jesus took Peter, James, and John and led them up a high mountain by themselves. There he was transfigured before them. His face shone like the sun, and his clothes became as white as the light. Mark says, "His clothes became dazzling white, whiter than anyone in the world could bleach them." When the four of them made their way down the mountain, there is what seems a curious verse, "As soon as all the people saw Jesus, they were overwhelmed with wonder." The people had seen Jesus many times, why now should they be filled with wonder? It's because Jesus, like Moses still had some of the glory of heaven upon him. When Yahweh was walking around the city of Ur, he may have not stood out in any particular way, when he became friends with Abraham at first Abraham may have not realized who he was speaking to. So God may have shown Abraham a touch of his glory to let him know who he was talking to. When the martyr Stephen was talking to the men who were about to kill him he said, "The God of glory appeared to our father Abraham while he was still in Mesopotamia, before he lived in Haran." So that may be a clue that Abraham got to see some of the glory of God himself. We don't read that Abraham had poor eyesight, except for the fact that he didn't see the ram caught in the thicket until after the voice from heaven had spoken to him. But he was otherwise engaged at that point; also if God touches someone's eyes so that they are dimmed he is also able to open the eyes of the blind as Jesus demonstrated.

If God's appearance caused eye weakness he would only leave someone's eyesight poor for a reason. Either the person themselves would have a reminder of their encounter with the Lord, facilitating humility within their lives, or it would be used as a sign for others.

CHAPTER 21

Idols' Insidious Influence

NOW THAT JACOB WAS spending a little more time with Leah she quickly got pregnant again. Jacob's first and great love was still Rachel and so Leah named her second child Simeon saying,

> Yahweh heard that I am not loved and he gave me this one too.

Then she had a third child, Levi. It seems that whenever Jacob spent a night with Leah, she got pregnant; this was galling to Rachel who got so irritable about the state of affairs that in her anguish she cried out to Jacob,

> Give me children, or I'll die!

This was their relationship's first rough wave in previously untroubled waters, Jacob himself got angry and retaliated by asking if he was in the place of God. Leah had four sons by this time; the latest boy to be born was Judah, who was to be the next male in genealogical descent to Christ. Clearly God's hand was at work, he was about his business and all the children born so far were boys. God was establishing, or we could say building something that was going to last.

Since Abraham first spoke with Yahweh and was told that he and Sarah would become a great nation, around 175 years had passed, the fertility rate of the family this far was meagre . But suddenly it was all changing. The Mesopotamian custom of giving a wife's servant girl as a surrogate mother was the only alternative that Rachel felt she had left so she played that card, giving her maidservant Bilhah to Jacob. She probably did this when Leah was in her third or fourth pregnancy, the Genesis chronology is largely straightforward but with any story that's being told there has to be overlapping periods here and there. Rachel wouldn't want to wait too long in the "bearing children" stakes; she was highly motivated. Leah quickly followed suit, giving her maidservant Zilpah to Jacob. Each maidservant produced two sons.

In the space of 7 years Jacob would father 11 sons and one daughter (although the daughter could have been born later). That so many children were born is surprising considering the sister who held the reigns struggled to conceive. The rivalry between the sisters should have slowed the process down but we see some providence at work. On one occasion Leah had to resort to bargaining to get a night with Jacob, Reuben who was about 4 or 5 years old found some mandrake plants, the roots tend to look like human beings and were fun for Reuben to play with. There was also an ancient myth that they could help with human fertility; this was of much interest to Rachel, who said she would let Jacob spend the night with Leah in return for her son's mandrakes. What Rachel did with the plants we can't be sure because they are poisonous to eat, but with Rachel's' affinity for terephim (small idols) she may have used them as charms placed around the bed without Jacob even knowing. Leah had three more children before Rachel realized the mandrakes were worthless. Rachel placed her trust in the mandrakes but Leah appealed to God. Genesis tells us that God listened to Leah and her fifth son Issacar was born.

We get a little bit of insight into the contention between the two sisters when Leah says, "Wasn't it enough that you stole my husband? Now will you steal my son's mandrakes, too?," which tells us that Rachel used her position to limit Jacob's time with Leah. After Leah's forth child, Judah, Rachel may have forbidden Jacob to sleep with Leah. That could be why there was a temporary cessation of births for Leah. Leah may have pleaded with Jacob to at least sleep with her maidservant, to which Rachel acquiesced as long as it was not Leah with whom Jacob spent the night. We then hear of the mandrakes incident which breaks the deadlock. It appears Rachel was more easygoing after that and Leah had a further son, Zebulun, and at some point later on a daughter, Dinah. The change in Rachel's attitude was noted and she also called out to God who heard her and finally after 7 years she gave birth to Joseph.

The term of 14 years that Jacob promised to work for Laban in return for his two daughters was now complete. Jacob asked Laban to send him on his way back home to Canaan. Jacob had some fear of Laban and knew he had to tread carefully, his father-in-law wouldn't want to let him or his two daughters and grandchildren go easily. Earlier we saw that he had a problem letting his sister Rebekah go. Also Laban always played up to his part as the shrewd businessman looking for an angle from which he could benefit, so he tells Jacob that through divination he has learned that Yahweh has blessed him because of Jacob. Divination was one of the problems in Ur and Haran, Laban sounds as if he's fully into the craft, he may have used Yahweh's name as a lure knowing that Jacob had an affinity with Yahweh. It didn't take divination for anyone to see that God's hand of blessing was on Jacob. He'd received the blessing from Isaac and it was strong; what Jacob put his hand to got blessed, "earth's richness" was part of it.

Jacob did need some substance with which to provide for his eleven sons, one daughter, and four wives, and recently Jacob had had a dream during one of the animal mating seasons. In the dream he saw streaked, speckled, or spotted goats mating. Then an angel spoke to him and told him to notice what kind of goats were mating. It was a sign, and Jacob noted it, God was about to do something.

Jacob acted upon the dream, he told Laban to let him have the goats and sheep that were of abnormal color as wages for his continued service. These particular type of animals were in the minority so Laban agreed, and to make sure that the deck was stacked in his own favor, Laban told his sons to remove all the sheep and goats that weren't plain, which would leave Jacob with only plain animals. The deal was then: if any of those plain goats or sheep gave birth to animals that had streaks, spots, speckles, or were dark they would belong to Jacob. Laban put the mottled animals three days journey away from the plain flocks, which would ensure there was no possibility of mating between the two flocks. To hide the fact that Jacob was working with inside knowledge, he conformed to the idea that's been believed as a type of "old wives tale" in past generations, which was that visual impressions at the time of conception affected the outcome at birth. He took branches and cut white stripes into them and placed them before the animals when they came for water. The ruse worked, Laban thought Jacob was working hard at getting himself some animals with a method that was known among real herdsmen to be useless. Lambing could take place in those climes twice a year and there were 6 years that Jacob worked for animals as wages so after two rutting seasons Laban saw that something was actually working for Jacob because the streaked sheep were multiplying fast. So for the next 5 years, Laban changed the deal. Laban didn't realize that whatever he did wasn't going to work for him, because God was working with Jacob.

Laban's sons appear late in the story, we don't hear of them earlier, they may have been born to him late in life. They were not happy with the state of affairs, somehow Jacob was ending up with a lot of animals and the sons complained, "Jacob has taken everything." This wasn't true of course, but Jacob knew the remark spelled trouble and that meant he needed to make good his escape back to Canaan. Jacob spoke to Leah and Rachel, "Your father has cheated me by changing my wages ten times." The sisters thought that their father Laban treated them as foreigners and that his sons were now his main concern, so they told Jacob to do as he thought best, they were with him. Common adversity was bringing the warring sisters together.

The undertaking would be large, but the family decided they wanted to leave and make their way 400 miles to Canaan. They had much livestock now but they also had employees who could help with the long journey. Jacob and Rachel saw their opportunity when Laban went to shear his sheep; Jacob waited until then because he wanted to make good his escape without attracting Laban's attention who might try any means to stop him. Rachel saw it as an opportune time to steal her father's terephim.

Idolatry crept into humanity as Satan began to influence people's behavior. Originally in Genesis chapter 1 God said, "Let the land produce living creatures according to their kinds," then God said, "Let us make man in our image." Men appear on the scene at the completion of creating the animals, and the text doesn't refer to the land producing again. Humans arrived after a long list of animals, the animals originated from the ground and we came from the same stock, according to Genesis chapter 1, and so we are connected to the long list of animals that originally came from the ground. Genesis chapter 2 reminds man that we too came from the dust of the ground just like the animals before us. We are different to them because we are made in God's image. God blessed humanity and had a relationship with the early humans who were living at that time. He would speak with them telling them to be fruitful, and to move on into all the earth, he told them not to let any created thing rule over them. He spoke with them about the best things to eat. As small families began to spread out from what a number of archaeologists say is Africa, the home of the first Homo sapiens, they moved northeast. Many of them were hunter-gatherers, they followed the animals to where the Fertile Crescent begins in Egypt and then on into

Mesopotamia and Europe. Some began to farm the fertile land, others followed the animals they were hunting across Asia, then crossed the Bering Land Bridge that connected Siberia with Alaska, and finally moved down into America about 11,000 BC. Jody Hey, a professor of genetics at Rutgers University calculated that as few as 70 people crossed over into America.[1] The professor's calculations are also consistent with archaeological evidence.

God had a relationship with early man, they were obeying his command to fill the earth and subdue it. God walked with man and helped him, telling him what he needed to know. I don't think we should view it as strange that God should walk on the earth that he created. The creation of the material world was a massive project, when its foundations were laid and it all started taking shape "the morning stars sang together and all the angels shouted for joy" (Job 38:7). We are made in his image, which means that God was able to be manifest in the same form as us. God is Spirit and the creation serves him who made it. We sometimes spiritualize the meaning of being made in his image, and there are several ways we can view it, but the simple text of Genesis tells us we are made in the image of God and image means optical, it is something we see. He walked on earth that he may reach out to us. In those early days of humanity we needed help, direction, and guidance, he gave it to us and so did his angels. How did men come to believe in God in the first place? The idea of God and his angels goes right back into the far reaches of the people groups who live on earth. The stories changed a little from generation to generation, because some of the angels who were on earth to help chose instead to hinder men rather than help them. There was one angel in particular who started to rebel.

Let's think about how Satan is first introduced to us in Genesis: "Now the serpent was more crafty than any of the wild animals the LORD God had made." The way the serpent is introduced strongly suggests that he has some history of craftiness, and that the storyline in Genesis needs to tell us this before it continues. Let's look at it another way. If we were explaining the story of Oliver Twist to someone we might say, "Now the Artful Dodger was a cunning boy who pretended to befriend Oliver." That sentence would impart a lot of information in a short time: we can infer that the Artful Dodger has a previous history of defrauding people and is able to recruit innocent new boys and turn them into cunning worldy-wise boys like himself. There is a clue in his name, "Artful Dodger"; his real name

1. Hey, "North America Settled," lines 14–17.

is Jack Dawkins, but the Artful Dodger nickname gives us a lot of information. Just as the word "serpent'" gives us information, Satan is able to take innocent humans and turn them into crafty worldy-wise creatures like himself. What happened in the garden of Eden was a microcosm of what was happening and had been happening in the wider world. Adam and Eve ate from the tree of the knowledge of good and evil. Figuratively this had been happening on a larger scale for sometime.

"Now the serpent was more crafty," because he'd been at this work of deception for some time. The word "was" refers back to what has happened previously, "was" implicitly includes some of the serpent's history, it alerts us to "watch out" and "be careful" because this creature may try something crafty. God allowed the scenario in the garden to play out because it relates to us all.

God loved early man but there was someone who made it his work to be a corrupting influence in the world. Satan wasn't the only one either, but he was their leader. In the last book of the Bible, Revelation, we read about a sign that appears in heaven: an enormous red dragon sweeps a third of the stars out of the sky and flings them to the earth. We understand that the imagery is pointing to angels who did not keep their first estate. With so many angels that were hindering and not helping it's not surprising that stories about God and angels got distorted. The Greeks believed in many gods, and had numerous myths about them. These beliefs may have become prevalent if angels were thought of as gods; righteous angels refused to be worshipped though. When the Apostle John experienced his revelation he said, "when I heard and saw, I fell down to worship at the feet of the angel who showed me these things. But he said to me, 'Do not do that. I am a fellow servant of yours and of your brethren . . . worship God.'" But not all angels had that humble attitude and some courted praise. Isaiah tells us that the "morning star" said, "I will make myself like the Most High." Lucifer lead early man astray and eventually God spoke to the serpent in the garden of Eden and took away Satan's ability to stand.

The stories of gods and angels remained, men made icons, idols, and images of what they looked like. *These gods can help us*, was the prevalent thought among men. It's partly true, some angels could help us and some from time to time still do, although the earth is pretty much populated now and by and large we help each other. However, in the days of the patriarchs the deception remained and Rachel clung onto her little images.

In the Septuagint, Deuteronomy 32:8–9 informs us that God divided the sons of Adam according to the number of angels, but the Lord watched over Jacob's people. This allows us to see that angels helped in the early days of human civilization: they had a particular commission to watch over Adam's offspring, but it was the Lord himself who kept his eye on the seed that was contained within the family of Jacob.

Angels looking after cities also fits in well with the ancient Sumerian religious texts, explaining that gods and humans lived together on earth. Each city in the fledgling city-states of southern Mesopotamia was thought to have its own god.[2] We can probably see how this belief arose. If as Deuteronomy 32 tells us angels were linked to Adam's other offspring and set their boarders, then tales of god-like beings who looked after each city would be passed down to subsequent generations.

2. Guisepi, "Ancient Sumeria," line 419.

CHAPTER 22

Two Angry Men and a Wrestling Match

IT DIDN'T TAKE TOO long for news to reach Laban that his daughters and Jacob had started to make their way back to Canaan, and he was soon in hot pursuit. Laban didn't have herds to drive either, and he was angry, so his progress would be quick. When he laid his head down at the end of the last day of pursuit:

> God came to Laban the Aramean in a dream at night and said to him, "Be careful not to say anything to Jacob, either good or bad." (Gen 31:24)

Jacob would have thought long and hard about his escape, he needed to get the time of year correct, so that the flow of the Euphrates would be low, and usually during August to September the Euphrates reaches its lowest point. Jacob's herds would be able to pass over at one of the fords. He would have also made sure that the herds were grazing in a southward direction, so they had a head start. All the land from Haran to the Euphrates River would be legitimate grazing land, but once Jacob actually crossed the river that would put an entirely different outlook on what he was doing. Laban wouldn't have thought Jacob was doing anything odd taking his flocks down south but as soon as he crossed over the river Euphrates this would send a signal to Laban that something was amiss, flocks were not taken across the Euphrates unless they were on a special journey. News of who crossed the river would travel around the area; people like to know who is coming and going. It took three days for the news to reach Laban that Jacob had "crossed over"; it took Laban seven days of pursuit. The two parties finally came face to face on land east of the Jordan River, in the hill country of Gilead. Poor Jacob—an angry man had tracked him down from behind and further up the road was, what he presumed would be, another angry man: his brother Esau. God needed to step in and help Jacob.

The day after his dream Laban finally caught up with Jacob and he remembered that God had told him not to say anything good or bad to Jacob. Instead Laban said, "I have the power to harm you"; and that was what Jacob had always been afraid of. Jacob replied, "I was afraid because I thought you would take your daughters away from me by force." The dream had its effect and Laban was careful not to threaten or bless Jacob, but he did have a few questions: "Why did you steal my gods?" Jacob was unaware that Rachel had stolen the gods and told Laban that if he could find anyone who had his gods among Jacob's company then that person would not live. Rachel had a short window of opportunity to own up and hand the gods back, but she wanted those idols so when Laban and his team made a thorough search Rachel sat on her camel and said, "Let not my lord be angry that I cannot rise before you, for the manner of women is upon me." What Rachel said might have been true but if she was a thief she probably had no compunction about telling lies either. Laban knew the terephim were sacred objects and surely no one would sit on them, especially a woman in menstruation, but Rachel was desperate to hold on to them. When Laban's search was fruitless, Jacob felt angry and gave Laban a piece of his mind. At this point Laban tried to calm things down by suggesting they make a deal. They set up a pillar and a heap of stones and shared a meal, both men agreed not to pass the stone to harm the other. Laban, now bereft of his gods, called on Yahweh to watch them both. They spend the night there and early the next morning Laban made his way home, poorer (or so he thinks) for not having his gods, but richer for having heard God's voice in a dream.

The angry man chasing Jacob had been sent back home appeased, Jacob can breathe a sigh of relief, but there's still one more angry man to face. When Jacob was still in Haran Yahweh had said to him, "Go back to the land of your fathers and I will be with you." As Jacob makes his way towards the Jabbok River valley, which is the route to where the river Jordan can be crossed, he meets some angels; he'd seen angels before when they climbed the ladder in his dream, now he saw them while he was awake. God had promised to be with Jacob and meeting the angels let him know that Yahweh was keeping his word. The angels camped not far from where Jacob camped, Psalm 34:7 tells us that, "The angel of the LORD encamps around those who fear him." Jacob called the place Mahanaim, which means "two camps."

Jacob asked some of his employees to make their way to Edom, southeast of the Dead Sea to find his brother Esau. He wanted his men to humbly explain what had been happening these last 20 years, that Jacob may find favor with Esau. His messengers would need 10 to 14 days to get back from their 40-mile journey directly south; the terrain wasn't easy to negotiate and they may have had to go around some of the hill country. From there they had to locate Esau and eventually make it back to Jacob with what seemed like bad news: Esau was marching out to meet Jacob with 400 men. Jacob was shaken to his core. He took evasive measures and split his company into two groups, so that at least one of them may survive. Then he prayed in true humility: "I am unworthy of all the kindness and faithfulness you have shown to me. Save me from my brother, I'm afraid he'll attack me and the mothers and their children." Jacob selected gifts with which to appease Esau to let him know that his intentions were brotherly. He sent all his family and lastly his possessions over the ford of the Jabbok River, by which time darkness had fallen. He wanted some time by himself so he stayed on the northern side.

What happens next has caused much wonder, not to mention perplexity in those who read it. While Jacob is alone on the north of the river, at some point during the night "a man" wrestles with him. Why is that odd? Because we immediately ask several questions, "Which man?" "Where did he come from?" "Why does he want to wrestle and not talk?" "Isn't wrestling a strange thing to do?" The whole scenario sounds a bit weird. It will help us if we remember that Jacob is getting to know Yahweh, and earlier that day Jacob had prayed about his fear of Esau, he had faith of some sort in God but fear was still in his heart, and "the fear of man is a snare." Yahweh had promised to be with Jacob and visits him during the early morning hours. Jacob had seen Yahweh before, standing at the top of the ladder in his dream, but it's dark now and Jacob can't see who it is, so at this point in the story all we know is that it's a man. Jacob had been a wrestler or heel-catcher from his youth, that's what the name Jacob means, so now Yahweh has to change that. How the wrestling started we can't be sure but if Jacob was sleeping and he awoke to see the form of a man close by, his first instinct might be to grab the man in a headlock thinking he was a thief. Particularly in Jacob's heightened awareness of 400 men about to bear down upon him.

So let's suppose that's what happened, Jacob grabs the intruder and let's remember that Jacob is from Adam's stock and has some strength at his disposal, but he finds that this man is able to fight back, they are locked in clinch after clinch. We again find ourselves wondering about this scenario, would God actually wrestle and get that close to a sweaty man, skin upon skin in a rough fight? We could wonder the same kind of thoughts about Jesus: he fought, he made a whip and chased out the money merchants. He also got close to the crowds who pushed against him, and we read that when he was gathered relaxing with his disciples there was one disciple who was reclining on Jesus's chest. So I think the answer is yes, Yahweh would get down and into a wrestling match if it was important to do so. As the light begins to break Jacob is still refusing to break his grip. The other man says, "Let me go, it's daybreak." So we could be correct in supposing that Jacob started this wrestling match, the other man was simply trying to break free the whole time. Maybe the other man did simply want to talk but Jacob started the fight. It is Jacob's nature not to let go until he gets what he wants, and submission in this wrestling match comes when Jacob gets his demand of being blessed by his opponent and Jacob tells him so. So the man asks, "What is your name?" The question isn't for Yahweh's benefit, it's to remind Jacob what his name means. The man then says, "Your name will no longer be Jacob, but Israel because you have struggled with God and men and have overcome. Israel means "he struggles with God." God appeared as a man and Jacob prevailed. In Hosea 12:4–5 we read about Jacob: "In the womb he grasped his brother's heel; as a man he struggled with God."

Jacob wants to know the man's name, the man won't say but does bless him. Once Jacob gets the submission he deems appropriate to end the wrestling match he lets go of the man. He can now get a good look at his opponent, the sun is rising and Jacob realizes who the man is. He names the place Peniel, saying, "I have seen God face to face, yet my life has been preserved." Peniel means "face of God."

Jacob must have thought, *What a night!* While crossing over the Jabbok ford he notices that he's limping; there was a price to pay for wrestling with Yahweh. But he was probably feeling a lot less apprehensive now. He sends his gifts on ahead, no longer as a means of pacifying his brother but as genuine gifts that Esau may share in his blessing. When the twins finally get within meters of each other, Jacob bows low seven times as was the custom, but Esau has no time for such conventions, he runs to his brother greatly moved and hugs him, kisses him, and weeps aloud. Jacob weeps too; it's a reuniting befitting two brothers who need to bury the past, show forgiveness, and love each other as brothers should.

Esau heads back home. Jacob takes his time moving his flocks after their long journey. He builds some stalls while still on the east of the river Jordan and also builds a house for his family. If Jacob's troupe crossed the Euphrates in August, winter would soon be upon them so the shelters would come in useful. Jacob and his family spent the winter in Succoth, a place he named himself, meaning "shelters." When the spring came Jacob would have continued following the route that Abraham, his grandfather had taken before him: over the Jordan and northwest along the Wadi Farah, which these days has a decent road called the 57, but Jacob would have had to make the climb on foot or with camels. The route climbs 800 meters in over 20 miles and when he reached the top he settled within sight of Shechem, which is what Abraham also did. Yahweh had appeared to Abraham at Shechem and told him that his offspring would own this land. Abraham built an altar there staking his claim.

Jacob bought the land from the ruler of Shechem, Hamor; all those years later he bought it on behalf of his grandfather Abraham. This was important because Stephen in Acts 7 tells us that Abraham didn't receive any of the land—not even enough to put the sole of his foot on. "But God," continued Stephen, "promised him that he and his descendants after him would possess the land." Notice that Abraham would inherit the land, scripture says, "he and his descendents after him"; while Abraham was on earth he received nothing. And yet God had told Abraham that he would be given all the land he could see (Gen 13:15). Jacob was buying the land not only on behalf of himself but also Abraham, as Stephen remarks later in his speech about the fathers being buried in Shechem: "Their bodies were brought back to Shechem and placed in the tomb that Abraham had bought from the sons of Hamor at Shechem for a certain sum of money." Abraham had purchased some land in Hebron but not in Shechem. This is a fascinating hypothesis that Stephen is bringing out. What does this mean? Abraham was still around at the time of Jacob even though he was dead? Jesus explained it by saying, "Have you not read what God said to you, 'I am the God of Abraham, the God of Isaac, and the God of Jacob'? He is not the God of the dead but of the living." Matt 22:29–23 continues, "When the crowds heard this, they were astonished." Stephen is saying the same thing. Joseph's tomb can still be seen in the modern city of Nablus that equates to the ancient city of Shechem.

The field and cave that Abraham purchased was for a special purpose, not given as an inheritance. And although Jacob purchased land the real inheritance of the land was still to come. Both Abraham and Jacob purchased land, but buying land is different to being given land as an inheritance.

Chapter 23

Kidnapped and Raped

THE TRACT OF LAND near Shechem was now officially in the hands of Abraham's family, they settled there for a few years and Jacob's sons began to grow strong and get to know the area. These were strong young lads who weren't afraid of hard work, and this is most likely the time they dug the famous "Jacob's Well"; Jesus spoke to the Samaritan woman there. The well is dug in limestone rock; some work would be required to dig it. Henry Maundrell visited it in 1697 and said,

> It is dug in a firm rock, is about three yards in diameter, and thirty-five in depth, five of which we found full of water.[1]

The well can still be seen in the town of Balata, a Palestinian village and suburb of Nablus. It currently lies within the complex of an Eastern Orthodox monastery.

The eleven brothers had been born in Mesopotamia but Canaan was now their new home. Their sister Dinah was a young teenager and being from Adam's line was fair to behold. The local men, as usual, quickly noted this fact. Jacob hadn't wanted to get too close to the local community, he knew that he and his family were different to them, but there were times when mingling couldn't be avoided. Being the only female in a large family of boys, Dinah would naturally want some female companionship, so she went to visit some of the local women, she may have had a friend or two and was paying them a visit. The ruler of Shechem, Hamor, had a son who was named after the town they lived in, Shechem, he saw Dinah's beauty

1. Maundrell, *Journey from Aleppo*, 53.

and forcibly took her to his house and raped her. Dinah must have been quite young because as a full-grown woman she would have been able to fight back, she would have inherited the same strength that Rebekah had, and all the women before her back to Eve. We also know she was a young girl because she was born around or shortly after Joseph's birth at the end of the 14-year period that Jacob worked for his two wives in Haran. Joseph was 17 years old when he was taken to Egypt and we are not yet at that point in the story, so Dinah was young, maybe only just into puberty.

Dinah was held against her will in Shechem's house. When her brothers found out they were seething. Shechem was besotted with Dinah and although he held her captive he tried to show her some tenderness too, he wanted to officially take her as his wife and asked his father to help. They both went to see Jacob and his sons and suggested that Jacob and his family should become part of the local community and trade and intermarry with them. They would be happy to give any gift, however large, if only Dinah could be Shechem's wife. The brothers, some of whom were in their early twenties, were fuming and wanted revenge so they cunningly agreed to the proposal as long as the men of the town would be circumcised. Shechem immediately agreed and got the deed done at once. But how would they sell this fairly demanding request to the other men of the town? Hamor and Shechem gathered the male townsfolk and gave them their sales pitch, which had two major selling points: first, Jacob and his family had a lot of animals that could be integrated into the life of the town. Secondly, Rachel was beautiful, Leah was also beautiful although she had poor eyesight, but no one would know that unless they were told, and Dinah was beautiful. We don't know about Bilhah and Zilpah, but if three of the women were fine looking and strong then there's every reason to suppose there would be more fine looking females to follow. "And," said Hamor and Shechem laying down the deal-clinching phrase, "we can marry them!" They also mentioned the small price the men of the town would have to pay for all this. Hamor and Shechem's presentation had the desired effect and the men of the town agreed. Hamor probably said, "Okay, let's get this done and we'll give the men some recuperating time too."

Jacob was almost certainly perplexed and concerned about the whole situation. He didn't want any trouble with the local people but he was getting railroaded into intermarriage, which he knew wasn't right. God had previously told Abraham that his descendents would come back to the land at the appropriate time because the sin of the Amorites had not yet reached its full measure, which lets us know the Israelites would bring some sort of justice to the region. Child sacrifice was a feature of idol worship, the Bible speaks of it and so do clay documents that have been found that read: "he will burn his oldest son to Sin," "he will burn his oldest daughter to Belit-Seri."[2] The Lord used the early Israelites to administer retribution to some of the excesses of the people who were moving far away from the original plan God had for humankind. Hamor wasn't an Amorite he was a Hivite, but all the same, men cannot go around raping females and holding them captive. Something needed to be done.

Jacob should have taken the situation in hand by demanding that Dinah be returned home immediately and that Shechem face trial and be sentenced accordingly. If that wasn't done then Esau's 400 men would be marshalled along with Jacob's family and employees, and just like Abraham set his nephew Lot free from his kidnappers and was prepared to take whatever consequences followed, Jacob would also free Dinah and make sure Shechem faced justice one way or the other. But Jacob sometimes let fear get hold of him and dictate his behavior. So two of Dinah's full brothers, Simeon and Levi, who were about 21 and 20 years old, took matters into their own hands. While the men of the town of Shechem were healing they used their Adamic strength and slaughtered each and every one of them including Hamor and Shechem, and they rescued Dinah from Shechem's house and took her home, telling the rest of the family what they had done.

The town of Shechem may not have been a well-populated place, but was home to a number of families who had suddenly lost their menfolk. Then the rest of Jacob's sons took the women and children, flocks, herds, and donkeys. Jacob upbraided Simeon and Levi because now he and his family would be a stench to the Canaanite people living nearby. The two young men replied by saying, "Should he treat our sister as a harlot?"

2. Johns, *Assyrian Deeds*, 351, 352.

CHAPTER 24

Love Story

BEMUSED AND APPREHENSIVE, JACOB wondered what to do next. Suddenly God stepped in and solved Jacob's dilemma by telling him to go to Bethel where he had first appeared to him, and make camp there.

> Go up to Bethel and settle there, and build an altar there to God.
> (Gen 35:1)

Bethel was a good 20 miles south, along the ridge route that Abraham had walked. Jacob may have thought that he was settled in his strip of land near Shechem, why had trouble followed him? Was it something to do with Rachel's terephim? Rachel had brought something into the camp that made the security of Jacob's household defective. God would make sure he covered the whole camp if he was asked to, but if there was an area that was kept from him then it was similar to locking most of the house before you go to bed for the night but not locking all of it; leaving a window open may encourage an intruder. Jacob's camp had been broken into and defiled. God had in the past spoken to Jacob and wrestled with him as Yahweh, someone familiar and approachable, now Jacob began to see God in a new majestic light. A little of God's glory was being revealed to Jacob. The Lord also gave Jacob a gentle hint about the last time he was in Bethel, saying, "when you were fleeing from your brother Esau," which reminded Jacob of the proposal he had made that if he returned safely back to Bethel then Yahweh would be his God. Immediately Jacob gathered his company of people together, he could now see the importance of having only one God and giving him undivided devotion, he told his household to rid themselves of their strange gods. There may well have been some new gods among them held by the women taken from Shechem and maybe a few from Haran that some of Jacob's employees had brought with them, and there would be Rachel's terephim. So they gave Jacob all their foreign gods and he buried them under the oak tree at Shechem. The whole camp's security was now in God's hands and God caused a numinous dread to fall on the surrounding townspeople so that everyone left Jacob's troupe well alone as they made their way to Bethel.

Jacob had been back in Canaan about 9 years or so, at first he was based near Shechem where he settled and from where he would have occasionally made the 2-day journey south to Hebron to visit his father Isaac. We hear nothing of his mother Rebekah and must presume she had died, however when Rebekah first left Haran to become Isaac's wife, she had a nurse, we didn't at that point in the story have a name for the nurse. But the lady in question made a big impression on Jacob because he would have spent a lot of time with her as a youngster and as a man in his time in southern Canaan. We only find out her name is Deborah when she dies. The name is Semitic so she could have been related in some way. Terah's family bred very closely. Abraham's brother Nahor married his niece, Milcah, his brother Haran's daughter, and they had eight sons including Bethuel who became Rebekah's father. Nahor also had a concubine named Reumah and together they had four sons. Twelve sons altogether, there would probably have been daughters too; perhaps Deborah was one of the females born to Reumah. We know that Deborah lived long. She was about 150 years old when she died, and it was probably on one of Jacob's trips to see his father that he took Deborah back with him to spend her last days with him. He would have been keen for his children to meet his mother's nurse who he was so close to.

Jacob had set up the stone he used as a pillow the last time he'd spent the night in Bethel about 30 years before. God had kept his side of the deal and brought Jacob safely back to the same place. Now Jacob built an altar, which was always more in keeping with what Yahweh had taught Adam's family. It was here that Deborah died. Jacob was greatly affected and buried her under an oak to the south of Bethel; he called the tree "oak of weeping."

In Jacob's distress God appeared to him again and reiterated Jacob's change of name to Israel. God also said that the land he gave to Abraham and Isaac he was also giving to Jacob. This is interesting because Isaac was still alive at the time God said this, so the land would belong to two people at the same time. And not only that, we have seen that Jesus saw Abraham as still living, so the land was owned by three people at the same time. After God had spoken to Jacob, "God went up." Jacob's revelations were getting increasingly breathtaking, the same type of ascension that Abraham witnessed now filled Jacob with wonder and he again responded by setting up a stone pillar. The trouble with the stone pillars was that they could easily become a stumbling block gaining more attention than they actually deserved. We can understand Jacob wanting to mark the spot where something wonderful occurred, just as Peter on the Mount of Transfiguration blurted out that they would build three booths for Jesus, Moses, and Elijah as memorials. God was not interested in stones or booths being built as memorials, which could themselves become objects of worship, in fact God would later tell the Israelites on more than one occasion not to set up stones, "do not erect a sacred stone, for these the LORD your God hates" (Deut 16:22). You can't really say it any plainer than that. The stones that were erected became high places in Israel and the good kings were commended for shattering them. "He (Hezekiah) removed the high places, smashed the sacred stones and cut down the Asherah poles. He broke into pieces the bronze snake Moses had made, for up to that time the Israelites had been burning incense to it" (2 Kgs 18:4).

Before God ascended in front of Jacob he had told him to "be fruitful and increase in number." Jacob must have thought, *I already have eleven sons and a daughter, I thought my days of "multiplying in number" were over.* But they were not; soon Rachel was pregnant.

The family had made plans to move lock, stock, and barrel 40 miles further south to where Isaac lived in Hebron. As they came within sight of Bethlehem Rachel came into labor. The family may have been taken by surprise and the birth may have been a premature difficult one. Rachel had previously passionately said, "Give me children, or else I die," and now she had children (for this was her second) and she breathed her last. Jacob buried her near Bethlehem and set up a pillar to mark her grave. Jacob named his newborn child Benjamin, and stayed close to the area. There was a tower called Migdal Eder near south Bethlehem that was used by shepherds for keeping an eye on their flocks, and Jacob pitched his tents south of the tower. He would be grief-stricken and may have wanted to stay close to Rachel's burial place. Rachel was not old; she was still of childbearing age.

Rachel's handmaid Bilhah probably took on the role of Joseph and Benjamin's mother. She was originally employed to look after Rachel's interests and Joseph and Benjamin were certainly Rachel's concern, so now they would be Bilhah's concern, she would be the natural choice to take up the role of mother. Shortly after this we find Joseph outside in the fields with the sons of Bilhah and Zilpah but not Leah's children. Rachel slept with Jacob as his main wife, Jacob could visit the tents of his other wives as we saw earlier, but Rachel spent the night as a matter of course with Jacob. If Bilhah took over that role rather than Leah, Jacob's choice may not have been accepted well by Leah or her sons. It's at this juncture we hear that Reuben slept with Bilhah. His motivation may not have been lust or love but the defiling of Bilhah so that his mother would take her rightful place as the legal wife and not allow a concubine to usurp her position. When Jacob issues his final blessings to his sons, he says of Reuben, "you went up onto your father's bed, onto my couch and defiled it," which seems to indicate that Bilhah was sleeping with Jacob in his bed at the time.

Jacob now made his home in Mamre near Hebron where his father Isaac was still living. Esau had some herds and flocks there and although he had made his home in Edom he still kept a watchful eye on his father. All animosity between the two brothers had now disappeared and had been replaced by mutual respect. Esau made the decision to move his animals so that Jacob wouldn't have to.

Jacob's relationship with God had grown. He had heard his father Isaac speak about God's involvement in their family's history, and as a young boy up to the age of 15 would have heard his grandfather Abraham speak of his experiences with Yahweh. Then Jacob saw Yahweh in a dream, and heard him introduce himself as, "Yahweh, the God of your father Abraham and the God of Isaac." Then Jacob met Yahweh in person. After that Jacob saw a manifestation of God and God ascended before him. He was getting a gradual revelation of who God was.

When Yahweh first walked about southern Mesopotamia people may have heard of him, they had names for him, the Sumerian's called him Enki. The Akkadian's who lived a little further north than the Sumerians called him Ea. The Amorites who moved from the westlands to Mesopotamia called him Mar.tu. The Amorites saw him as a hero, a strong young man, endowed with power, the one who shines brightly, he annihilates evil and deeds of violence, he is the god who makes the right decision, and gives enduring existence to the right.[1] God was working chiefly with Adam, the surrounding peoples wouldn't have had the insight that Adam had, but

1. Haldar, "Amorites' Position in Society," 69.

they would be aware and intrigued. When Adam left the confines of the garden he would relate what he knew about Yahweh to the surrounding communities, the local people may have caught glimpses of Yahweh or his co-workers now and again as they planted saplings and pruned them as they grew in the garden. In our modern world we have sterilized our view of how things happened in Genesis. If some day we get a chance to talk to God about what happened in the early days of human civilization, we may say something like, "Lord, you know when you were walking in the cool of the day, were you actually walking?" And the Lord might reply, "Yes." And we might say, "Is that why Genesis says you were walking?" And his reply might be, "Yes."

If we got to talk a little more about Genesis with God, we may like to ask, "Lord, thank you for being patient with me, but when we read in Genesis that you planted a garden, I didn't think it meant you actually planted a garden." And the Lord might reply, "Why not?" And our reply might be, "Well I thought you would do it . . . you know . . . like pow! And it would be there, like CGI graphics in a movie or something." The Lord may then ask, "How should I have written it?" And we'd say, "Well, it may have been helpful to us if you'd written something down about how you planted a garden." And God's reply might be, "How do you normally plant a garden?"

God reaching out to humankind is a theme running though Genesis; it's a love story, a relationship with turbulent ups and downs. We end up with a desire to ask obvious questions that seem to answer themselves but still we feel the need to ask them: "Did God really have lunch with Abraham?" "But God doesn't need to eat does he?" "Then why was he having lunch?" "Was he doing it to be friendly, just like two friends might have lunch together?"

Abraham invited God to lunch on behalf of humans everywhere. It's not just Abraham who God is happy to eat with, Jesus said, "Behold, I stand at the door and knock; if anyone hears my voice and opens the door, I will come in to him and will dine with him, and he with me" (Rev 3:20). We see the favor returned when several days after the resurrection Jesus stood on the edge of the water and called out to the boat that Peter, Thomas, and few other disciples were aboard, asking if they'd caught any fish, they answered with a glum, "No." Jesus suggested lowering their net on the right side of the boat and when they did, it filled up quickly. As the fishermen made their way to shore they saw some coals on fire with fish cooking above them and some bread. Jesus said, "Come and have breakfast, and bring some of those fish too." Abraham's invitation to eat was returned; Jesus also fed 5,000 and 4,000 men on other occasions. He did this to make sure we know he was eager to return the favor and pursue the relationship between God and humankind.

The more familiar we get with the book of Genesis, the more we begin to build up a picture of what Yahweh is like, we see he is willing to walk with us, eat with us, and talk with us. We notice he is artistic, creative, a hard worker, and industrious. We see he has a love of drama and the creative flair to communicate important truth through it. He is kingly, stately, and a judge, but is also gentle, loving, and willing to look for the best in men and women. He sentenced Cain, not to death, but away from the area, he did not treat him as his sins deserved. It wasn't until Cain's line had become totally corrupt and that the wickedness of man (Adam) was great on the earth, and that every inclination of the thoughts of his heart was only evil continually, that the Lord decided to call a halt to the proceedings. The page had become completely black, useless for writing on. Only Noah was righteous. The situation is similar to when the Lord said in Isaiah 65:8 that there is still a little good juice in the cluster of grapes that have mostly gone bad so the husbandman won't destroy all the grapes. Or as Matthew quoted, "A bruised reed he will not break, and a smouldering wick he will not snuff out." He will encourage a smouldering wick as long as there's the smallest chance it will break out into a flame. Genesis tells us about the earliest history of the universe, earth, and humankind; men probably wrote it on skins, papyrus, copper, and maybe clay; they wrote because God inspired them. But the story that God is most interested in writing is the one he writes on human hearts, that's where his passion lies, he writes upon our hearts and it is left up to us to read what he has written and then to respond.

CHAPTER 25

The Serpent Shifts Schemes

Stay alert! Watch out for your great enemy, the devil. He prowls around like a roaring lion, looking for someone to devour. (1 Pet 5:8 nlt)

SINCE ALL THE FOREIGN idols had been removed and God was now protecting Jacob's family, external forces were unable to bring trouble to the seedbearers. But if the serpent changed his plan of attack and focused his main strategy on internal wrangling and jealousies then he may have some success.

Joseph always stood a good chance of being Jacob's favorite child, simply because his mother was Rachel, Jacob's first love. So it's a small wonder the other brothers were disgruntled when Jacob had a richly ornamented coat made for Joseph. Favoritism in a family is not good and parading it is worse; Jacob was making a rod for his own back. To make a bad situation worse, Joseph started to have dreams that he told his brothers about. He'd seen sheaves in one dream, it was harvest time and suddenly Joseph's sheaf stood upright and the sheaves the brothers had been making bowed down to Joseph's sheaf. The brothers hated him all the more; they couldn't speak a civil word to him. We might think that Bilhah's sons, Dan and Naphtali, might possibly give Joseph some brotherly support and advice, after all he tended to hang around with them now that their mother had adopted him, but Joseph had already made sure that any close bond with Dan or Naphtali was nipped in the bud by telling his father about some bad behavior his two brothers committed in league with Ziplah's sons. Then Joseph had another dream where the sun and moon and eleven stars all bowed down to him.

He told his father, who was bewildered and rebuked Joseph, incredulously asking if it meant he and Joseph's mother, who was now Bilhah, along with Joseph's brothers would actually come and bow down to Joseph: "What kind of dream is that?" The whole scenario seems designed to leave Joseph without support, not unlike Christ whose disciples all abandoned him, and even Christ's Father turned his face, leaving Jesus to cry out, "My God why have you forsaken me?" We get the feel of a movie script beginning to take shape; another drama begins to emerge.

Fresh grazing land and water for the flocks meant the brothers needed to take the animals north to the area where Shechem lies. Joseph was the only grown-up brother who hadn't gone with the others to Shechem; he stayed at home along with his baby brother Benjamin in the homely tents of his father's household, no doubt adding to the list of reasons for resentment. Jacob asked Joseph to make the journey to see if all was well with the grazing and to bring a report back. So wearing his "coat" he started out. We can't say that Joseph did much wrong in any of this. Firstly, he told his dreams faithfully as God had given them to him. Some people may think he should have kept his dreams to himself, but if he'd allowed the whole drama to play out and then tried to tell people years later that he'd had a dream about it all, who would believe him? Announcing his dreams before they came true let people know that God was at work. Secondly, he did bring a bad report about Dan and Naphtali and also Ziplah's children Gad and Asher, but we don't know what it was they were doing and the situation may have needed taking to a higher authority. Thirdly, he couldn't help being his father's favorite. And fourthly, when asked by his father to go to Shechem to see how his brothers and sheep were doing he agreed straight away, knowing that by now his brothers were pretty hostile towards him. He was a faithful and good boy.

It took Joseph a while to locate his brothers but after asking about their whereabouts he saw them in the distance 15 miles further north than planned. Water could have been the reason the brothers and flocks were now situated in Dothan, there were many water cisterns in the area and some of them contained water. The brothers saw their opportunity to get rid of Joseph and quickly planned what to do before he arrived. Simeon and Levi were already adept at killing men, the other brothers were happy to see Joseph killed and his body to be thrown into one of the nearby cisterns. "Yeah, then we'll see what becomes of his dreams," they barked. But just like the hero in a movie is saved at the last minute, Joseph is rescued from death by his oldest brother Reuben, who manages to convince the rest not to be hasty and shed blood. So they grabbed Joseph, manhandled his coat away from him and threw him into one of the cisterns that had no water in it. Then they sat down to eat, leaving Joseph to shiver and starve; hatred had done its job of making their hearts callous. Reuben's timely mediation helped because blood was not shed. It was another of Leah's sons, Judah, who helped with the next phase of Joseph's rescue by suggesting they sell him to Ishmaelite traders who happened to be travelling to Egypt by the coastal trade road known as the "way of the sea," which doesn't go past Hebron where Jacob lived. A little profit wouldn't go amiss either and they'd still be rid of their irksome and infuriating brother. So they swiftly decided to seize this stroke of good fortune; Joseph was sold and soon found himself on his way to Egypt.

Reuben, who had already run completely out of favor with his father, wasn't present when the sale took place. Being the eldest, he assumed responsibility for his younger brothers, and wanted to keep Joseph free from harm if possible but didn't want to appear that he was weak or going against the grain of what the majority of the brothers wanted. He knew that Simeon and Levi didn't mess around when it came to violence, so he had to tread carefully. He made it appear as if he was nonchalantly heading away from the cistern Joseph was trapped in but actually took his sheep in a big circle, and when he returned to find Joseph missing cried out, "Where can I turn now?" He must have felt that if ever the true story came out, in his father's eyes he would be anathema. Not only had he slept with one of his father's wives, he had now lost his father's favorite son.

The brothers had to cover their crime so they slaughtered a goat and dipped Joseph's coat in the blood. Judah, feeling wretched because of his involvement in the sale of Joseph and knowing the grief it would cause his father, separates himself from the brothers before they complete their journey home to Hebron. At some point on the journey he falls in with another traveller named Hirah and "went down from his brethren" heading due south from Dothan to Adullam. The rest of the brothers took Joseph's bloodstained coat and presented it to their father when they arrived home, leaving him to come to his own conclusions, thus their sins were covered by the blood of a goat, or so they thought. Jacob was inconsolable. His sons attempted to assuage his grief, but how could they possibly comfort their father? Knowing what had actually happened and leaving their father to think the worst, there would be very little sincerity or empathy in their consoling; criminals comforting their victim were unlikely to be successful. The text also mentions that his daughters also tried to comfort him, they weren't hypocrites like their brothers, but Jacob refused their consolation too. We know Jacob had one daughter, Dinah, it's possible he had more, one of his three remaining wives may have bore him a daughter. Or more probably, the text could mean that some of his sons were now married and their wives are classed as daughters.

The next scene focuses on Judah and not any of the other brothers, which is a testimony to the fact that the book of Genesis is inspired. The writer of Genesis didn't know which genealogical route the promised seed would take, but he who breathed into Adam and upon the Genesis text did.

The scene we have just watched describing the mistreatment and sale of Joseph has changed, leaving the viewer wondering what will happen, and like any good movie the story will be picked up later, but now there's an important development. Eleven years have passed since the family arrived in Canaan; Reuben is now 24 years old, which makes Judah about 20. Judah's new friend, Hirah was a Canaanite. The members of Abraham's family were careful to keep themselves a safe distance from the Canaanites; they were carrying the precious seed and needed to safeguard it. Judah may not have realized it but he was the chosen vessel through which the seed would be carried. The serpent used the sale of Joseph to start breaking up the family and singled out Judah for special treatment. It's as if the serpent, who is a spiritual being, could see something we humans couldn't see. Judah had something within him that made him of particular interest to the serpent. Once in Adullam the serpent made sure that Judah was introduced to the daughter of Shua, they got married and within a short space of time had three boys. This was not to plan, Abraham had strictly specified that his son should marry only in his family line, Isaac too with Jacob, and now Jacob had lost control of the situation and Judah who was the chosen seed-bearer had married a Canaanite woman and they soon had offspring: sons Er, Onan, and Shelah.

Judah tried to settle down and make life as normal as possible. He arranged for an early marriage for Er, and chose a girl with the Semitic name of Tamar, which means "date palm." The Targum of Jonathan says she was a daughter of Shem. (A Targum was used as an Aramaic version and explanation of the Hebrew Scriptures to the Jews who didn't speak Hebrew.) Shem lived to be 600 years old but he would have died before Judah arranged Tamar's marriage to Er. These pieces of genealogy could mean that she descended as a daughter from Shem's line with a few people in between her and Shem, similar to Jesus who was called the son of David even though there were people in between David and Jesus. Some people think she may have been a Canaanite but given her name and the outcome of the story it looks like providence is working to protect the seed and there's a probability that Shem was not too far back in her family's history. Shem lived long, so his offspring would inherit the longevity too, though not as much as Shem because their length of days was shortening with each successive generation; intermarriage would speed up the process. If Noah's grandson from Ham's line, Canaan, had intermarried and his offspring intermarried with the local peoples they would soon lose what they had. But if Shem had some offspring late in life, they too would live longer than Abraham and Isaac because they were genetically closer to the original source: Shem. So it is possible that Tamar was a long-living daughter of Shem but further down the line. Judah may have felt uncomfortable about the fact he married a Canaanite when he knew all the trouble previous family members had gone to to protect their genealogical line. So finding a daughter from Shem's line for his firstborn son may go some way to putting things right.

But there was a problem. Er was wicked, we don't know in what way, but he was young, probably headstrong, and had a measure of extra strength over and above his peers. It may be that the Lord allowed Er's own evil behavior to cause his demise. Whatever happened, he died young. Judah told his second son Onan to have intercourse with Tamar to produce offspring for Er. Onan may not have got on well with Er, which helps build up a picture of what Er was like, although we still can't be sure. But Onan thought to himself there was no way he was going to produce offspring for his brother, so he used the withdrawal method when he slept with Tamar, which also tells us a little about Onan's personality too. Onan didn't last long either and also died young. Genesis tells us that the Lord slew him. At some points in life we find, like Job, all we can say is that, "The Lord gives and the Lord takes away." Something had gone amiss with Er and Onan, Judah himself was beginning to see this now and didn't want his third son getting anywhere close to Tamar, so he cooked up a story for Tamar, telling her to wait for Shelah and when he's of age they can marry, but he had no intention of it ever happening. He sent Tamar to live in her father's house, which seems to suggest her next of kin father was still alive, so it wasn't Shem.

Er and Onan's mother also died. This must have been a traumatic time for Judah. Things were not working out well for him since he had left his father's household; something seemed seriously amiss. We can almost see what's coming in this story, Tamar is there for a reason, if she was part of Shem's line and not too far away from him then the integrity of the gene God placed in Adam could be preserved, if only Tamar and Judah could get it together. But how was that ever going to happen? There's no way Judah would sleep with his daughter-in-law. But that is in fact what we find happens in the story. Tamar didn't want to be childless; she soon realized that Shelah wasn't going to father children for her, so she took action herself. Disguising herself as a shrine prostitute at sheep shearing season, and using her posture, she attracted Judah's attention. She would be careful to change her normal mode of speech too, she wore a veil and Judah was taken in.

All sorts of moral questions appear before us, but perhaps it's sufficient for us to say that darkness can never overcome light, and as bad as we humans sometimes get, God is always able to grow something worthwhile in the soil of human behavior.

Judah offers to pay Tamar the price of a goat, but she is a clever lady and wants Judah's seal and cord plus his staff as security. Once the deed is done Judah went on his way, he asked his friend Hirah to take the goat to the woman. But the woman could not be found. Hirah asked some of the local men where the shrine prostitute could be found and they told him that there was no shrine prostitute in this area. Hirah told Jacob, who said, "Okay let's drop it now before we become a laughing stock, she can keep my seal." Three months later Judah sees an excellent opportunity to get rid of the jinxed Tamar for good. He hears that somehow she has got herself pregnant and is accused of prostitution. Judah already has some standing in the local community, it was his sheep that were being sheared and now he is asked to judge in the case of Tamar. He decides to "bring her out and have her burned to death!" Tamar, knowing this might happen, produces the seal with its cord and staff, which of course belong to Judah saying, "I am pregnant by the man who these belong to." The case collapses and Tamar goes free, giving birth to twins Perez and Zerah. Perez would be next in the line towards the Messiah.

CHAPTER 26

Points of Interest

> God spoke to Israel . . . "Jacob! Jacob! . . . I will go down to Egypt
> with you." (Gen 46:2, 4)

THERE IS SOME SKEPTICISM about the timeline of Judah and Joseph's stories running concurrently, implying that there wasn't enough time for Judah's story to unfold before he moved to Goshen in Egypt with the rest of the family. Looking at a possible timeframe may help. Judah settled down near Adullam at about the same time that Joseph was taken to Egypt, so we can work out approximately how much time passed. Judah seems to have married quickly and if his first son Er was born within a year, Er could have married Tamar when he was 18, and that would be a total of 19 years so far. It looks like Er died quite quickly after his marriage, and if Onan's death was about 2 years after his brother's death, that would be 21 years. If Judah's three sons were all born over a 4-year period, it would take Tamar about 4 years to realize Shelah wasn't going to marry her. (Two years for Shelah to come of age, and two years for Tamar to realize the wedding wasn't on the horizon.) So from Onan dying to Tamar tricking Jacob we can say 4 years, giving a total of 25 years for Judah's excursion. We can conclude that there isn't a problem with Judah's timeline—25 years is sufficient to allow for all that Genesis describes concerning Judah's actions in the vicinity of Adullam.

If we look at it from Joseph's perspective we know he was 17 when he was taken to Egypt and 30 when he started working for Pharaoh, that's 13 years. Pharaoh had a dream that Joseph interpreted and was made manager of the whole land of Egypt. Joseph was introduced to the people of Egypt as their new prime minister by a tour of the country in a special chariot. He also made a tour of the country to issue instructions and put into place the necessary infrastructure required for the tax and storage of food in the 7 years of plenty. So let's say there was a 5-year period for Joseph's introduction and the building of necessary storage facilities throughout the cities of Egypt. Plus the actual 7 years of plenty, that is a total of 25 years. When Joseph reveals himself to his brothers he tells them 2 years of famine have passed so we can add those 2 years, which gives us 27 years. Judah had gone back to Jacob's household by this time, probably partly because of the famine and partly to put things right with his father for his excursion into the Canaanite population. Leaving us to conclude that there isn't a problem with Judah's timeline running concurrently with Joseph's.

If we look at the timing from Jacob's perspective, Joseph was born at the end of the 14-year period Jacob worked for his wives. Jacob worked a further 6 years for his flock then came back to Canaan, so Joseph would have been 6 years old when they made their way to Canaan. Joseph was 17 years old when he was taken to Egypt. He met his brothers about 27 years later when he would have been 44 years old. There was probably a 2-year period while Jacob travelled to Egypt with his animals and settled in Goshen before he finally stood before Pharaoh when he was 130 years old, leaving a total of 29 years for the stories of Judah and Joseph and the settlement in Goshen to unfold. Each of the three timeline viewpoints— Judah's, Joseph's, and Jacob's—work well together, the numbers add up, leaving adequate time for their stories to unfold. (These numbers also tell us that Jacob was about 70 years old when he first met Rachel at Haran and that Isaac was roughly 130 years old when Jacob left for Haran.)

A further complaint against the chronology of the stories comes when we read that Perez had two sons, Hezron and Hamul, because they are included in the list of persons who settle in Egypt from Canaan. They were of course born after the actual migration, but before Jacob's death hence they are included in the record of 70 people in Egypt. Stephen, in his final speech in Acts chapter 7 quotes the Septuagint and mentions 75 persons, which includes some extra grandchildren.

In Genesis the story of Joseph takes up about the same number of chapters as Abraham's story. Joseph's adventures make fascinating reading. We won't go through it but we can bring out a thought or two that may be of some importance.

Pharaoh was interested in the fact that Jacob had lived long, he asked Jacob about it. The life expectancy of the Egyptians was not long, occasionally a pharaoh would make it into old age but the average life span was shorter than it is today.[1] Jacob may have impressed the pharaoh with his age of 130 but Jacob's melancholy humor added, "My years have been few and difficult, and they do not equal the years of my fathers." Pharaoh had probably heard of the "long-livers" but now he had met one. Jacob played it down: "It was all the more years to have trouble and strife. And anyway I haven't lived as long as my fathers before me, now they really did live long." Jacob had grown by getting to know Yahweh. Jacob did not waste any time with Joseph but told him all he needed to know. "Jacob said to Joseph, 'God Almighty appeared to me at Luz in the land of Canaan,'" and Jacob then passed on the stories and wisdom he had learned from the LORD. We may have a hint that Jacob's insight of the LORD had increasingly become greater when we read towards the end of Genesis, "Israel's (Jacob's) eyes were failing" (Gen 48:10). He certainly seemed more settled and had some wry phrases at his disposal. When the famine began in Canaan and the family learned that there was grain in Egypt we hear Jacob's laconic rebuke to his sons when they learned there was grain in Egypt: "Why are you standing around looking at each other"? The comment conjures up a picture of the grown-up sons of Jacob looking nonplussed and a little foolish, until their father speaks up. It probably brought a few smiles to the faces of their womenfolk.

In Canaan the idolatry of the surrounding people was always going to be a temptation for Jacob's family, he had managed to get rid of all the idols and buried them back at Shechem, but perhaps we can see some divine reasoning with the whole family being taken south to Egypt. The Canaanite or Mesopotamian gods would not be a problem in Egypt, Jacob's family could become devoted to the one true God and he could teach them lessons they needed to learn.

Pharaoh let Jacob and his family settle in Goshen, which he called the "best part of the land." Jacob lived a further 17 years. Jacob's life had been a gradual move towards God, he was now inspired by God's Spirit and wrote a song about each of his sons. Each stanza had something to say about the sons and prophetically about their posterity too, the sons who were set to become the twelve tribes of Israel. In the song Simeon and Levi are remembered for what they did to the men of Shechem:

1. Ruiz, *Spirit of Ancient Egypt*, 15.

> Let me not enter their council,
> Let me not join their assembly,
> For they have killed men in their anger
> And hamstrung oxen as they pleased.
> Cursed be their anger, for it is fierce.

Judah, who will be a forefather to Christ, is told that his brothers will praise him and that his hand will be on the neck of his enemies. If we see Christ in this prophecy, we see the reinforcement of what the LORD said to the serpent back in the garden of Eden; the divine seed was still on course to grow into a human man who would crush the head of the serpent on behalf of all humans. At various points in Genesis we have seen the serpent slyly and silently hidden in the long grass, working toward destroying the seed God planted in the human race. But by the time we reach the end of Genesis, somehow the Lord has managed to outmaneuver the serpent at each attack. Jacob in his song also mentions that the scepter will not depart from Judah, "he will always rule." He will tether his donkey to the choicest vine, his colt to the choicest branch, speaking of Jesus as he rode into Jerusalem on a donkey and colt; branches were spread out before him. The branches were palm branches too, echoing back to the garden where the Mesopotamians had the story of the date palm tree that had the man and woman on either side with the snake in the background. Now Christ was treading down these palms, he was destroying the work of the devil. Jacob also told Judah that his robes would be washed in the blood of grapes, prophesying that bloodshed was in store for his seed. And Jesus who was the seed would also have read this song, he knew he was from Judah's line; he knew he was the promised seed. These words would help Jesus as he moved towards the cross.

Since God first deposited "the life" into Adam we have seen different aspects of Christ in the genetic links of the chain. The beauty of the women points to the beauty of Christ: he is fairer than ten thousand. The strength of the men and women involved points to the strength of Christ: he was strong and resolute to complete the work he had to do, he set his face as a flint and would not turn back. The "long years" of the people point to him who is alive forevermore, his seed was among them, giving them outward attributes that show us something of the Son that was to be born from their line. Local people noticed that God was with these people in some special way, some were thought of as kings or judges. Jacob goes on to mention that Judah will have eyes that are darker than wine. Previously we saw Leah with weak eyes, Isaac and Jacob too, and now Judah's eyes are said to be dark. The character of a judge has to be one of impartiality, bribes and corruption have hindered humankind's progress toward civilization and the Bible has a lot to say about it. You may have seen the statue of justice outside a law court. The figure is holding a pair of scales and a sword and is blindfolded; a true judge will not look with favoritism on anyone but will judge justly. Isaiah speaks of Christ saying, "He will not judge by what He sees with His eyes."

Gradually all the attributes (and negative aspects like weak eyes) of being in the line to Christ faded away. Long life, strength, and beauty faded as Christ's birth got closer; once Christ was born he was all of those things. The attributes were actors in the drama and now the reality was among us. The signs were no longer needed.

Jacob instructs his sons upon his death to take his body and place it in the cave of Machpelah; all those who were buried there so far were seed-bearers. Abraham, Sarah, Isaac, Rebekah, Leah, and Jacob would follow. Although Jacob loved Rachel she was not buried there, Leah had finally taken her place in death as Jacob's first wife.

There would be more attempts to destroy what God had planted in other books of the Bible. But what we have learned in Genesis informs us that God who began the good work is able to take it on to completion. God has a way of keeping a rescue plan safe and secure for when it's needed. When Mordecai was encouraging Esther to speak to the king he said, "If you remain silent at this time, relief and deliverance for the Jews will arise from another place." The line to Christ will be protected and overshadowed by God's hand; he is always able to get things back on track. To those looking on it seemed like Judah might wreck the plan by marrying a Canaanite, but God had Tamar in reserve. There would be other reservists too. The scenario of Lot's daughters being impregnated by their father seems too imprudent to be useful and yet the close family genetic ties may be useful for being kept in reserve. The eldest son of Lot's daughters was named Moab, father of the Moabites. Six generations along the line from Judah's son Perez we get a man called Boaz from Judah who married a woman called Ruth who was a Moabite, taking her place in the line to Christ.

Yahweh first breathed into a man, which began the links in the genetic chain to Christ, then the Holy Spirit and power of the Most High overshadowed a woman, Mary, and she gave birth to a son. The work was completed; God started the process and finished it. And now all humankind benefit from having God with us—Emmanuel.

Genesis tells us about genes, we all had our beginnings made from the earth except he who is from above. His beginnings were not from the earth; he already existed before the universe came to be. As John the Baptist said, "The one who comes from above is above all; the one who is from the earth belongs to the earth . . . The one who comes from heaven is above all."

Appendix

Why does Genesis refer to the city of Ur as "Ur of the Chaldees" when the Chaldeans arrived later than the timeframe Genesis was supposed to be written in?

Good question! Genesis is supposed to be very ancient and yet the Chaldeans only began to occupy Ur from around 1000 BC. If Genesis was written in the 2nd or 3rd millennium BC the writer wouldn't refer to Ur as being Chaldean.

There is an explanation: "Ur Kasdim" is the way "Ur of the Chaldees" is written in Hebrew, and "Ur Kasdim" is ancient. The book of Jubilees informs us that a Semite named Ur rebuilt the city after the Flood and he named the city after himself and his father, so in Hebrew it is known as Ur Kasdim. However, when the Greek Septuagint was written in 300 BC Ur had long been occupied by the Chaldeans so the Septuagint translated "Ur Kasdim" as "Ur of the Chaldees" which would resonate with its readers because they had heard of the Chaldees. English bibles usually follow the Septuagint's lead when referring to the city of Ur, although its real name is Ur Kasdim.

When Sarah was with Abimelech how could three months be long enough to notice that no one in the community had got pregnant?

They noticed because the problem could have been with Abimelech's inability to have intimate relations with the slave girls in his household. They may have said "What's up with Abimelech? He's not approaching any of the girls lately!" That's probably why God advised Abimelech to ask Abraham to pray for him, that he may be healed and live.

Are there any more scriptures referring to adoption that could possibly refer to Adam?

Adoption is a theme that runs through the Bible. For example Romans 8:15 says, "the Spirit you received brought about your adoption to sonship. And by him we cry, 'Abba, Father.'" If we think of Adam as an illustration we see that Adam did receive a measure of God's Spirit because God breathed into him. He also received adoption into God's family: God was his father and planted and provided an area for Adam to live in. Adam was an example of what God can do for each one of us. For instance Psalm 27:10 says, "For my father and my mother have forsaken me, But the Lord will take me up." (nasb). We can view this verse prophetically regarding Jesus, the second Adam, we can also see it as a reference to the first Adam. Abandoning a child is a rare occurrence but it does happen. David wrote the Psalm and he was still living happily at home with his father Jesse as a young man. Jesus asked his father, "Why have you forsaken me?" But the mother of Jesus was not far away. The theme of a baby being abandoned by both parents and the Lord taking care of him, seems to have happened at some point; the Bible uses the scenario for us to learn lessons and also seems to allude to an historical event. Adam fits the criteria for being that baby if humanity has been on the earth for longer than 6000 years.

The King James Version of the Bible translates Genesis 2:13 by saying the river Gihon travels through Ethiopia and Ethiopia is a long way from Southern Mesopotamia.

Most Bibles translate the river Gihon as winding through the land of Cush. Ham fathered Cush, and Cush was the father of Nimrod. Nimrod ruled in Mesopotamia (Genesis 10:6–12). It's most likely that Cush gave his name (Sumerian "Kish") to a city and to the area. Later, the name Cush is found in Ethiopia (Psalm 68:31) Ham's offspring eventually moved south and an area in the upper Nile region was also known as Cush. But the Gihon river travelled through the land where Ham's son Cush lived—the land of Cush—which was in Mesopotamia, where Cush's son Nimrod ruled.

Bibliography

Abbas, Mohammed. "Drought Threatens Peace in Iraq's Marsh Eden." *Reuters* (February 3, 2009). Online: http://www.reuters.com/article/2009/02/03/us-iraq-marsh-water-idUSTRE51201M20090203.

Alexander, Denis R. "Can a Christian Believe in Evolution?" *Evangelical Alliance* (May 1, 2005). Online: http://www.eauk.org/church/resources/theological-articles/can-a-christian-believe-in-evolution.cfm.

———. "Is it Possible to be a Christian and Believe in Evolution?" No Pages. Online: http://www.bethinking.org/does-evolution-disprove-creation/is-it-possible-to-be-a-christian-and-believe-in-evolution.

Allan, Tony. *The Dawn of Civilization: Prehistory to 900 BC.* Reader's Digest Illustrated History of the World. Edited by Christian Noble. Vol. 1. London: Reader's Digest, 2004.

British Museum. Babylonian tablet no. 74329. Copied by A. R. Millard, translated by W. G. Lambert. Kadmos, vol. 6. Circa 2000 BC.

———. "Foundation Figure of Ur-Nammu." No Pages. http://www.britishmuseum.org/explore/highlights/highlight_objects/me/f/foundation_figure_of_ur-nammu.aspx.

———. "Third Dynasty of Ur (Ur III)." No Pages. http://www.britishmuseum.org/explore/highlights/articles/t/third_dynasty_of_ur_ur_iii.aspx.

Budge, E. A. Wallis. *The Babylonian Story of the Deluge and Epic of Gilgamish.* Revised by C. G. Gadd. The Legend of Gilgamish, tablet 11. British Museum, Department of Egyptian and Assyrian Antiquities, October 15, 1929. Online: http://www.sacred-texts.com/ane/gilgdelu.htm.

Carleton, P. *Buried Empires: The Earliest Civilizations of the Middle East.* London: Edward Arnold, 1939.

Chiera, Edward. *Sumerian Epics and Myths.* Chicago: University of Chicago Press, 1934.

———. *Sumerian Texts of Varied Contents.* Chicago: University of Chicago Press, 1934.

Churchin, Leonard. "Old Age in Sumer: Life Expectancy and Social Status of the Elderly." *Florilegium* 2 (1980) 61–70.

Clay, Albert Tobias. *A Hebrew Deluge Story in Cuneiform: And Other Fragments in the Pierpont Morgan Library.* New Haven, CT: Yale University Press, 1922.

Constable, George, ed. *The Age of God Kings: TimeFrame 3000–1500 BC.* Alexandria, VA: Time Life Books, 1987.

Crawford, Harriet. *Sumer and the Sumerians.* Cambridge: Cambridge University Press, 1991.

Bibliography

Fischer, Richard James. *Historical Genesis: From Adam to Abraham*. New York: University Press of America, 2008.

Gamel, Kim, and Sinan Salaheddin. "Drought Strikes Iraqi 'Garden of Eden' Marshes." *Associated Press* (April 15, 2009). Online: http://www.cleveland.com/world/index. ssf/2009/04/drought_threatens_iraqi_garden.html.

Gill, John. *An Exposition of the New Testament*. 3 vols., 1746–1748. London: Mathews and Leigh, 1810. Commentary on Luke 3:36. Online: http://www.biblestudytools.com/ commentaries/gills-exposition-of-the-bible/luke-3-36.html.

Guisepi, Robert A. "Ancient Sumeria." No Pages. Online: http://history-world.org/ sumeria.htm.

Haldar, Alfred. "The Amorites' Position in Society." In *Who Were the Amorites?* Vol. 35. Leiden: E. J. Brill, 1971.

Hallo, William W. "Antediluvian Cities." *Journal of Cuneiform Studies* 23, no. 3 (1970) 57–67.

Hallo, William W., and William Kelly Simpson. *The Ancient Near East: A History*. New York: Harcourt Brace Jovanovich, 1971.

Hamblin, Dora Jane. *The First Cities*. New York: Time-Life Books, 1973.

Harte, Julia. "Drought and Dams in Biblical Garden of Eden." *National Geographic News Watch* (April 11, 2013). No pages. Online: http://newswatch.nationalgeographic. com/2013/04/11/drought-and-dams-in-biblical-garden-of-eden/.

Hey, Jody. "North America Settled by Just 70 People." Live Science. No pages. Online: http:// www.livescience.com/289-north-america-settled-70-people-study-concludes.html.

Hottinger, Johann Heinrich. *Smegma Oriental*. Vol. 3, part 2. Heidelberg: Adriani Wyngaerden, 1660.

Jacobsen, Thorkild. "The Harps that Once. . . . : Sumerian Poetry in Translation." The Eridu Genesis. New Haven, CT: Yale University Press, 1987. Online: http://www. piney.com/EriduGen.html.

Johns, C. H. W. *Assyrian Deeds and Documents*. Cambridge: Deighton Bell, 1898.

Kramer, Samuel Noah. "Sumerian Myths and Epic Tales." In *Ancient Near Eastern Texts: Relating to the Old Testament*, edited by James B. Pritchard, 37–59. 3rd ed., with supplement. Princeton, NJ: Princeton University Press, 1969.

———. *The Sumerians*. Chicago: University of Chicago Press, 1963.

Lloyd, Seton. "The Oldest City of Sumeria: Establishing the Origin of Eridu." *Illustrated London News*, September 11, 1948.

Lovett, Richard A. "Bible Accounts Supported by Dead Sea Disaster Record?: New Evidence Suggests Body Once Vanished, Could Again." Meeting of the American Geophysical Union, San Francisco, California. *National Geographic News* (December 8, 2011). Online: http://news.nationalgeographic.com/news/2011/12/111208-dead-sea-bible-biblical-salt-dry-science/.

MacDonald, D. "The Flood: Mesopotamian Archaeological Evidence." *Creation/Evolution* 8 no. 2 (1988) 14–20.

Mark, Joshua J. "Eridu." In *Ancient History Encyclopedia* (July 10, 2010). No pages. Online: http://www.ancient.eu.com/eridu/.

Maundrell, Henry. *A Journey from Aleppo to Jerusalem: At Easter, A.D. 1697*. London: C. and J. Rivington, 1823.

Mayell, Hillary. "Climate Change Killed Neandertals, Study Says." *National Geographic News* (February 9, 2004). Online: http://news.nationalgeographic.com/ news/2004/02/0209_040209_neandertals.html.

Morton, Julia F. "Date: Phoenix dactylifera." In *Fruits of Warm Climates*, 5–11. Miami, FL: Morton, 1987. Center for New Crops and Plant Products, Purdue University, West Lafayette, IN. Online: http://www.hort.purdue.edu/newcrop/morton/Date.html.

Owen, Bruce. "Mesopotamia: Neolithic and Early Complex Cultures." Anthropology 341: Emergence of Civilizations, notes 10. Sonoma University, Rohnert Park, California, 2009. Online: http://bruceowen.com/emciv/a341-9s-10-EarlyMesopotamia.pdf.

Pearlman, Jonathan. "Kidney Grown from Stem Cells by Australian Scientists." *The Telegraph*, December 16, 2013. http://www.telegraph.co.uk/news/worldnews/australiaandthepacific/australia/10520058/Kidney-grown-from-stem-cells-by-Australian-scientists.html.

Plutarch. "Sayings of Spartans." In *Moralia*. Translated by Frank Cole Babbit. Loeb Classical Library. Vol. 3. Cambridge, MA: Harvard University Press, 1936.

Realhistoryww.com. "Ancient Man and His First Civilizations: Sumerian Cities." No Pages. Online: http://realhistoryww.com/world_history/ancient/Sumer_Iraq_1a.htm.

———. "Ancient Man and His First Civilizations: The Ziggurat." No Pages. Online: http://realhistoryww.com/world_history/ancient/Misc/Sumer/the_ziggurat.htm.

Rogers, John H. "Origins of the Ancient Constellations: The Mesopotamian Traditions." *Journal of the British Astronomical Association* 108, no. 1 (February 1998) 9–28.

Ruiz, Ana. *The Spirit of Ancient Egypt*. New York: Algora, 2001.

Safer, Fuad. "Eridu." *Sumer* 6 (1950) 28.

Smith, George. *The Chaldean Account of Genesis: The Near East: Classic Studies*. New edition by A. H. Sayce. Eugene, OR: Wipf and Stock, 2007.

Smith, R. Payne. *A Bible Commentary for English Readers*. Edited by Charles John Ellicott. Vol. 1. Genesis to Numbers. London: Cassell, 1897.

Stanley, Bruce E. "Ur." In *Cities of the Middle East and North Africa: A Historical Encyclopedia*, edited by Michael R. T. Dumper, and Bruce E. Stanley, 382–84. Santa Barbara, CA: ABC-CLIO, 2007. Online: http://books.google.co.uk/books?id=3SapTk5iGDkC&pg=PA382&lpg=PA382&dq=inhabitants+city+of+ur&source=bl&ots=8tTIc7Pb6t&sig=dURBDnO44UWDyM3qBcy_Np_evYE&hl=en&sa=X&ei=857HU_XDMcfHoQXJqYDwDw&ved=0CEoQ6AEwBg#v=onepage&q=inhabitants%20city%20of%20ur&f=false.

Stol, M. "Private Life in Ancient Mesopotamia." In *Civilizations of the Ancient Near East*. Edited by Jack M. Sasson. Vol. 3. New York: Charles Scribner, 1995.

Thomson, William M. *The Land and the Book: The Holy Land*. Vol. 2. Yew York: Harper and Brothers, 1865. Online: http://babel.hathitrust.org/cgi/pt?id=njp.3210102691107 1;view=1up;seq=17.

Ur, Jason A., et al. "Early Mesopotamian Urbanism: A New View from the North." *Antiquity* 81 no. 313 (September 2007) 585–600. Online: http://nrs.harvard.edu/urn-3:HUL.InstRepos:4269009.

Vivante, Bella, ed. *Women's Roles in Ancient Civilizations: A Reference Guide*. Westport, CT: Greenwood Press, 1999.

Wayman, Erin. "Lack of Water Threatens 'Garden of Eden.'" *Earth Magazine* (April 15, 2009). Online: http://www.earthmagazine.org/article/lack-water-threatens-garden-eden.

Yaron, Reuven. "Varia on Adoption." *Journal of Juristic Papyrology* 15 (1995) 171–83.

Printed in Great Britain
by Amazon.co.uk, Ltd.,
Marston Gate.